Advance Praise for *Hidden Healers*

Hidden Healers cuts through the many myths associated with incarcerated women to highlight the actual battles they have to face every day within a criminal legal system never designed for them. The book is both a riveting personal account of Dr. Covington's commitment to gender-responsive correctional reform over the last 30 years and an amplification of the voices of women who have had to endure repeated systematic harms. The little-known gem that *Hidden Healers* poignantly reveals is how often women, despite all this, come together to support one another in the day-to-day struggles to provide genuine hope, healing, and meaning. It will be a go-to book in my library for many years to come.

EMILY J. SALISBURY, PHD
Director, Utah Criminal Justice Center
Research Director, Women's Risk Needs Assessment Lab
Associate Professor of Social Work
University of Utah

Women make up only about 10 percent of America's imprisoned population, so men get most of the attention—from a prison system designed with testosterone in mind, and from those who study that system. Stephanie Covington, a psychologist and social worker, has spent three decades helping incarcerated women help one another cope with trauma. Her empathetic and readable portrayal of women's lives in and after prison deserves a wide readership.

BILL KELLER
Founding editor, The Marshall Project
Former columnist and editor, the New York Times
Author: What's Prison For? Punishment and Rehabilitation in the Age of Mass Incarceration
Southampton, New York

Hidden Healers is an important book because it reveals the absurdity of calling our justice system for women "just." It is not an easy book to read because Stephanie Covington, one of our country's wise women, is merciless in her descriptions of what it is like for a woman to be sent to jail or prison. At the same time, the reader is accompanied on this journey by incarcerated women who are the "hidden healers," clearly demonstrating the time-honored caregiving that women provide for each other under adverse conditions. This book should be a mandatory part of the curriculum of every law school in the country.

SANDRA L. BLOOM, MD
Associate Professor, Health Management and Policy
Dornsife School of Public Health, Drexel University
Philadelphia, Pennsylvania

~

As important as her earlier works have been, the voices of the women with whom she has worked and from whom she has learned makes this her most personal and most important book. Dr. Covington writes in an informed and impassioned voice about what she has learned and the women she has learned it from, in thirty years working in prisons and jails. Hers is a voice of intelligence and compassion, pragmatism, and hopefulness, honed by the sharp edges of the reality of our prisons and jails. A must-read for everyone interested in prisons and jails today.

MARTIN F. HORN
Secretary of Corrections, Commonwealth of Pennsylvania (ret.)
New York City Correction Commissioner (ret.)
Distinguished Lecturer, John Jay College of Criminal Justice (ret.)
New York, New York

~

Hidden Healers documents what I have witnessed when accompanying Dr. Covington on prison visits: women feeling seen as she validates their situations, histories, and collective voices. Dr. Covington's portrayals of the pain and isolation experienced as a result of confinement also clearly articulate the need for continued advocacy. She reminds us that advocacy work within prison does not negate or minimize abolitionist views. Rather it speaks to the duality of our obligation: continuing to work with those caught in this draconian web while dismantling oppressive systems.

SHERYL KUBIAK, PHD, MSW
Dean, School of Social Work
Center for Behavioral Health and Justice
Wayne State University
Detroit, Michigan

Dr. Stephanie Covington has yet again developed an insightful way of thinking about women and their healing journey. With clarity and care she identifies and magnifies what we often do not see. *Hidden Healers* celebrates individuals who generate hope and inspiration with no expectation of recognition: invisible healers who without formal training make a pivotal difference for another through a moment, a day, or years of kindness and perception. These informal and unlikely individuals know that healing begins when a woman feels worthy and supported.

ANDIE MOSS
Founder and CEO
The Moss Group, Inc.
Washington, DC

Hidden Healers is a gift to those of us who care about women in prison. In sharing her keen insights into the unnecessary suffering created by women's imprisonment, Dr. Covington highlights those who bring compassion into one of our cruelest institutions. Within the context of her own experience with this world, Dr. Covington provides both the cold, hard facts of the gendered harm of imprisonment and the hope and clear guidance needed to envision alternatives. A must-read.

BARBARA OWEN, PHD
Professor Emerita, California State University, Fresno
Author: In the Mix: Struggle and Survival in a Women's Prison
Co-author: In Search of Safety: Confronting Inequality in Women's Imprisonment

Stephanie S. Covington's book, *Hidden Healers*, should be required reading for anyone interested in the realities of women in prison. This book is the *real deal.* As a formerly incarcerated woman who spent fifteen years in prison, I found *Hidden Healers* to be true to life, depicting what that system is like and how it needs to be changed. Women face so many different challenges in prison, and Stephanie Covington's exhaustive interviews with women in the United States and throughout Europe allow their voices to bring to light the many issues women face before, during, and after prison and their recommendation for a reenvisioning of the entire system.

BEATRICE CODIANNI
Co-founder of the National Council for Incarcerated and Formerly Incarcerated Women and Girls

Stephanie Covington's goal is to make the invisible visible. Not only does she accomplish this, she calls for a social justice response that acknowledges that prisons are harmful and not conducive to healing. This is a must-read for policymakers, practitioners, advocates, scholars, and all who are compelled to "do one small thing" to promote alternatives to imprisonment.

BARBARA BLOOM, PHD
Professor Emerita, Sonoma State University
Co-director, Center for Gender & Justice
Petaluma, California

The issues of female imprisonment are the same the world over: abuse, trauma, domestic violence, addiction, and navigating how to mother from inside concrete walls. Dr. Covington writes with authority and compassion about all of these issues in *Hidden Healers*. Despite the challenges laid out in her latest book, we do know what the answers are—we just need to be bold enough to take the action required.

LADY EDWINA GROSVENOR
Founder of Hope Street
Founder of One Small Thing
London, England

~

Through compelling interviews with women who have lived experience, Dr. Stephanie Covington has given us a glimpse between the bars of the American criminal legal system. Her interviews with justice-impacted women amplify the voices of the silenced and show how women use their relationships with each other to create resiliency, build on their strengths, and triumph against all odds.

ASHLEY BAUMAN
President
Bauman Consulting Group
Loveland, Ohio

~

Dr. Stephanie Covington addresses women in the criminal justice system in her new book, *Hidden Healers*. However, what is really explored is "the criminal legal" system that evades justice at every turn. Our society continues to turn a blind eye to the reality that incarcerated women face every day and in every state. In conversation with multiple stakeholders within the prison system, Dr. Covington describes the tremendous impacts of grief, generational trauma, sexual assault, and isolation. Through searing personal anecdotes and cutting-edge research, this book equips criminal legal system practitioners, treatment providers, and policymakers with the knowledge and impetus to address the root causes of women's incarceration and create pathways to healing and not prison.

MIMI TARRASCH
Chief Program Officer
Women In Recovery/Women's Justice Programs, Family & Children's Services
Tulsa, Oklahoma

~

Stephanie continues to be a leader in both advancing and transforming the criminal justice system—committed to highlighting and training around the areas of gender responsivity and trauma-informed care. Her work is unparalleled in this space, and she truly is an expert we've all come to rely upon and be inspired by.

DOUG BOND
President & CEO
Amity Foundation
Los Angeles, California

After working in the criminal legal system for over 25 years as a criminologist, I am grateful for the opportunity to continue to learn about things I claim to be an expert on. *Hidden Healers* is a very moving and personal account of Dr. Covington's journey with this system and the people behind its walls. She brings attention to the realities of daily life in prison and the research that supports the recommendations for change. She debunks the stereotypes with such clarity that you cannot pretend you don't get it! Incarcerated women become something more than subjects in these pages: they become people once more.

NENA MESSINA, PHD
Criminologist, University of California, Los Angeles (ret.)
President and CEO
Envisioning Justice Solutions, Inc.
Simi Valley, California

Women in prison are often called forgotten offenders in a system whose practices are dominated by concerns over male inmates. Driven by fears of male violence and the possibility of escapes, prison rules make women's experience of incarceration far worse than is necessary. In this important addition to her earlier work, Covington lets us hear the actual voices of women who have served time in prison. Her long history of working with justice-involved women makes *Hidden Healers* must-reading for those seeking to understand what this group of women needs to succeed and stay crime free.

MEDA CHESNEY-LIND, PHD
Professor Emerita
Department of Women, Gender, and Sexuality Studies
University of Hawaii at Manoa

This book clearly displays the years of work Dr. Covington has spent aiding incarcerated women. She shares with us another side of incarcerated women that is usually unknown. Even in prison, women have the ability to remain compassionate, empathetic, and helpful to each other in the face of their own trauma. These characteristics enable their healing in a system that often remains ignorant and unforgiving.

DAWN S. DAVISON
Former Warden and Correctional Consultant
Los Angeles, California

Hidden Healers is a brilliant and rattling study of women's journeys into imprisonment, their stories of abuse and pathways into crime (often born of psychological trauma), their unnecessary degradation and humiliation upon arrival in prison, and their ongoing pain from the daily grind of imprisonment. Yet it is also a story of women's survival and support for one another. Stephanie Covington captures the different ways women transform their lives against the odds and help to heal one another. The great strength of this book is that Covington tells it like it is. Compelling and incredibly moving.

LORAINE GELSTHORPE, PHD
Professor, Institute of Criminology
University of Cambridge, United Kingdom

~

It is not enough for us to be concerned about mass incarceration and to advocate for criminal justice reform. Like creating a powerful photomosaic, Dr. Covington shares the details of women's lives—before, during and after incarceration—so that we can really grasp the big picture of what is not working and what needs to change. Accurate, compelling, compassionate.

ANN L. JACOBS
Formerly Executive Director
John Jay College Institute for Justice and Opportunity
Women's Prison Association
New York, New York

~

Read this thoughtful book and be inspired to take action to transform our broken criminal legal system. Stephanie Covington, who draws on her extensive expertise and profound experiences working with incarcerated women, is just the guide we need to begin that journey.

REBECCA EPSTEIN
Executive Director
The Center for Gender Justice & Opportunity at Georgetown Law
Washington, DC

~

"The US population has been taught to fear incarcerated people and to believe they 'deserve' any punishment that is meted upon them," writes Stephanie Covington in her new book, *Hidden Healers: The Unexpected Ways Women in Prison Help Each Other Survive*. "In addition, Americans have been told that when more people are put away, the people living out in community are safer." In this captivating book, told through the experiences of women who have been in prison or are still there, not only does Covington blast those myths to smithereens, she reveals the healing work she's been doing in US prisons for the last 35 years. Covington provides many useful, truly useful, ways for to you to help replace this inhumane travesty of a system with an approach that truly heals.

JANE STEVENS
Founder of PACEs Connection
Publisher of ACEsTooHigh.com

Hidden Healers offers a critically important and poignant insight into the lives of women and their families—what pushes them into the justice system, their lived experience while inside, their experience transitioning out of it. What reverberates off the pages is the profound harm and cost not only to them, but to their children, communities, and society. This book issues a call to action to envision and make real a new way forward while also providing resources and discussion questions to support us in learning and doing more!

JEANNETTE PAI-ESPINOSA
President, National Crittenton
Portland, Oregon

Dr. Stephanie Covington's book *Hidden Healers* sheds light on human experiences that are often difficult to express verbally. As I reflected on my own experiences in prison, I could relate to the feelings of powerlessness expressed in the book. Reading about these experiences hit me unexpectedly hard. I hope Dr. Covington's book catalyzes a human-centered approach to intervention and resolution.

EL SAWYER
Co-director and producer of the film Pull of Gravity
Co-founder, Media in Neighborhoods Group
Philadelphia, Pennsylvania

Hidden Healers guides the reader on a journey through the criminal legal system from sentencing through incarceration to release. But it is unlike any other book you will read about women in prison. It conveys the terror and isolation of a first night in prison, the disgust of prison food, the desperation of women trying to mother whilst in prison, the tragedy of being unable to grieve loss, the shame of giving birth under sentence, the insecurity caused by inadequate healthcare, and the emotional resilience needed to merely survive from one day to the next. For each of these challenges, there are stories of women reaching out to offer practical and emotional support and human connection in institutions designed to dehumanize. Read this book for an accessible introduction to the working of the criminal legal system, a critique of the harms it inflicts on women, and uplifting stories of women coming together to survive.

MADELINE PETRILLO, PHD
Senior Lecturer in Criminology
University of Greenwich, United Kingdom

Great thanks to Stephanie Covington for providing a chilling look into the traumatic lives of women in prison. Written in simple, clear language, it provides graphic detail about the tragic reality of the lives of incarcerated women. It requires an open mind, a series of deep breaths, and a willingness to jump into the black hole of justice and punishment American-style. The author explains that most women populating our country's prisons and jails were born into poverty, many suffered racism, and all are victims of horrific trauma having to do with their environment. *Hidden Healers* is a book that begs for a painstaking evaluation of our collective thinking that has allowed our "justice" systems to continue to retraumatize the women (and men) in our prisons. When we fail to scrutinize our core beliefs about what it means to do justice, we cannot reduce our incarcerated population or the crime and violence that feeds it. *Hidden Healers* is powerful.

ROBERT REED
Executive Deputy Attorney General for Special Initiatives
Pennsylvania Attorney General
Chair, Pennsylvania Reentry Council
Philadelphia, Pennsylvania

Hidden Healers is an essential resource for anyone working with or advocating for incarcerated women. It explores the urgent need for change to address the carceral system's deeply harmful impacts. It also illustrates how women connect with and support each other, formally and informally, to heal.

MARILYN VAN DIETEN, PHD
Senior Advisor, Center for Effective Public Policy
Project Director, National Resource Center on Justice Involved Women

With grace, clarity, insight, wisdom and compassion, Dr. Covington shines a light on one of the darkest and most misunderstood corners of our communities. In the voices of women who have been there, she illuminates the systems that perpetuate the harms. Truths such as "all prisons are bad; some are just worse than others," and "we should be working both to better support incarcerated people today and to dismantle and completely rethink the system for the future" bring to light the complexities of the problems we face and the question of "where do we go from here?"

LORRAINE ROBINSON, MSW
Former Executive Director
Ka Hale Hoʻala Hou No Na Wahine (the home of reawakening for women)
Honolulu, Hawaii

I read Stephanie Covington's book *Hidden Healers* with deep appreciation. The challenges women in prison face and the ways they survive, with the right help and through Covington's self-help training, is inspiring. The book is also a witness to the bitter failure of the United States' correctional system to meet the women with humanity. Women in prisons are a hidden group. They are a minority in the very gendered correctional system and, as in my country, the data about them is also hidden. The book is both a sharp reminder of how much work is needed to reinvent the correctional system and a testimony to the strength and healing power of the incarcerated women we get to know through Covington's insightful overview.

KRISTÍN I. PÁLSDÓTTIR
CEO, The Root (Rótin) Association on Women, Alcohol, and Addiction
Iceland

Building on a remarkable thirty-year career in this space, Dr. Stephanie Covington's new and timely book brings the hidden voices of justice-involved women to the fore, particularly significant in an era which has seen a sharp incline in their imprisonment rates globally. Exploring both the complexity and diversity of relationships formed among women in prison, Covington highlights how women survive in a flawed and dehumanizing environment that strips them bare—figuratively and literally. In stories that will be familiar to those who work on behalf of women involved in the criminal legal system and eye opening for those who do not, Covington's accessible, truthful, and always compassionate *Hidden Healers* is bound to gain new allies and, most important and urgently, help advance alternative responses that heal instead of harm. No matter who you are, let's all do "one small thing."

MANDY WILSON, PHD
Anthropologist, Research Fellow, and Justice Health Program Lead
National Drug Research Institute
Curtin University, Western Australia

Hidden Healers

Hidden Healers

The Unexpected Ways Women in Prison Help Each Other Survive

STEPHANIE S. COVINGTON

WILEY

Published by John Wiley & Sons, Inc., Hoboken, New Jersey.
Published simultaneously in Canada.

For general information on our other products and services or for technical support, please contact our Customer Care Department within the United States at (800) 762-2974, outside the United States at (317) 572-3993 or fax (317) 572-4002.

Wiley also publishes its books in a variety of electronic formats. Some content that appears in print may not be available in electronic formats. For more information about Wiley products, visit our web site at www.wiley.com.

Library of Congress Cataloging-in-Publication Data

Names: Covington, Stephanie, author.
Title: Hidden healers : the unexpected ways women in prison help each other survive / Stephanie S. Covington, Center for Gender & Justice, Del Mar, CA.
Description: Hoboken, New Jersey : Wiley, [2024]
Identifiers: LCCN 2024000267 (print) | LCCN 2024000268 (ebook) | ISBN 9781394254392 (paperback) | ISBN 9781394254415 (adobe pdf) | ISBN 9781394254408 (epub)
Subjects: LCSH: Women prisoners–United States–Psychology. | Women prisoners–United States–Social conditions. | Women–Violence against–United States. | Prison psychology–United States.
Classification: LCC HV9471 .C68 2024 (print) | LCC HV9471 (ebook) | DDC 365/.430973–dc23/eng/20240201
LC record available at https://lccn.loc.gov/2024000267
LC ebook record available at https://lccn.loc.gov/2024000268

Cover Design: Wiley
Cover Image: © NatalyFox/Shutterstock, aristotoo/Getty Images

Set in 10/12pt AdobeGaramondPro by Straive, Pondicherry, India
SKY10070023_032024

Prisons do not disappear social problems,
they disappear human beings.

—Angela Davis

To the women still inside who are unseen and unheard

Contents

Acknowledgments

FIRST AND FOREMOST, this book would not be a reality without the women I interviewed. The willingness of formerly incarcerated women to remember and share their experiences with me was a gift and provides the heart of this book. Those who have worked in the system have also contributed their insightful stories. I am so grateful for every interviewee's openness to this project and their support in creating *Hidden Healers*.

Over the years I have undertaken many writing projects. Each one has been unique and each one has benefited from a wonderful team. The *Hidden Healers* team continues this tradition with both new participants and some from the past. Thank you to Gina Walter at PageMill Press for excellent transcription and helpful feedback. Another new team member is Vanessa Carlisle, who played a major role in making this book a reality. She not only participated in all of the interviews, she organized each section and incorporated my years of experience. She's been a great writing partner. Kathryn Robinson provided skillful polishing as well as enthusiasm for this project. I also want to thank those who read the various drafts and made important suggestions: Barbara Bloom, Becky Novelli, Barbara Owen, Penny Philpot, and Sharon Young. A special thank you to Michele Zousmer for the use of her photographs.

Then there are the three who have worked with me on other projects. Laura Waligorski not only manages the office with great skill, she managed to fulfill my odd requests for the minutia needed for a manuscript. Roy M. Carlisle at PageMill Press receives a major thank you from me as well—he edited my first book, published in 1988, then decades later asked me to write another. I told him there *was* a book I'd been thinking about for upwards of fifteen years, the project of my heart, but that I'd decided not to do it. He talked me into it, and how pleased I have been to write *Hidden Healers*.

And the last and most important thank you is for Penny Philpot. She has supported me and my work in so many ways for over thirty years. Each project bears her imprint.

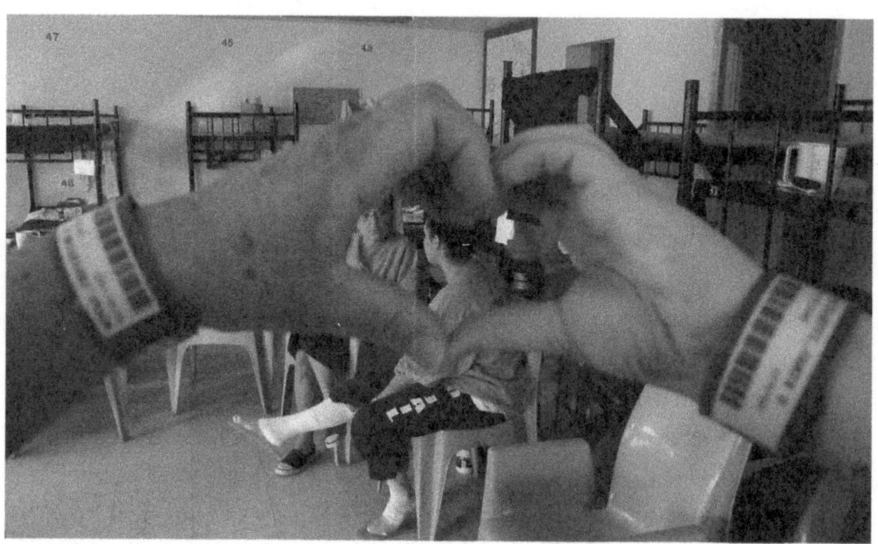

Source: Michele Zousmer.

A Note from a Hidden Healer: It's Time for Change

FOR OVER TWENTY years, I was trapped in repeated cycles of incarceration, molestation, and degradation. Homeless when I was on the outside, relegated to a number and forced into a two-by-two cage when I was on the inside—I cycled through layers of trauma and pain I neither acknowledged nor understood.

Prison is not an environment conducive to healing, but for me, the opportunity to heal presented itself there. I participated in a pilot program that used *A Woman's Way through the Twelve Steps* by Dr. Stephanie Covington, who had already gained a reputation within her fields of addiction and trauma and was expanding into programming for incarcerated women. Prior to Dr. Covington and her colleagues Dr. Bloom and Dr. Owen, no one working with incarcerated women talked about how trauma lived under the skin and in our DNA. That book helped me to understand my history of trauma and opened me up to cry about what I'd been through. I connected with other women who had similar experiences. I learned that when we start to share our pain with each other, we can help each other.

That is the important work that Dr. Covington offers. She gives us a chance to look both inward and outward, to accept responsibility for what was our doing and to understand the harm that came to us that was *not* our doing. I benefited directly from the work she did, and I would not have been able to rise above my pain without her work. I'm just one of the many sparkles from the diamond she created.

Today I am the founder and ambassador at the Time for Change Foundation. The mission of TFCF is to empower disenfranchised low-income individuals and families by building leadership through evidence-based programs and housing, creating self-sufficiency, and thriving communities. Since we started in 2002, we have helped reunite 315 children from foster care with their mothers, and we have helped over 1,700 homeless women and children become self-sufficient through our supportive housing and innovative programs.

The Time for Change Foundation is now considered the model of excellence across the globe for empowering disenfranchised families transitioning from homelessness and recidivism. Additionally, I'm the president and CEO of the Center for Housing Advancement and Motivational Projects where I train probation, parole, and other community-based organizations to effectively implement evidence-based programs and services … the programs and services that actually *work*.

I went from being homeless to building affordable housing for low-income women. I went from breaking laws to making laws, and now I work with others to do the same. Inspired by public health, I created a social-ecological epidemiological model coined "The Disease of Incarceration" to articulate incarceration as a public health issue—a model that was accepted by the American Public Health Association. Using this model for our programmatic services and interventions has yielded tremendous success, with great impact in the lives of the people we serve.

Fighting against "ex-con" stereotypes has always been a challenge; I remember not getting calls back from government applications that I submitted. Today those same governments contract millions of dollars to me. Being in a position to actually help those coming from prison has been my greatest reward. I get to make helping tangible, where folks can actually receive the help they need, because we take care of the bureaucracy on the backend.

I've also had to push up against people who didn't want to see formerly incarcerated folks reenter. There may be an empty lot sitting around for fifty years doing nothing but collecting trash, but the minute I have a housing project to build on it, millionaires are rolling out of bed to come fight me in a city council meeting. Systemic racism and sexism affect every level of change we are trying to make, but our fight is relentless, and we don't stop. It's the air that we breathe; it's the pursuit of justice for all.

I was stunned when Dr. Covington told me her book was going to be titled *Hidden Healers*. Hiding isn't something we do intentionally; it's the result of a society that renders people like me—Black, beautiful, brilliant—invisible. We're right here; we always have been. There are so many brilliant women who can do so much. We live, we exist, we have value, and our work matters. By holding up the experience and ideas of formerly incarcerated women, we now have programs that work, we know how to reduce recidivism, and we have solutions.

It is time for change. Our voices have been heard, our evaluations are in, and our impact is undeniable. I'm grateful for the support Dr. Covington's work has offered over the years and for the transformation this book is a critical part of. We are the help we have been waiting on—women helping women.

Kim Carter, *timeforchangefoundation.org*
January 2024
Author, *Waking Up to My Purpose*
Featured in the film, *Tell It Like a Woman*

Introduction

YOU TURN YOUR face to the sun as you shuffle behind a woman in a bright orange jumpsuit. Your ankle chains scrape the ground. You try to match your steps with both the woman in front and the woman behind you in line. You savor the warmth in the air for a moment before you step carefully into an old van with metal seats. You are cuffed to a metal chain around your waist, attached to the woman next to you, and you do not have a seat belt. Your bench mate stares through the metal grate over the window.

You are on your way from the county jail to the prison where you will live for years. Even knowing your sentence, there is no way to know exactly how many years. You hope to earn time off, but you know there could be trouble inside that adds time or changes in the laws that affect you. You try to slide your glasses back up your nose with your forearm, lifting your cuffed hand and ducking your head, without disturbing the woman pressed into your side. They made you throw away your contact lenses. They made you throw away your street clothes. You have no personal effects coming with you to prison. Every time your mind reaches for something familiar it comes back with nothing. You focus on that moment of sunlight, that moment of warmth you felt, as the van seems to get colder and colder.

You haven't been in a moving vehicle for over a year. The van is moving too fast. It seems too close to other cars. Every turn slams you into either a person or the window as you slide along the metal bench. Your heart races. It will be better in prison, you reassure yourself. It has to be. You want to smell green grass. You want to see the sky. You want to wear regular shoes, not the plastic slides you've had on for months. Prison is better than jail. Everyone told you so. But nothing about this feels better.

When the van stops, you enter a large, spare waiting room with a dozen other women. You are ordered to take off your jumpsuit and underwear and throw them into a plastic trash bin, and you stand, huddled and naked, waiting for the officers to come back. One uniformed woman officer returns and tells you all to line up with your hands on the wall and bend over, then squat and cough. You do your best to avoid looking at the women next to you. You think, *At least I'm not getting searched alone somewhere.* This feels humiliating, but safer.

They send you in groups to the shower. The water goes from cold to scalding, then back again. When asked for your prison number, you recite it. You receive a uniform: baggy pants and a smock made of thick, rough canvas. But here, you get closed-toed shoes! And then you wait in a holding cell. For hours. You are hungry, but you were transferred during mealtime, so you won't be offered food again until tomorrow. You are cold, but you've been issued all your clothes. You steal a few looks at women around you—some from the same van, some from other facilities. A few of them seem agitated, maybe experiencing symptoms of drug withdrawal. A few of them know each other, seem at ease, and chat like they were sitting in their own living rooms. A few, like you, are staying quiet and watchful.

After weeks of living in the reception center for your processing, it's your turn to talk to the counselor, who has a reputation for hitting on the women he sees. His job is to assess you for physical health needs, mental health needs, and your potential for violence. His assessment determines where you are housed and whether you receive regular medical or mental health services. You don't want to be singled out for unwanted attention, so you try to answer his questions clearly and truthfully. He seizes on a few very personal details from your file. He tries to get you to "open up." He asks you if you think he's handsome. You avoid a full answer. You hide your disgust.

Later on, you'll hear from another woman that she became sexually involved with this counselor when he hit on her because she was afraid he'd place her in a more dangerous housing unit if she didn't. You will encourage her to file a report. She won't, because the counselor would see it, and she fears retaliation. You wonder how many women he has preyed upon without consequence.

The day you are assigned permanent housing you have butterflies in your stomach. You are going to meet someone with whom you will share unprecedented intimacies: every bodily function, every poor night's sleep, every emotionally intense visiting day. You hope she is kind. You hope she is sober. You hope she is calm. You hope you can maintain some boundaries and also treat each other well. You carry your small plastic bag of belongings acquired during your weeks in the reception center—a pair of underwear and a ChapStick from the commissary—and wait for the officer to unlock the door to your new cell. "Hey there," an older woman's voice reaches you. "Your stuff goes in the locker on the left."

As you adjust to your new situation, you begin to feel the strain of daily life in prison. You have not spoken to anyone here about why you are incarcerated, but somehow many of them know, and you feel exposed and raw. There is one male officer in particular who likes to give you extra chores and make crude remarks to you while you do them. When a woman is sick, he makes you mop it up, telling you to just keep bending over. The smell of decades-old floor wax, bleach, and vomit makes you lightheaded and you can't wait to shower. You have never processed the trauma that brought you here. Your body begins to show your stress: your hair thins, your skin goes patchy, you feel somehow both hungry and bloated all the time. You struggle to get through each day, measuring time by the one communal phone: two hours until you can speak to your daughter, then another twenty-four.

You have not yet been assessed for job skills that might be useful to the prison's internal ecosystem. A few experiences using the drugs available inside have not yet become a habit you have to address. You have not yet developed intractable digestive issues from the cafeteria's food. You have not yet spent the night in tears after a visit with your daughter and your mother, who is still angry with you for putting her in this situation.

For a while you suffer alone, because you have not yet found the other women living in the prison who can help you make it through your time.

In this story you are both brave and lucky. In this story, despite the pain and exhaustion of surviving daily life in prison, you will find a small circle of women you can trust. You will find them in a support group, or sitting together in the dayroom, or laughing in line for the shower, and you will feel safer when you are with them. You will find women who want you to work a program, to keep your eye on securing a release date. You will find women with whom you can share your story. With their help, you will survive, and because of their care, you will begin to heal.

Ask yourself: What do you know about women in prison? There are plenty of myths and stereotypes, sensational media portrayals, and insensitive jokes, but what do you really *know*? Prisons belong to us, like schools, hospitals, and other public services. We are responsible for what happens in them. Yet unless you have been there, or been close to someone who has, it is likely you know very little about women in prison.

This lack of information is a problem. It contributes to widespread injustice and fractured communities. It is time for us living on the outside to understand more about what happens inside women's prisons and how women survive the brutal experience of incarceration. Is it easy to read about? No. Many of the scenarios you will encounter throughout this book are horrific and will be triggering for some. But I believe that for those who can, exposing oneself to the realities of our criminal legal system is critical. It is important to examine our own beliefs and assumptions about how the criminal legal system works, who is incarcerated, and what happens while they are inside.

It is one thing to suspect our current system isn't working in the abstract. It is another to encounter stories directly from women who have lived through it. We cannot change something we are unaware of. This is true in our personal lives and equally true for social issues. Each of the women I interviewed for this discussion has had a unique path, but they all agree that the way we do "justice" in this country is unconscionable. As a result of hearing more of their stories, I hope you will be motivated to take practical action and join us in making change.

My Time Inside: Black Mountain, North Carolina, 1987

Over thirty-five years ago, I talked my way into a three-day prison stay in the Black Mountain Correctional Center for Women, a (now closed) minimum-security facility in North Carolina.

This is a view of the yard at the former Black Mountain Correctional Center for Women with housing on the left and the administration building on right.

Source: North Carolina Department of Public Safety.

I wasn't being held there against my will, like everyone else. I was there to observe and to learn. As a social worker, a psychologist, and especially as a trauma and addiction specialist, I was there to confront the pervasive silence, the cultural void, which keeps most of us from knowing how incarcerated women lived. I wanted to understand how it was that I knew nothing about women in prison. I wanted to address their invisibility in my professional and personal life. Freedom was deeply important to me, and I felt compelled to understand what it was like to live without it.

At the time, I was seeing clients in private practice, speaking at conferences, and providing consultation to women's treatment programs. I had been in recovery and sober for almost ten years, during which time I divorced my husband, embraced my identity as a lesbian, and earned a doctorate degree in psychology. In the year before my stay at Black Mountain, I was speaking at one of very few conferences on addiction where women's issues were centered, advocating for gender-responsive programming for women in the community. I saw an attendee with a different name tag than the rest: it said *warden*. I introduced myself.

The warden told me she worked at the nearby women's prison in Black Mountain. She also told me she was bringing six honorees from the prison where she worked to my talk that evening. That night, standing among that group of women, all I could think was, *Why are you in there and I'm out here?* It was a huge realization of my privilege.

While I was drinking, I certainly broke laws. I had driven under the influence of alcohol many times. Once in my early twenties I was enabled by my father, who fixed my mother's car in secret after I'd gotten into an accident. It had been just the luck of the draw that I hadn't hurt myself or someone else more seriously. Standing in a circle with women who were currently living inside a prison, I felt the certainty that anyone could get caught up in the system. Then it struck me that even if I had harmed someone during my active addiction, I was white and had resources, and my trial and incarceration would have reflected that privilege too.

I was still naive about the criminal justice system, but I knew there was something very wrong with the fact that incarcerated women had not been on my radar until that evening.

About a year later I was sitting on a thin mattress atop a metal cot in a grimy beige room with two other roommates. I already wished they hadn't taken my hand lotion at the gate. I could bring in a toothbrush, but no shampoo or conditioner. We each had sixteen inches of closet space. No chairs. One very small window on the high end of a blank wall. I didn't know what to expect. Why did I fight so hard to do this? Would anyone talk to me?

Although I didn't ask them to, my roommates volunteered their stories. One of my roommates had done sex work and had been in and out of the criminal system many times. The other was a woman who had been stealing for her kids after a divorce left her destitute. I remember the small, dirty lamp we had because she would turn it on at night to read her Bible.

They asked me how I got there, and I told them the truth: that I had talked the warden into letting me stay inside the facility for a few days. I told them that I had done work for women's recovery programming but had never worked with women in prison, and because I knew nothing about it I felt I needed to come inside. They were surprised, but they kept my project to themselves and we got along well.

I wore the uniform: a pair of boxy pants and a wide shirt that reminded me of hospital scrubs cut for a large man. I walked with my roommates to meals, and I got in trouble for trying to close our door at night because the lights in the hallway never went off.

If I hadn't been so interested in observing everything, I would have been bored out of my mind. There were long stretches of hours with nothing going on. My observation then, and something that the women I interviewed for this book all tried to describe, is the way prison is both a place of terrible pain and tremendous waste. It is paradoxically both traumatic and mind-numbingly uninteresting. It is not something that can be made into a metaphor, because there is actually nothing that is "like prison." Prison is an all-encompassing experience.

Some of the regulations made absolutely no sense, and then they would change unpredictably. On the second day, the morning alarm that should have startled us all awake never went off. We all slept through breakfast, and there was no apology, no discussion. I always felt slightly off because there was no way to get it right. We had to be present for count, do chores, eat bland and unappetizing food, and watch television in the dayroom. Some women could afford cigarettes and junk food from the commissary. Everything inside was monochromatic—beige, brown, gray, and not quite filthy but never truly clean. The wax on the linoleum floors sealed in the grime, like you see in an old school.

I was lost and felt small. It was so clear to me all along that the only way I managed was because of the other incarcerated women telling me how. They asked me if I had a roll of toilet paper. I said, No, isn't there any in the bathroom? No, they said. Absolutely not. You have to have your own roll. They asked me if I had shower shoes; I did not. Was I supposed to? Yes, of course, or you'll get fungus on your feet. They told me to go to the front office, because they had things in the closet I could ask for. They told me I was not to use the bar soap on my face, because it would take my skin off. We use that soap for our sneakers, they told me.

I entered a conversation with a woman in the hallway, and I asked her to come into my room to sit down and talk. She told me no, of course she couldn't do that. She told me she was a lesbian. "It means they watch me really closely here," she said. I hadn't known there was a rule against going into another person's room. It made sense when I thought it through, but no one had told me. There was no way to know anything until you stumbled into it. I must have seemed extremely strange to her.

On the day I left, the warden had a barbecue where I got to thank the women I had gotten to know for helping me through the experience. When they found out I was a psychologist and social worker, they had a lot of questions. One of them privately asked if I could give her some advice. She had a two-year-old and was afraid her husband was sexually abusing the child. She was afraid to tell anyone because the child would be taken away and sent into the foster care system, and she would lose her. So she was trying to decide if she should tell someone and lose her child or not say anything and sort it out when she got out of prison. This is not the kind of decision most people will ever have to face. It was heartbreaking. Over the years I have heard many stories, from many incarcerated women, that are equally heartbreaking.

When I left Black Mountain I knew I wanted to work with women in prison, I just didn't know how. I wasn't connected to anyone in the system. As I readjusted to my life outside, I was struck by how surreal it all seemed. I was newly aware of how much people on the outside take for granted: wearing their own clothes, closing a door, turning off a light. I let the experience simmer for a few days. Shortly after, I began trying to help set up some reentry support for women leaving the Black Mountain facility. Slowly, my work grew from there.

I would never say I have lived the experience of incarceration— that would be arrogant and ridiculous. I have had the experience of living for a few days inside a prison. I had my life, home, and work to come back to, and I knew I could leave at any time. What I will say is that my experience was like shining a flashlight in a dark room. I saw a little sliver of something. That something started me on a path.

Incarcerated Women Are Made Invisible

The conditions inside American prisons are disastrous. Overcrowding, poor-quality food, lack of health care, and lack of access to phone calls and visitation are all so common they are considered normal. Many Americans hold erroneous beliefs about how our criminal legal system works, so they do not understand the way lengthy pretrial detention and plea bargaining affect millions of people and their communities.

Individuals who experience incarceration live under a lifetime burden of stigma, which affects their job prospects, connections with family, and long-term health outcomes.

While all people in prison are hidden and made invisible to the community, women are doubly so (1). First, in a corrections industry built for men, the needs of women and gender-diverse people are not prioritized and are often outright ignored. Second, women are invisible to both the outside world and to the system they live in. Although the number of women incarcerated in the United States has risen 700 percent since 1980, women still make up only about 8 percent of the overall incarcerated population (2).

Women returning to community after incarceration often feel they must hide their history in order to find decent work and housing, which reinforces their invisibility. The stigma endured by people with criminal histories is robust and constantly present in American media, policy, and law. When women speak out about maltreatment inside prison, they are often met with such comments as, "You shouldn't have been there in the first place," "It's your fault, you put yourself there," or "You should have thought about that before you did what you did." They do not receive thorough attention to their situation or to the legacies of harm that made them vulnerable to incarceration. From inside, women speaking out about conditions in prison—through phone calls or mail, all of which is monitored—is considered a transgression deserving of more punishment.

Women impacted by our criminal justice system suffer a secondary stigma because of their gender: they are seen not just as bad people because of their contact with law enforcement, but also as *failed women*. Intense, often violent sexism is levied at incarcerated and formerly incarcerated women. Many formerly incarcerated women already do not want to talk about their experience inside because of how painful it was. When they try, people do not listen. They are silenced at every turn.

My first goal in *Hidden Healers*, then, is to take readers on a journey inside this occluded world, to shine a light on what must no longer remain hidden. It begins with Part One, "Entering the System," an overview of the criminal justice system for women in the United States. Although this book is intended for an audience that has had little contact with courts, jails, and prisons, those who are more experienced will still find useful information pertaining to the specific experiences of women in a system originally designed for men, especially when it comes to discussing trauma as a pathway to incarceration.

In Part Two, "Living Inside," we explore daily life inside women's prisons and how women help each other to navigate the pressures of mental and physical health concerns, visiting, parenting, relationships, and more. Part Three, "The Journey Home," is a look at women's experiences in parole systems, reentry services (or lack thereof), and rebuilding life after incarceration. In Part Four, "What We Can Do," we enter the work of envisioning alternatives to incarceration and taking action to support projects already under way.

JUST THE FACTS

Male versus Female Incarceration

In 2019, 92 percent of all incarcerated people in the United States were male.

Rate of Rise in Female Incarceration

Since 1980 the number of incarcerated women has grown by 700 percent—double the rate of men.

Numbers of Women Incarcerated in Prisons and Jails

As of a March 2023 report, 162,000 women and 10,700 girls are incarcerated in the United States (3). Of the incarcerated women,

» 72,000 are in prisons,
» 76,000 are in local jails, and
» 14,000 are in federal prisons and jails.

Numbers of Women in Community Supervision

Incarcerated women represent just 18 percent of women under correctional control; 808,700 women are on probation or parole.

Racial/Ethnic Breakdown

Incarcerated women are

» 53 percent white,
» 29 percent Black,
» 14 percent Latina,
» 2.5 percent American Indian or Alaska Native,
» 0.9 percent Asian, and
» 0.4 percent Native Hawaiian and Pacific Islander (4).

Education

Of incarcerated women, 53 percent did not finish high school.

Childhood Adversity

- 12 percent of incarcerated women report homelessness before they turned eighteen.
- 19 percent of incarcerated women were in the foster care system.
- 43 percent of incarcerated women came from families that received welfare or other public assistance.

Almost half (45 percent) of incarcerated women had been arrested by age eighteen.

Parental Status

- 58 percent of incarcerated women are parents of minor children, versus 46 percent of incarcerated men.
- 39 percent of incarcerated mothers with minor children live in single parent–led households, versus 21 percent of incarcerated fathers with minor children.
- 52 percent of incarcerated women lived with their children prior to their imprisonment, versus 40 percent of incarcerated men.

Because of this, incarceration of women is more likely to uproot children, terminate parental rights, and permanently break up families (5).

Type of Offense

For women within state prisons,

- 45 percent are serving time for a violent offense,
- 20 percent for property offenses,
- 25 percent for drug offenses, and
- 10 percent for public order offenses.

Within local jails, fully 61 percent of incarcerated women are not yet convicted.

Before the Arrest that Led to Their Incarceration ...

- over a quarter of women (26 percent) experienced homelessness, versus 16 percent of men, in the year before their arrest;
- over half (53 percent) of women were unemployed in the month before their arrest;
- over half (58 percent) of women met the criteria for a substance use disorder, a significantly higher rate than for men, in the year before their arrest; and
- over three quarters (76 percent) of women had some indication of a past or current mental health problem, a significantly higher rate than for men, in the year before their arrest (6).

Trauma in Prison, Trauma of Prison

Within five years of my three-day prison stay, I had completely shifted my professional focus to developing an understanding of the needs of incarcerated women. For the next thirty years I wrote curricula, books, and papers on trauma, addiction, and recovery with a focus on women in prison. I conducted trainings for staff, ran therapeutic groups for prison residents, and consulted with administrations. I worked to change policies, secure grants for research, and offer high-quality programming to women who live inside prisons. I am proud that a women's residential treatment house operated by the Nelson Trust in the United Kingdom has been renamed "Covington House."

The US population has been taught to fear incarcerated people and to believe they "deserve" any punishment that is meted to them. In addition, Americans have been told that when more people are put away, the people living out in community are safer. These myths are rooted in racism, classism, sexism, and the many other -isms.

For many justice-impacted women, incarceration is both a personal and a historical trauma. The violent histories of slavery, residential schools for Native American children, internment of Japanese people during World War II, and other acts of systemic racism have all impacted communities for generations and contribute in many ways to the dynamics we see in prisons today. Imprisonment has generational impacts, especially for women with children.

At the beginning of my work with incarcerated women, I had much more faith in the possibilities of prison reform. I am still a consultant and trainer for many different Departments of Corrections, which I consider to be one way to reduce the harms of incarceration. Since the early days, when concepts like *trauma informed* and *trauma responsive*[1] were not yet popular buzzwords, I have spent countless hours trying to convince prison staff and administrators to acknowledge and understand the effects of trauma.

[1] My trauma-focused work takes place on three levels: ***trauma-informed services*** include information we need to know about how trauma impacts people, ***trauma-responsive services*** include what we need to do (policies, practices, and environmental concerns) when we work with trauma survivors, and ***trauma-specific services*** are the programs we need to provide.

Indeed, as someone who has been working within the system for decades to advocate for change, I feel I am well positioned to make the claim that women who survive their imprisonment do so despite the criminal legal system, not because of it. What I've learned in this work is that the current criminal legal system—including the complex set of reentry requirements—does much more harm than good.

I no longer advocate for prison reform because I no longer believe the US criminal system can be fixed. It must be completely dismantled and rethought from the ground up. The question of what happens when harm is caused in a community is never answered by the harms that are then caused in prison.

That said, this book is not a map to an abolition solution. There are many people doing the important work of articulating the vision of abolition, and some I've learned from are listed in the resources section. Although systems are interlinked, I will not directly address issues in the civil system, such as immigrant detention, or the justice systems of sovereign tribal nations. I simply haven't worked in those systems. I would love to see information like ours emerge from someone who has.

How Women Survive Prison

Donna was in jail for two months awaiting trial when she found out she had cancer and needed surgery. During the course of her treatment, she received a long-term prison sentence and began serving her time. She recovered from surgery inside prison. As part of her recovery, Donna was prescribed a clear liquid diet. Prison staff told Donna they could not accommodate her needs. They told her she should "just drink water." She calls that moment "the bottom of my life."

Donna survived because the women she lived with inside the prison came to her aid. "They took care of me," she said. "We get each other through it." Friends close to her provided Donna with soups and other liquids she could drink by spending their own commissary money, a form of gift that is technically disallowed. They made sure she got her medication on time by threatening not to leave her cell until staff responded.

On visiting days Donna's friends would come to her cell before her children arrived and help her bathe, comb her hair, brush her teeth, and put on makeup so she wouldn't look too sick for her kids. If she broke down after her kids left, her friends would write her cards and spend time talking with her. They hugged her, another form of social support that is against prison rules. Donna survived because the women she met inside helped her, and they helped her despite the risk of being disciplined.

It was in response to stories like Donna's that *Hidden Healers* began to take shape for me—to document the brutalities within the criminal legal system, yes, but even more as a testimonial of the many affecting ways, large and small, that women help each other to survive them. These reflections come from interviewing formerly incarcerated women and my own observations from many years of developing and running therapeutic programming for incarcerated women.

Given their trauma I am amazed by the resilience, kindness, wisdom, and strength that women living in prison have consistently brought to my life and work, and even more important, to each other. Many formerly incarcerated women are able to develop what some professionals would call post-traumatic growth, a set of positive psychological changes that can emerge from a major life crisis. Post-traumatic growth does not happen in a vacuum. Several factors facilitate the process: receiving care from supportive people, approaching versus avoiding grief, and recognizing that a person needs to be in control of the timing of their recovery process (7).

During my stay at the Black Mountain facility, I witnessed how the women I met were in terrible pain. I saw their lives being wasted by incarceration rather than restored. I saw that they had to rely on each other in ways I'd never considered before, adapting to the stressors of unpredictable prison environments by using what they have to help themselves and each other. They make shower shoes out of maxi pads when there aren't enough plastic shoes. They use their clothing to make pillows for aching necks and knees. They repurpose food from the kitchen or commissary to make dishes to share that remind them of home.

They respond to the pain of incarceration, both theirs and other women's, by being of service. Many of them continue to expand their strengths and be of service to others after their release. Although not all of the women inside a prison find opportunities to begin healing, many more do than the stereotypes would suggest. This they do in spite of their environment and in the face of incredible odds and obstacles.

Women experience a great deal of loss and pain in custodial settings. Often the best (and sometimes only) person to talk to and share your pain is another woman.

Source: Michele Zousmer.

The Language We Use

In his book *Just Mercy: A Story of Justice and Redemption*, Bryan Stevenson famously said, "Each of us is more than the worst thing we've ever done." When people outside prison use words like *convict*, *felon*, *inmate*, and *offender*, we are identifying someone by their status in the criminal legal system, which is often the same as labeling their entire person by the worst thing they've ever done. It is similar to labeling their entire person by the way they have been stigmatized via their race, class, neighborhood, group affiliation, or gender. These labels get attached to a person forever.

This is also the language of the corrections industry, which is overtly punitive despite occasional nods at rehabilitation. Although incarcerated women will often refer to each other using this language, this does not give permission for others to use it. Throughout our discussion I will use *incarcerated women*, *prison residents*, *justice-involved* and *justice-impacted women*, and *women living inside a prison*. My intention throughout *Hidden Healers* is to avoid stigmatizing language, to stay accessible to a broad audience, and to be accurate.

Although many people are used to the phrase *criminal justice system*, I have begun to replace this phrase in my own work with *criminal legal system*. We have a legal system that criminalizes people who are already impacted by racism, poverty, and the effects of trauma, such as substance use concerns and mental health issues. Overall, that system is not about justice. At the same time, because the term *criminal justice* is so common, I sometimes use *justice impacted* to refer to the millions of Americans who are in custody, under supervision, or experiencing secondary effects of incarceration. I think terms like *prison industrial complex* and *criminal punishment system* are accurate ways to describe our current system, even though I tend not to use them for simplicity and accessibility in my own work.

Corrections refers both to the industries that surround and support the prisons and jails, and to the staff and administration who run facilities. It is ironic to me because nothing gets "corrected" by prison. However, for accuracy I attempt to call personnel by their titles, such as *corrections officer* (*CO*), *warden*, *captain*, and so on. Sometimes incarcerated women will refer to *guards* or even *cops* when they are talking about corrections officers, and I have tried to maintain some consistency and clarity throughout while preserving their voices.

Everywhere, prison systems operate on a gender binary. All people are perceived to fit either the category of "woman" or "man," and they are housed according to their sex assigned at birth. This means there is no foundational understanding of, or respect for, the needs of transgender, gender nonconforming, and nonbinary people. The experiences of transgender, gender nonconforming, and nonbinary people are unique to each individual in the system. Although some are open about their identity, many are not, because it is not safe for them to come out of the closet. Across the country, transgender women are often housed in men's prisons, and transgender men regularly go uncounted, even if their friends inside use he/him pronouns. Transgender people are often placed in solitary confinement, ostensibly for their own protection. Each transgender, gender nonconforming, and nonbinary individual must constantly evaluate their safety, and most facilities are not safe places to stand out.

Here it is important to point out that the absence of transgender, gender nonconforming, and nonbinary people in *Hidden Healers* does not reflect the writer's intent, but rather a few practical issues. First, although they are disproportionately targeted by police, incarcerated transgender people are overall a small percentage of the population.

Second, being out of the closet as transgender, nonbinary, or gender nonconforming is not always safe, so I have not had many incarcerated contacts who were openly transgender. I decided to acknowledge this up front, rather than risk tokenizing someone I didn't know well by asking them to speak to "the trans experience" as it may differ from that of cisgender women. Trans women and men have participated in my programs, and I am currently writing a curriculum based on feedback from LGBTQ+ communities in an effort to make sure that people of all genders have access to programs that address their needs.

I use the word *women* throughout this conversation to refer to people living in a prison designated for women because the vast majority of those I've worked with, and everyone I interviewed for this project, identifies as a woman, to the best of my current knowledge. Some of them are members of queer, lesbian, and bisexual communities; some would rather not be labeled at all.

When making generalizations, there are always nuances that get missed. I have tried to qualify and acknowledge this throughout. In an effort to acknowledge the personal risk those questions can bring, I did not ask anyone to give me information about their gender or sexuality. Those interviewees who did discuss their relationships, gender, or sexuality offered the information on their own.

The Voices in *Hidden Healers*

This overall discussion is simultaneously about women's prisons in general as I've perceived them over thirty years, and about the lived experiences of the women I interviewed. I interviewed twenty-one formerly incarcerated women, two program coordinators who are paid by grants to work inside prisons, one former and one current warden at a women's prison, and two academic colleagues whose research has supported the needs of incarcerated women. Interviewees gave me permission to edit their words for clarity, and I have done my best to preserve their voices, viewpoints, and stories.

Unfortunately, talking about prison means that some emotional difficulty is going to arise. A trauma-informed interview is one where interviewees are allowed to direct the conversation, make choices about what they want to share, and are not pressed to give details or tell stories that harm them to recall. All interviewees were asked to go at their own pace, and I did not ask anyone to share specific traumatic events with me, although many of them volunteered stories that they were ready to tell. I did not ask anyone to share the story of their arrest, trial, plea bargain, or sentencing, although some did offer that information. Because this was not a research study I did not collect demographic details, but it is important to disclose that the interviewee pool was diverse in race, ethnicity, age, class, geography, life experience prior to incarceration, and time spent inside.

Our discussions here are not about each woman's "crime story." I did not ask why they were incarcerated, because it is none of my business. It is also part of the culture for many women living inside prison not to ask about a woman's specific crime but to let women tell their stories when and if they decide to. All the personal information shared was volunteered by the interviewees.

Interviewees ranged from women who had been jailed for small drug-related misdemeanors to women who had received life sentences for violent events where a life was lost. Some of them had traumatic childhoods, some did not. A very few came from stable middle-class homes, whereas some experienced food scarcity and homelessness prior to incarceration. A few had been through juvenile justice systems prior to their incarceration as adults.

When I asked my interviewees to tell stories about how women help each other inside prison, I did not get the stories I expected. I expected rich descriptions of specific and impactful actions, longer narratives with characters and details. Instead, most of the women I spoke to remembered themes and snippets. On reflection I feel this was very important.

Formerly incarcerated women do not want to "go back" and remember, even when they are asked to do so for a reason they support. When they try, the memories are not encoded in a beginning/middle/end progression. Both the desire to leave the memories in the past and the way the memories show up in snippets are characteristic of trauma. Imagine a woman getting out of an abusive relationship who doesn't want to go back in time to describe all of the details. Even when she describes the people who supported her through that time, she has to return to that time in her mind. It is painful, and that affects memory.

My interviewees told me about tiny, consistent actions that added up to a culture of care, not cinematic plot points or big reveals. The prison system is brutal and dehumanizing, and the ways women take care of each other while enduring it are through practical, material, and deliberate actions taken every day.

Hair is important to many women. It is not uncommon to struggle with haircuts and hair color, as well as obtaining basic hair products. Every facility has different rules and regulations regarding hair, including whether a woman can touch another woman's hair.

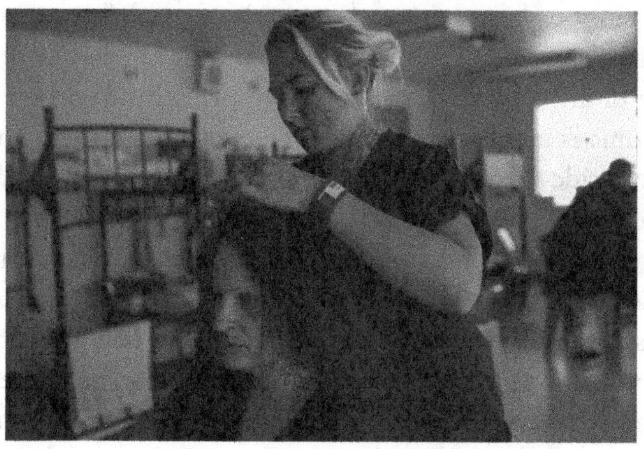

Source: Michele Zousmer.

My purpose in this book is to amplify the voices of women who are stigmatized and rendered invisible. I asked them to share their lived experience to show not only their strength and resilience, but also the gifts they have shared with others on the inside and are now sharing on the outside. Nearly all the formerly incarcerated women I spoke to have found meaningful work in advocacy or direct service, which is how I was able to connect with them. These hidden healers are addiction counselors, abolitionist activists, reentry specialists, artists who share their skills with currently incarcerated women, therapists, coaches, and so on.

Of course, many formerly incarcerated women do not go on to work in advocacy or direct service, and may never speak of their experience. The traumatic effects of incarceration can last a lifetime, and for many women the safest way forward is to put that part of their life firmly in the past. Three of the interviews represented in this book were with women who broke long silences to support this project. Their courage is a gift to the conversation.

Throughout our discussion interviewees are referred to by first names only, some of which have been changed to protect their privacy. Exceptions are those women who have already made their stories public: Kim Carter, founder and ambassador of the Time for Change Foundation who wrote the "Note from a Hidden Healer"; Beatrice Codianni, a longtime community organizer and activist for sex workers' rights; and Robin Cullen, a 2020 Connecticut Hall of Change honoree for her work supporting incarcerated women. For most of the interviewees, certain details about their lives are included while their locations and other details have been changed or generalized.

Ultimately, there is no formal recognition for the women who helped Donna survive her cancer recovery by buying her broth on commissary, helping her clean up for her children, and comforting her when she was struggling. They didn't perform those acts of kindness for personal gain; they did it because they thought it was right.

Donna's situation and the ways her friends came to her aid are not uncommon. What is uncommon is for people outside the system to see or hear about it. There are very few experiences as powerful as truly feeling seen. Women who help each other survive the painful, often brutal experience of incarceration and rebuild their lives should be seen and respected for the work they do, by everyone in their communities.

As we prepare to encounter the brutal realities of our criminal legal system in the following section—much of which is disturbing and difficult to envision—let us keep our attention fixed on the inspiring ways women continue to support each other, no matter what.

PART ONE:
Entering the System

Introduction to the Criminal Legal System for Women in the United States
Pathways to Prison: Understanding Trauma and Addiction
First Days

Many if not most women involved with the criminal legal system enter as girls. Some years ago, I and my colleague Dr. Barbara Bloom at the Center for Gender & Justice were hired to assess the juvenile justice system in a southwestern state. Over the course of a year and a half we assessed their custodial services, community services, mental health services, and so forth. We learned that the girls in this state's custodial facility were predominantly girls of color with histories of sexual and physical abuse and problems with alcohol and other drugs. Many of them had run away from home. There was a disproportionate number of LGBTQ+ and gender-diverse girls in the facility. These profiles matched the profiles of the women in the adult system at large.

The girls in the juvenile system become the women in the adult system. They may have spent time in juvenile probation, detention, or any number of the prisons for youth that have names like "training school." If our facilities and programs were working for youth, then we would not see this pipeline of incarceration stretching into adulthood.

Even more important, the girls' risk of getting into the system doesn't start when they are adolescents—it starts when they are born. The girls at greatest risk of entering the juvenile system come from communities of color experiencing poverty and a lack of services and from families experiencing domestic violence and addiction. Our discussion may focus on women entering prison as adults, but the risk of entering the system begins much earlier for many, and that is why simply fixing up adult prisons will not address the deeper problems that land women there.

In addition to recognizing the risk factors that begin a woman's journey into the criminal legal system, it is important to understand how the system works to capture and keep women involved. In this section we will discuss the functioning of the criminal legal system in the early days of a woman's journey.

Contrary to what many believe, the vast majority of incarcerated women did not receive their sentence via a jury trial. The main method by which women receive their sentence is through plea bargaining. We will take a look at the implications and consequences of this and other important features of the system as women navigate it. We will discuss what makes a women's prison similar and different from a men's facility and examine the role of trauma and addiction in women's incarceration.

The complexity of the criminal legal system can be overwhelming. Imagine attempting to navigate it on the heels of a significant trauma, without access to adequate support. Next, add the physical experience of entering a jail or prison. I will never forget the ways I have seen women arrive at prisons and jails, shackled to each other in locked vans and buses. I have seen them chained together at the waist, with their hands also shackled. To enter a new facility, they must line up and be strip searched. The degradation and humiliation begin before women even get in the door.

Introduction to the Criminal Legal System for Women in the United States

The contemporary prison is expected to deal with the failures of other social institutions, an expectation that the prison is both philosophically and practically unable to meet.

—**Barbara Owen,**
In the Mix: Struggle and Survival in a Women's Prison

When I first went to prison, or "the gated community" as I like to call it, the counselor there told me: "You do realize you're going to leave here in a pine box." And that was a slap up the back of my head.

—**Brandi,** *personal interview*

It's Not Like TV

When I asked my interviewees what they wanted people to know about the criminal justice system, many said, "It's not what you see on TV." Although *Orange Is the New Black* is currently the most widely recognized television representation of incarcerated women, nearly all of my interviewees mentioned it as a negative example. Yes, the show humanized some of the characters through backstory; yes, it nailed a few of the lesser-known details of everyday life, like the way women learn to make shower shoes out of sanitary pads. However, the women

I interviewed said the lack of representation of the ways women support each other in prison, not to mention the increase in sexual drama and violence as the seasons progressed, added up to a show that only added to the stigma.

On the other hand, Piper Kerman's 2011 memoir *Orange Is the New Black: My Year in a Women's Prison*, which inspired the television series, is a thoughtful description of many of the dynamics and daily realities of Kerman's experience and did not need to rely on sensationalism.

One thing Kerman made very clear was how meaningful her race and class privilege were during her incarceration. She was one of a minority of incarcerated women who could rely on community support, family, and financial resources while she was inside. She experienced and reported that being white got her better treatment from openly racist corrections officers. Beatrice Codianni, who was incarcerated with Piper Kerman and appears in the book under a pseudonym, told me, "The TV show, I can't watch. But I think the book is right on."

Beatrice grew up in a low-income area and has seen firsthand how stigma affects generations of people. "I just want to fight against bullies," she said. "I want to fight against a system that oppresses people. I will do that until my dying day. I'm seventy-three. I still have fight in me. So, you know, it's not over!" Beatrice's jet-black hair and exuberant energy show that age hasn't slowed her down. Beatrice entered prison because of her association with the Latin Kings when she was in her forties. She served fifteen years and spent them all advocating for herself and others to receive adequate medical care, access to reading materials, and other rights.

Beatrice speaks openly about the difficulties of living inside a prison and the effort it takes to make even small policy changes. "I took the Bureau of Prisons to court against cross-gender pat searches," she told me. An action like this is monumentally difficult. But Beatrice was adamant. "I was gang raped when I was twelve," she told me. "Every time a corrections officer would come behind me and make me put my arms up and spread my legs for a search, he would put his hands under my breasts, and I was retraumatized." Beatrice won an exemption that required a female corrections officer to conduct her pat downs, and this opened the door for other women who had a history of trauma to apply for the same exemption.

On the outside, Beatrice founded the Sex Workers and Allies Network (SWAN), a harm reduction organization that advocates for the decriminalization of sex work. Beatrice is the managing editor of Reentry Central, a nationally recognized website on reentry and criminal justice reform issues. She is a cofounder of the groups Real Women Real Voices, the National Council for Incarcerated and Formerly Incarcerated Women and Girls, and the Women's Resettlement Working Group. She is also on the Connecticut Bail Fund's community advisory board. Her life has been devoted to advocacy and justice for marginalized people.

When Piper Kerman's memoir *Orange Is the New Black: My Year in a Women's Prison* was adapted into a television show, Beatrice and a few other formerly incarcerated women who had lived alongside Kerman formed an educational group called "The Real Women of Orange is the New Black." They spoke out at universities, church groups, and community organizations to raise awareness about the issues facing incarcerated women. "The book is right on, but the show was made for entertainment, not to educate people," Beatrice said. "We tried to fill the gap." Violence and sexual jealousy among women may get ratings, but life inside a real women's prison is both more mundane and more painful than television can depict.

Women who live inside face daily struggles that don't lend themselves to intriguing plot twists—but when we zoom out and look at the system in its entirety, it is truly a shocking story we have to tell. The system we have was not inevitable, and it can be undone. But in order to contemplate what to do next, we have to know what we have in operation right now.

Who Gets in "The System"?

Internationally I've seen that wherever I go, the most oppressed women in the country are overly represented in the prison system. In New Zealand I saw high numbers of Māori women. In Australia it was Aboriginal women. In Germany it was women who had emigrated from Turkey. In the United Kingdom women who are called "foreign nationals" are incarcerated at higher rates than British citizens. In Canada, First Nations women and other marginalized women are disproportionately incarcerated. Imprisonment is a worldwide indicator of the prejudice held by a majority. If the most disadvantaged women are overly represented in the prison system, then that system is not about justice.

Overwhelmingly, American women's prisons house poor women of color. Black women are twice as likely to be arrested as white women. Black women make up 30 percent of the population of incarcerated women. Latina women are 1.4 times more likely to be arrested and incarcerated as white women. Of course, prisons keep some demographic records, because policy and advocacy campaigns are often built on those records. However, the records are not standardized across state systems, and they often lump together a number of minorities. All ethnicities aside from white, Black, and Latina—roughly 10 percent of all incarcerated women—are lumped into one category: *other.*

After years of work from policy makers and activists, some states are beginning to keep more detailed records. Advocacy groups have investigated rates of incarceration for Asian American and Pacific Islander (AAPI) communities and discovered how difficult it is to find members of these "othered" communities in the system once they are inside (1). Although Native American, Alaska Native, and Native Hawaiian women are a small percentage of the population overall, they are disproportionately represented in certain geographical locations (2).

As I mentioned earlier, all prisons operate on a gender binary, so everyone living in a women's prison is categorized according to their sex assigned at birth, not their self-identity. We do not have much data on the number of trans, nonbinary, or gender nonconforming people who live in women's prisons, although what we do have indicates that they are disproportionately represented as well.

Housing, programming, clothing, safety, and medical care for transgender people are issues of ongoing and immediate concern, but as of this writing, most corrections departments are not addressing those concerns in an organized way. Even in California, where the issue of safety for incarcerated transgender people has finally been addressed by new policy, resistance to housing trans women in women's facilities has come from diverse corners, including from some incarcerated cisgender women.

One major reason for the difference between real life for incarcerated women and what we see on television is that the real criminal legal system is extremely complicated to navigate. It is not the clear pathway from arrest to trial to incarceration indicated by police procedural shows. Once a woman is inside, she doesn't just serve her time and get released. There are many different issues that can arise to affect how long her sentence is, including the possibility of "good time" (a reduced sentence based on her behavior inside) or an extended sentence because of trouble she gets in. Many scholars and activists liken the criminal legal system, and especially the prison system, to a maze: many ways in, very few ways out, and a lot of dead ends on the inside.

There is no single criminal legal "system" in the United States. There is a plethora of autonomous systems including a federal system, fifty state systems, and around eighteen thousand local systems (3). This diagram indicates the process in one system.

Figure 1. Entering the system.

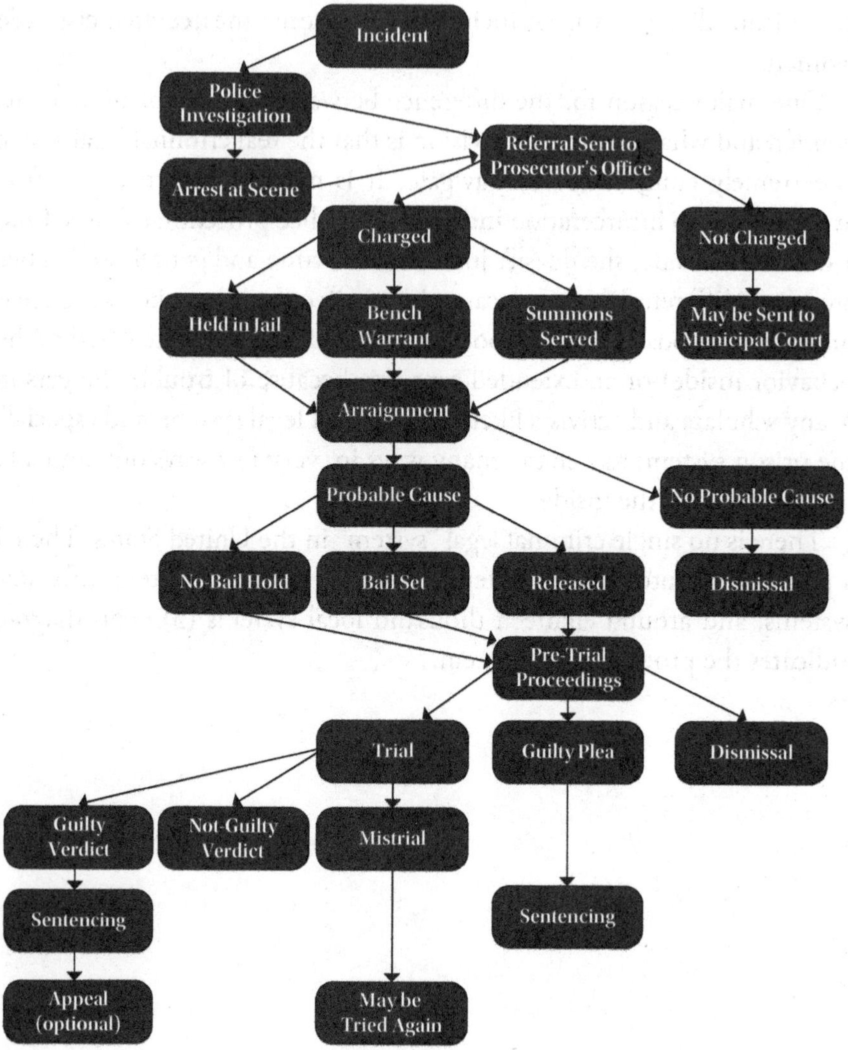

Incident
Police Investigation
Arrest at Scene
Referral Sent to Prosecutor's Office
Charged
Not Charged
Held in Jail
Bench Warrant
Summons Served
May be Sent to Municipal Court
Arraignment
Probable Cause
No Probable Cause
No-Bail Hold
Bail Set
Released
Dismissal
Pre-Trial Proceedings
Trial
Guilty Plea
Dismissal
Guilty Verdict
Not-Guilty Verdict
Mistrial
Sentencing
Sentencing
Appeal (optional)
May be Tried Again

Source: Reproduced by permission from Jefferson County, WA, website, 2023, https://www.co.jefferson.wa.us/1243/How-the-Criminal-Justice-System-Works.

Cash Bail and Plea Bargains

After being arrested, a person suspected of a crime goes to jail to await notification of their charges. If a person cannot make bail or is not offered bail, they are held in jail after being *arraigned* (the court proceeding where a defendant is notified of the charges filed against them) and until they are convicted and sentenced. This is known as *pretrial detention*. If subjected to pretrial detention, a person's likelihood of taking a plea deal goes up 46 percent (4). Jails are full of people who have been arraigned but not convicted of a crime, and women are more likely to spend their pretrial time incarcerated because they are less likely to be able to make bail than men are.

One factor is that when men need to make bail, they often have women gathering—mother, sisters, wife, or girlfriend—to raise that money. Women who need bail usually do not have men or other family members gathering together to raise funds for them. A woman who needs bail also often needs someone to care for her children, and she may not be able to get both bail funds and childcare from her family. Sometimes women lie to the police and don't tell them they have children. They do this hoping their oldest child will be able to manage the rest of the kids for the next few days until she is released on her own recognizance (an option for lower-risk defendants); otherwise her children may be sent into the foster system.

Because of how obviously prejudicial it is toward those who can't afford bail, the cash bail system has been replaced by most countries in the world. The United States still uses it. Though California is one jurisdiction that's working to reform the practice, the cash bail practice is one of many ways women are disadvantaged in an already rigged system.

Another practice that disproportionately affects women is plea bargaining. We know that more than 90 percent of criminal cases that end in conviction are the result of plea bargaining, not jury trials (5). This fact alone should give us pause.

The plea bargain process is informal and private: it happens behind closed doors among lawyers, judges, and the accused. Overall, the odds of receiving a plea offer from the court that includes incarceration are almost 70 percent greater for Black people than white people (6). Still, taking a plea is often a better deal for women, regardless of their race, because women of all races are more likely to have their most severe charge dropped during the plea process than men are (7). For most women the cost of enduring a trial is simply prohibitive—they usually cannot afford a private lawyer and nearly 80 percent of them have children to plan for. So even if they are innocent or believe they should have a lesser charge, taking a plea deal often makes material sense for them. It gives them a sense of what they can expect going forward, and it seems to cut their losses.

This was the case for interviewee Patricia, who spent five years incarcerated because she took a plea. She told me it was the hardest decision she ever made, but she did it for her daughter. If she hadn't taken the plea and had lost her case, her sentence would have been much longer. "So I did plea," she said. "Because otherwise I couldn't guarantee to my daughter that I would come out in time to actually see her grow and be there to raise her."

Let's say one of the rare women who decides to go to trial does win, and—even more rare—is found not guilty and released. If she was unable to make bail pretrial, she may have been incarcerated in jail for two years while fighting her case, and there is no formal system to support her afterward in rebuilding her life, reconnecting with her children, or getting a job. This is the situation for a woman who has "won."

After pleading guilty to felony or misdemeanor charges (or a combination) and taking a deal—or after losing at trial—women are sentenced by a judge. Then they are sent to a temporary holding area—often called a *reception center*, sometimes a separate housing building within the prison—while they await their transfer to the prison unit where they will serve their sentence.

Differences between Jail and Prison

Jails and prisons are operated by different arms of a byzantine custodial system. *Jails* are usually under county jurisdiction and are operated by sheriff's departments. *Prisons* are operated by a state or the federal corrections department. Of course, the names and purposes of jails and prisons vary across the United States and around the world. In general, jails are typically local and hold people for shorter duration in a pretrial or preconviction status, whereas prisons are almost always post-conviction facilities for longer stays. For this reason, prisons are more likely than jails to offer comprehensive programming for women. This system is not the same in other countries; in the United Kingdom, for example, there are no jails. All women convicted of a crime, no matter the severity or length of sentence, are housed in prison together.

Longer sentences for felonies require a transfer from jail to a state or federal prison, which can sometimes take months. Women who have been convicted of federal crimes including tax evasion, counterfeiting, wire fraud, and drug trafficking will go to federal prisons operated by the Federal Bureau of Prisons. Everyone else will go to state prisons operated by each state's independent department of corrections. In California sometimes we "joke" that in the California Department of Corrections and Rehabilitation (CDCR), the *R* is silent.

Because there are so few women's facilities in the context of the entire system, women are often sent to prisons that are quite far from their families and communities. Connecticut has one state facility. California has two. In some cases, women are sent to another state entirely. This is especially common for women in the federal prison system, because there are only twenty-nine facilities for women to serve all fifty states. In some states like California, prison overcrowding has led to women serving much longer sentences in jails.

Women living together in a dormitory-style room with bunk beds in a jail. Because there is a shortage of space for programming, all activities are in this dorm.

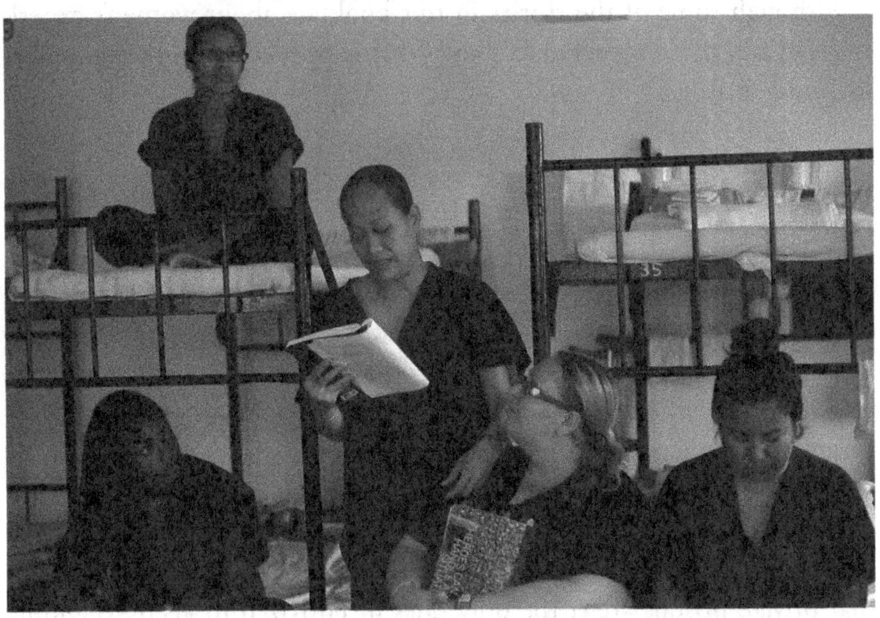

Source: Michele Zousmer.

Reception centers, where women are processed when they first arrive, are also places where women are unlikely to receive programming. This means that when she is first incarcerated, while she is trying to adjust, a woman may spend two months in a place where all the staff do is ask questions to figure out how dangerous she is, whether she has a mental illness, and whatever else they are assessing in the name of security.

One of my interviewees told me that the risk of violence is highest in a reception center, where people are "settling scores" over things that happened outside and have less to occupy their time. She witnessed one very brutal attack from one resident on another and remembered that the corrections officer allowed the attack to continue until the women involved were bleeding. The women I spoke with all agreed that violence was much less common once they were living together long term inside a prison.

I've worked to get *Healing Trauma*, a six-session intervention program that is peer facilitated, to be run inside reception centers and have been successful in a few women's prisons. In addition to the program content, the important benefit of getting a peer-led program running in reception centers is that women coming in can meet someone who has been there for a while, who can tell them how the place operates.

Although some of the stories in this book are about women's experiences in jail, most of them are about what happened when they were living inside prisons.

Who's in Charge

Prisons are paramilitary organizations. Corrections officers have a strict chain of command with titles like *lieutenant* and *captain*. In general, wardens are at the top. There are a number of different offices and jobs that intervene in the workings of a prison, such as health services, program coordinators, and counselors. Incarcerated women have to learn their system quickly.

Private prisons do house about 8 percent of our currently incarcerated population, and they do lobby to keep more people locked up. However, the Massachusetts think tank Prison Policy Initiative points to the fact that private prisons aren't the only ones incentivized to keep expanding the population of incarcerated people.

Private industry extracts profits from our public prison systems through services and goods: telecommunications (big markups on collect phone calls from jails and prisons), food (lower-quality food served inside at low cost), clothing (uniforms and shoes made cheaply in bulk), restraints (different sets for different purposes), and many others.

State and federal institutions are conglomerations of a publicly funded paramilitary authority plus a host of private contractors—all incentivized to keep expanding. This makes the prison system like a dilapidated old house with a poor foundation getting constantly remodeled, but without a plan. You've got stairs to nowhere and a door that opens onto a brick wall, but the builders keep working because they have been contracted to do so.

In addition to the formal structure of corrections, there is a power structure inside the prison that is developed by the women who live there. In my experience there is always someone in charge of the workings of daily life who isn't the warden. Every facility changes over time with new management, policies, and people coming through. This is one reason why women with long-term sentences end up with a lot of responsibility. They have the most institutional knowledge and experience, and so they often end up mentoring people coming in on how to survive.

Differences between Men's and Women's Prisons

> *Here's something that's incredibly important to understand about incarcerated women versus incarcerated men: incarcerated women are usually moms, and usually come from communities with very little resources. And so, if you have to ask out of necessity for someone to take care of your children, there's probably no money left for anyone to send you commissary, to come visit you, to send you magazines or underclothes, or any of the amenities that you would get from the outside. With men, women are taking care of them. Men usually have the amenities from the outside world, where women have to rely on themselves and one another. It's different.*
>
> —**Amy**, *personal interview*

Women living in prisons tend to be poorer on average than men. Many people do not realize how important financial support from the outside is to people living in prisons. As one interviewee put it: "If you don't got nothing, you ain't nothing."

To get their basic needs met inside, women have to rely on each other more than men do. Some of my interviewees viewed this as an inherent quality of their gender; they believe women are more nurturing and relational than men are. What I see is the combination of gender socialization and economic necessity. Men are already socialized toward dominance behavior, self-reliance, and repression of emotion. These are exacerbated by incarceration, which is all about dominance and control.

Women in prison are responding to a very different set of expectations and needs, and they are much more likely to build family-type bonds, to share resources, and to talk with each other about their struggles. Relying on each other is one of the ways women survive prison, regardless of how each woman may fit in with other gender norms.

Many people believe that women have become more violent in recent decades. There are more media portrayals of women who have used violence, but in fact the rates of violence among women have not changed much over time. Women are more likely to use violence with someone close to them than with a stranger. The percentage of incarcerated women who are in for violent crimes is about 38 percent in state prisons, compared to 58 percent for men (8).

In general, women's facilities have less documented violence than men's do. There are fewer attacks on corrections officers (COs), fewer altercations among residents, and there has never been a documented full-scale uprising or riot at a women's prison. At a men's prison, I've had to sign a form that said if there was a riot and I was taken hostage, I understood the staff would not rescue me. I've never had to sign that form at a women's facility.

What surprises people outside the field is that for corrections personnel, it is generally understood that working in a men's facility is preferable. I can't tell you how many times I've heard COs say, "Give me ten men for every one woman." Why is this? When you drill down on it, incarcerated women are seen as more difficult to manage. The generalization is that they ask why instead of simply following orders, and they overtly express their feelings. Prison staff have not been trained or provided the programming we know to be most effective for incarcerated women. In addition, for people working in corrections, it is harder to move up the professional ladder from the women's side than the men's.

In prison, women are more likely to cause harm to themselves than to others. Worldwide, self-harm is a leading cause of death for prison residents (9). Women's prisons have much higher rates of mental health concerns than men's. In the United Kingdom women are four times more likely to self-harm in prison than men are, with a significant uptick in self-harming behaviors across the board during COVID-19 lockdowns (10).

Even thirty years ago, when one of my interviewees, Rose, was incarcerated in Kent, England, she recalled that "there were a lot of distressed women. Sometimes self-harm was the only way to get the attention you needed." We will take a closer look at how violence, trauma, addiction, and mental health concerns shape the lives of women before they enter prison in the next section.

A major difference between American facilities designated for men and those for women is the way people are housed according to their level of risk. In most state systems men are assessed for their "dangerousness" or risk of causing harm to others in the facility via their crime of commitment, their record, and an on-site assessment. They are housed according to their risk level, which is why we have *minimum-security facilities*, *maximum-security facilities*, and different levels of freedom or constraint within those.

The population of incarcerated women, while growing exponentially, is still small enough in most places that all women are housed together, irrespective of their risk level. This means that women are forming relationships and working side by side across a number of differences in ways that incarcerated men are not.

Although it varies by region, men's and women's facilities often differ markedly in the types of programs available to residents. I am an advocate for and creator of gender-responsive programming that seeks to meet the specific needs of incarcerated women. *Gender responsive* does not mean I intend to reinforce gender norms, although it can be very difficult to communicate this within the prison system.

Effective gender-responsive services for women must create an environment—through site selection, staff selection, program development, content, and material—that reflects an understanding of the realities of the lives of women and girls and addresses their strengths and challenges (11). I am appalled when a women's facility calls their vocational programs "gender responsive," and then I find out they focus on cooking and sewing. What I've found is that many women's facilities struggle to provide adequate programming because they lack the funding, infrastructure, and political will to do so.

This gap between men's and women's facilities can have big consequences. One example comes from my own experience writing programs. About ten years ago I was consulting for a midwestern prison to improve their substance use disorder treatment. The state department of corrections asked me to write a therapeutic intervention program for women who had committed violent crimes. I had no experience or background in that area, so I declined. Then two events changed my mind.

First, I found out that the men's prisons already had such a program, and that men who completed it could go before the parole board early for a chance at early release. Women had no such option because they didn't have a comparable program. That was unconscionable. Next, before I left to return home, a prison resident approached me and said, "I hear you're going to write something for us around violence." I told her I had been asked, but I was not going to do it, and she started to cry. She told me she had killed her best friend of nineteen years, and she thought I was going to help her.

Flying home from that job, I carried her with me. How could I not? It occurred to me that I'd said no to the administration because the requested program was out of my subject area, but I could learn. So when I got home, I started researching. I contacted friends in the field and asked them where the programs were for women who had committed violent crimes. Over and over again I was told there weren't any. I couldn't find one being used anywhere in the United States or in any of the countries where I had contacts. This was in 2011.

I contacted the department of corrections that had requested the program and told them I would write it on two conditions: First, I needed to spend some time with the women living in the prison who had committed a violent crime. I needed to listen to them, to learn from them. My outside research would only go so far. Second, they needed to have a university-based researcher assess the program for its effectiveness.

Through focus groups, research, and pilot studies, I developed the program *Beyond Violence: A Prevention Program for Criminal Justice–Involved*

Women: a forty-hour evidence-based and manualized therapeutic program for women in criminal legal settings (jails, prisons, and community corrections) with histories of aggression and/or violence. It deals with the violence and trauma they have experienced, as well as the violence they may have perpetrated.

A randomized control study found that women who completed *Beyond Violence* experienced significantly less recidivism—25 percent at one year post-release—than women who completed a much longer comparison program designed for men, who returned at a rate of 47 percent one year post-release (12). (Here it is worth noting that many programs that call themselves "gender neutral" are in fact programs designed for men.) In the initial programming the groups were facilitated by staff. We began to offer the program elsewhere—and eventually in California with peer facilitators.

Prison residents who volunteer are interviewed and selected to attend the training pictured here. Then they participate in the intervention itself, led by a program coordinator. Upon completion they begin to co-facilitate in pairs.

Source: California Department of Corrections and Rehabilitation.

I made sure that peer facilitators were well trained and paid the highest wage possible. Although the program is not explicitly designed as vocational training, many former facilitators who have been released have gone on to translate the skills they developed running *Beyond Violence* groups into jobs as counselors in substance use disorder programs, services for those with physical health challenges and experiencing homelessness, and advocacy work. This program is also my contact point for many of the women I interviewed for this project, an unexpected gift that came from addressing an unmet need. I have been asked to develop and provide trauma-focused, gender-responsive services for men in prison due to the success we have seen in women's programming.

Unmet need is a recurring theme in the lives of women who experience incarceration. Older research from the Bureau of Justice suggests that both men and women who have experienced incarceration report higher rates of childhood physical and sexual abuse than the broader public. Newer research indicates that when questions focus only on physical abuse and intimidation as children, incarcerated men report higher prevalence than women.

What the data reveal, then, is that for men the physical violence and intimidation against them declines as they become adults and presumably grow bigger and stronger. It does not decline for women. For women who experienced physical violence and intimidation during their childhood, it is significantly more likely to continue into adulthood. Close to 90 percent of incarcerated women who reported childhood violence and intimidation also reported continued violence and intimidation as adults.

Figure 2. Victimization trajectories for men.

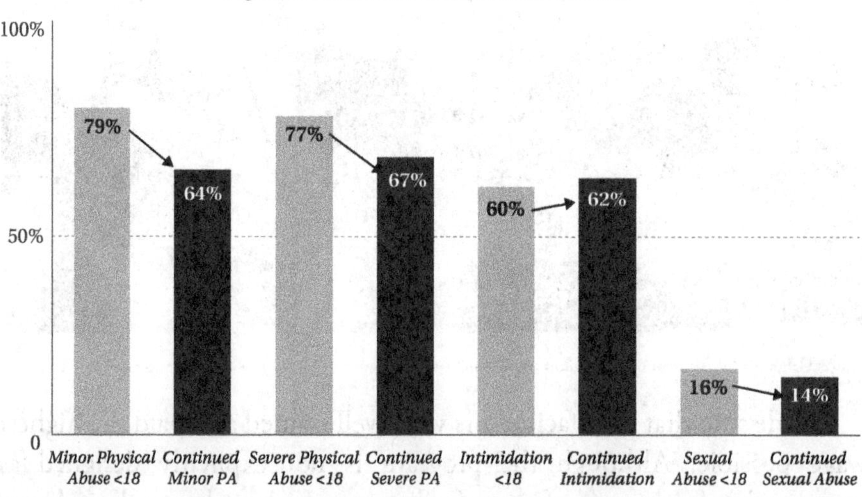

Source: Nena Messina, "An Experimental Study of the Effectiveness of a Trauma-Specific Intervention for Incarcerated Men." *Journal of Interpersonal Violence* 49, no. 10 (2023): 1399–1417. https://doi.org/10.1177/00938548221093280.

Figure 3. Victimization trajectories for women.

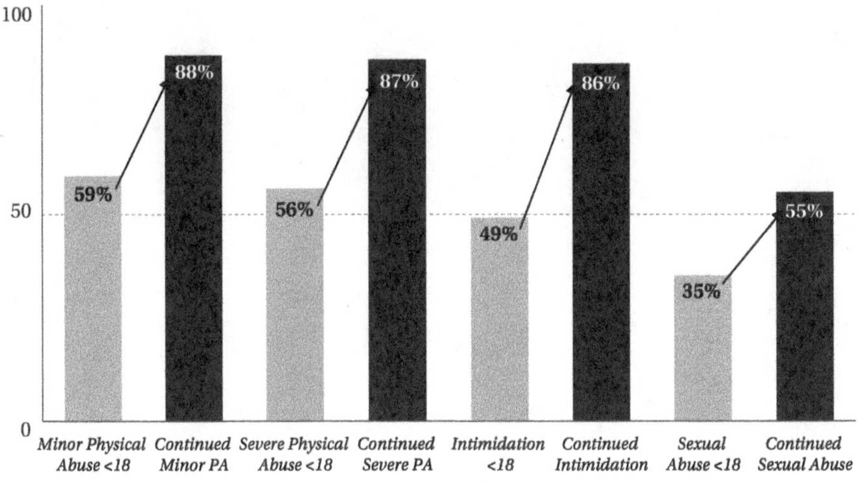

Source: Preeta Saxena and Nena Messina, "Trajectories of Victimization to Violence among Incarcerated Women." *Health and Justice* 9, no. 18 (2021): 1–12. https://doi.org/10.1186/s40352-021-00144-8.

In other words, although men experiencing incarceration live with significant violence, they are less likely to contend with an increasing level of violence as they grow from childhood to adulthood. For women it is a different story, as the level of violence and intimidation they face is likely to hold steady or increase. What happened prior to incarceration is important in understanding how to support women as they make choices about their lives coming home. In the next section we will take a deeper look at these pathways to prison, especially the roles of trauma and addiction.

Pathways to Prison: Understanding Trauma and Addiction

Because trauma is as much a chief cause of violence as the result of violence, our current fear-based system paradoxically generates more harm than it prevents, in never-ending cycles of trauma.

—**Zach Norris**,
Defund Fear: Safety Without Policing, Prisons, and Punishment

Back in our days, when we were growing up, we swept everything under the rug, you didn't tell anybody that you were in an abusive household, or your parent was getting beat up by the other spouse. You didn't say any of that, and so nobody knew things were amiss. I always thought that everybody's household was the same as mine, but I also knew we didn't talk about it.

—**Brandi**, *personal interview*

I GOT MY social work training at Columbia University in the 1960s. I often tell people that in all my coursework, there were only two sentences about trauma. The first was "Incest occurs in less than 1 percent of American families." The second sentence was "The majority of them live in Appalachia."

I was hearing and reading these prejudicial lies as a graduate student, so people who were running the social service agencies through the 1980s all had that same kind of training. Now the growing emphasis on trauma in social services is the result of decades of work to undo the stigma and silence so many were trained to believe in. It's taken a long time to get through the ignorance and denial.

Still, people in social services do not generally receive training specific to the needs of the formerly incarcerated or the needs of their children. We know that women involved in the criminal legal system are victimized at high rates before, during, and after incarceration, but the silence that surrounds this complex set of issues is nearly as pervasive now as it was when I first began working with incarcerated women thirty years ago.

I often tell people that if they want to know a criminal mind, they should go looking at successful businessmen or heads of countries. I'm sure you can imagine a few examples of people with access to resources and power who have exploited others to get where they are. Lacking empathy and taking advantage of people for personal gain is a much more serious set of crimes than what most people get incarcerated for, from my perspective. What's called the "result of a criminal mind" are often simple acts of survival. White-collar crime is not about survival; it is about amassing more and more resources at the expense of other people. *That* is criminal thinking.

It may be difficult for people who have not been exposed to much violence to understand how and why most violence happens, especially when it is caused by women. People don't like to think about violent women, and women who have used violence endure much more stigma than men who have.

As mentioned, women are much less likely to use violence against someone they don't know. There is always a story. Sometimes the violence is levied at a person who was abusing her. Sometimes her history of violence can be traced back to childhood sexual trauma, or it is how she feels she can protect her children. Sometimes there are very serious mental health issues occurring, and violence is the only way a woman sees a solution to her problems.

One of the saddest examples of this I have witnessed was a woman who killed her young daughter because she believed the child was safer with God. The mother was afraid that as the girl got older she would be sexually abused, just like she herself had been. So she decided to send her child to God.

How can someone make sense of this, who hasn't experienced what she had? Perhaps we can at least see that the community around this mother did not support her when she most needed it. She was not able to find or use resources that would have helped her to heal from her own trauma, and tragedy was the result.

People who live in prison have typically been seen as victimizers, not as victims themselves. Historically, this has arisen from the prevailing myth that crime is an individual problem. Conceived this way, there is no social or structural solution to the problem of crime.

The majority of women who enter the criminal legal system already have experienced significant trauma and are therefore both victims and victimizers. You have to hold both those realities, which is a huge shift, and not a comfortable one. It reveals something important about how systemic issues have terrible consequences in individual lives. Yes, people make choices. However, for the vast majority of incarcerated women, their choices were often painfully circumscribed by the traumas of poverty plus racism, sexual and physical abuse, and coping through disordered substance use.

What has happened is that we have criminalized behaviors associated with trauma.

I don't tend to separate conversations about addiction from trauma. In my experience it is rare to find a woman with a substance use disorder who doesn't also have a history of trauma, especially a woman impacted by the criminal legal system. However, historically, drug treatment programs did not address trauma. In the recovery field we used to be told that people shouldn't start talking about their trauma until they had one year sober. I think this is backward. A woman should receive support to work through her trauma as soon as she is ready to.

In many prisons drug treatment programs fill up, and even women who were ordered by a court to receive treatment can't get into a program. The Alcoholics Anonymous (AA) Twelve Step model is still the standard in many American prisons. Many people find solace and support in twelve-step groups, and they can be a powerful tool for recovery. I wrote *A Woman's Way through the Twelve Steps* because I had been helped by Alcoholics Anonymous and wanted to see women's experiences represented as tools for change.

Still, traditional twelve-step literature continues to use only male pronouns, and women need stories of other women's recovery and language they can relate to. Moreover, a fully realized treatment program needs to offer more for participants than the twelve-step recovery tools. We have years of research backing the use of medication-assisted detox, medical monitoring of symptoms, motivational interviewing, one-on-one case management, and so on. Many women are swept into the criminal legal system because of their drug use, but they may struggle to get treatment even if they want it, and they may never have a caring conversation with anyone in authority about *why* they started using.

The Sexual Abuse to Prison Pipeline

Most readers will be familiar with the concept of the "school to prison pipeline." It was assumed that the processes by which young boys were swept into juvenile detention and later prison also applied to girls. For boys, especially boys of color, failing in school is one of the most important risk factors for later criminal involvement.

Research at Georgetown Law found that when the experiences of girls and young women were assessed independently of boys, sexual abuse was one of the primary predictors of involvement in the system (13). In other words, the behaviors that land girls and young women in juvenile facilities, such as drug use, truancy, and running away, are also the behaviors most associated with the experience of sexual abuse and trauma.

I am grateful to Liz, a certified drug and alcohol counselor who facilitates evidence-based practice groups, for being willing to talk with me about how she got into the sexual abuse to prison pipeline as a girl. Her dark, curly hair was cropped ultra short, and her glasses framed her bright, smiling eyes. Many of the women she works with have histories like hers. She told me that her transformation isn't over, because "this is going to be a lifelong process for me."

Her life is a story of survival, and her current healing took incredible dedication. Liz lived in an orphanage from birth to two years old, when she was adopted by a family that subjected her to multiple forms of abuse. "I became a very angry child," Liz said. "I felt I had to be tough, to live in a state of callousness."

Liz ran away from her home in Tucson, Arizona, at age ten. She hopped a train and rode in a boxcar until the train stopped in Los Angeles. For many years she slept on the streets, survived off whatever she could find in trash cans, and eventually started using drugs to cope. When she was arrested at the age of fourteen, Liz lied about her age so she could stay away from her family. She said, "I didn't want to get sent back to Tucson, so I started lying about my age, so I could just go to jail when I would get caught for the crimes that I was committing."

Liz remembers years of cycling in and out of incarceration, and how every time she got started on a more successful path, she would get derailed. Her desire to survive and find a way to live free, outside of prison, eventually motivated her to seek a GED program in prison and then therapeutic programs. She participated in *Beyond Violence* and then became a facilitator for others.

"The cycle is super hard to break," Liz told me. "I had organizations reaching out to me with resources for years, but I couldn't embrace those resources and make a transformation until I was ready to get vulnerable. I needed someone to see me through the process of looking at what had happened to me and how I had responded. I blamed everyone else for a long time. So now I do tell the population that I work with that I'm formerly incarcerated, formerly addicted; I let them know that I've been in the same position that they're in right now. And I help them see that they have support."

It is a myth that only a licensed mental health professional can work with someone who has a trauma history. Prisons sometimes refuse to run peer-facilitated therapeutic programming for women in fear that a prisoner will have power over another prisoner. In some cases, mental health professionals are concerned the women will decompensate, experience a worsening of psychiatric symptoms, and become unmanageable if they start talking about what happened to them. Prison administrators say that the residents will need more care than they can provide. Sometimes they even claim that there is no treatment for trauma and that people just have to live with it.

My team has debunked this set of beliefs more than once with both quantitative/administrative data and qualitative/narrative data, but they persist. We have shown that peer facilitation is effective, and that even short interventions can improve outcomes (14). Thousands of women have successfully completed and graduated from *Healing Trauma*, a six-session brief intervention.

This is a group of women graduating from a peer-led trauma program wearing caps and gowns. For some women, this is the only graduation and certificate they have had in their lives.

Source: California Department of Corrections and Rehabilitation.

This is a group of graduates who are living in the secure housing unit (isolation unit). This photo has been photoshopped to change the background and remove the handcuffs and belly chains.

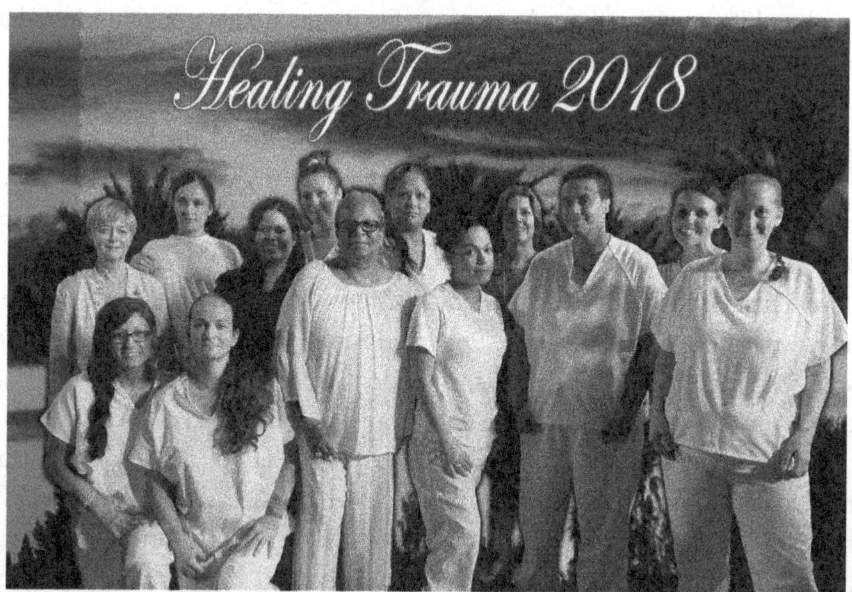

Source: California Department of Corrections and Rehabilitation.

Trauma is never erased, but it can be addressed. People can learn positive coping skills and learn how to manage their responses. There's healing work people can do without rehashing the details of their experience. They can gain insight into their own actions and learn what is theirs to take responsibility for and what happened to them that was not their fault. People must have choice in this process, and they must be able to go at their own pace. It takes time, effort, and investment.

With the exception of a small group of progressive wardens, administrators, and personnel, our current prison system as a whole does not view incarcerated women as people deserving of that level of resource. Nonmutual, nonempathetic, disempowering, and unsafe settings make change and healing extremely difficult. When women are able to put in the effort to self-educate, work through their pain, and rebuild themselves and their lives, it is largely because the other women around them support them in doing so.

Clearly, prisons are full of women with significant unmet needs. Once they are caught up in the system, however, they start having to navigate the demands of incarcerated life immediately, no matter what was happening for them on the outside. It takes time to settle into the culture and routines of a new place, but incarcerated women are expected to adjust as soon as they enter. Next, we will look at the disorienting experience of their first few days inside and hear their stories of how support from other incarcerated women got them through.

First Days

I remember going in and feeling like I was on Mars.

—**Patricia**, *personal interview*

THE STORIES IN this section come primarily from women who had never before been acquainted with the criminal system. This is not to say that returning for the previously justice-involved is easy; it is not. In California approximately 50 percent of people return to custody within three years after serving their first sentence (15). Returning to custody brings many difficulties. It is, however, nothing like being locked up for the first time.

For these individuals, the first days of being incarcerated—pretrial, or when they were transferred to their prison unit—were terrifying and disorienting. They had no idea what to expect. Researchers have found that withstanding *entry shock* is one of the most difficult tasks for incarcerated women. Attempts at suicide, self-harm, and the onset of self-destructive psychiatric disorders are most prevalent in the initial phase of confinement (16).

Although I have a different set of experiences with prison facilities than those who have been incarcerated, even my perception of any particular facility is very different now than it was when I first began my work with incarcerated women, because of how much more I know and how much more I have seen. When I first entered the Black Mountain facility in North Carolina as a guest for those three days in 1987, I was deeply intimidated. The place scared me even though it was a minimum-security facility, because it had a perimeter fence and I was totally unaccustomed to what a real prison looked like. I knew nothing about what to expect at a real prison; I only knew what I had seen in the movies.

Twenty-five years later I was invited back to give a talk to staff and administration of the North Carolina Department of Corrections. They considered me an expert because of the therapeutic programs I had developed and the articles I had written. By now I had experience with a wide variety of prisons and jails, including high-security, multistory facilities—truly frightening for both women and men. I was familiar with some of the worst conditions that outsiders were allowed to see. By comparison, Black Mountain now seemed more like any one of a thousand inexpensive motels, not intimidating at all. Still, just because I'd seen more and could now put the facility in a broader context, it did not take away from the way I felt and still feel about the injustice and disastrous consequences of incarceration on the whole, or the extreme dislocation I knew any woman would feel walking in for the first time.

Most of the time there is no orientation packet for jail or prison. You can't know what you don't know. Repeatedly, I've heard that you're lucky if anyone tells you anything without wanting something in return. In general, the stories I hear about how women help each other in prison take place after the first few days, in part because the first few days are very difficult for everyone to navigate physically, socially, and emotionally. Everyone feels lost. People may be in withdrawal from a substance, in shock from the experience of arrest, and unable to find any calm in the chaos.

Patricia, who had earned a PhD in clinical psychology before her incarceration, recalled her first few days in jail as incredibly scary. She did not know what to expect and had to learn everything on the fly. She told me that when she was first incarcerated, she didn't have her glasses, so in addition to all the expected anxieties of the experience, she was blind. "I had no idea who I was talking to, so I kept to myself," she recalled.

For Patricia, one of the most important things to figure out was the currency. She asked herself, *What do most people want in here?* She learned right away: "It was coffee and sugar. So I decided not to buy coffee or sugar. I told people I didn't drink coffee—so all of a sudden I no longer drank coffee! And truthfully that saved me. Many of the women around me were coming off something, so they wanted that coffee or that candy bar, and I avoided getting caught up." This move was important for Patricia's safety in that it allowed her some time and space to interact with other residents and get to know her new situation without the social pressure of bartering. "You're in survival mode in jail," she said, "especially at the beginning."

This is one of the differences between jail and prison that bears repeating: jail is designed for the short term; prison for the longer term. People in jail are awaiting trial, undergoing trial, or serving a shorter sentence (which can be anywhere from a few months to around a year or two, depending on the jurisdiction, although some stay for five years or more). The first days of incarceration in jail, post arrest, are very different for people who can afford bail than for those who cannot. If a woman has been arrested and detained and is awaiting trial, she may lose her job or custody of her children if she cannot post bail. Clearly, being unable to work while you await trial does not set you up well to afford a good defense, much less meet basic needs for your family.

The first days of incarceration are not only mysterious in terms of how to navigate the institution, but they are also often utterly devastating for women who have just been involved in a traumatic incident that led to their arrest, are now unable to see their children or families, and are tasked with making logistical decisions about their own defense. Because of the high turnover in jails, the women I spoke to for this book all told stories of isolation during their first days, if they could remember them. Sometimes they dissociated and were unable to process what was happening during the first few days, because of their drug use, trauma experience, or a combination of the two.

Patricia called jail "utterly dehumanizing and brutal," and many others echoed that description. Jails rarely carry educational or self-help programs the way prisons do, and often people incarcerated in jails are locked down twenty to twenty-three hours of the day, without access to a common area, cafeteria, or yard. We have many women in jails who haven't been found guilty of anything, haven't been sentenced, and are just waiting for the court. It is much more difficult to meet and bond with people in jail because residents are being moved around so often.

Many women, like Liz, do not seek to find a group to fit in with right away. "I was moved around every few months," Liz told me. "I kept to myself, didn't rely on anyone, and didn't form any trusting relationships with anyone for a long time."

The Transfer to Prison

By the time a justice-involved woman is entering prison from jail, she has completed her plea bargain or been convicted at trial. She can begin to try to settle into a routine once she is sentenced and transferred to prison, because she is now going to stay in one place for a while. However, even the notion of a routine or a predictable environment requires qualification, because for an incarcerated individual, the rules of daily life can change at any moment. Your routine does not belong to you and can be altered by any corrections officer at any time.

In California a woman moving from a jail to a prison will be shackled, often both to herself and to another woman, loaded onto a bus, and driven to one of California's two facilities for women, where she will live in the reception center until she is assigned to a unit. Even though there is a potential for more routine and predictability, the first few days in prison are extremely disconcerting, and women usually feel frightened by the new situation, not knowing what is going to happen.

By contrast, in England, prisons have a practice called "first night accommodations," which describe the place where women spend their first or second night when they come in. They stay in a single cell that is apportioned more like a room, and they get a night or two to adjust there before they go into the main part of the facility. The goal is to give women a slightly softer landing, so that when they enter the main facility they have had a little time to calm down and adjust. In the United States most first nights are spent in the company of many other women, sometimes in triple-decker bunks in rooms where the lights never go off.

Strip Searches

Another feature of first days is adjusting to invasive practices like strip and cavity searches. For Angela, a formerly incarcerated woman who now runs a life coaching business, "that first strip search at county jail let me know that my life would never be the same. It's one of the most dehumanizing things that they do. I was subject to that every week in county jail, where I stayed for four years and two months fighting my case."

The practice of strip searching is the subject of debate and is in constant challenge in the courts. In 2019 the Los Angeles County Sheriff's Department paid a $53 million settlement to avoid continued litigation on a 2010 case involving flagrant violation of women's Fourth Amendment rights during a large group strip search. The officers were yelling profanities at the women, demanding that they remove their tampons and throw them on the ground, having them stand naked in groups for up to forty-five minutes. Menstruating women were bleeding on themselves. The area where they were required to strip was filled with trash, and women could see and smell human urine, feces, and vomit. There has been a similar case in Illinois, highlighting the most egregious human rights abuses that can happen in the context of strip searches. But that doesn't mean that a "normal" strip search is okay, especially because research has repeatedly shown that such searches have not stemmed the flow of contraband in and out of prison (17). For residents, the point of a strip search is humiliation.

In fact, many women have told me that strip searches are one of the more degrading parts of the incarceration experience. They begin during your first days in jail, and Patricia summed up many people's sentiments when she told me that "strip searches are a way to break you." This is especially true for women with histories of sexual trauma. I once had a prison resident tell me that she was no longer going to have visits with her children because she could no longer go through the cavity search after visitation. She was a sexual trauma survivor, and to go through a cavity search every time she was leaving the visiting room was ultimately more than she could handle.

Although corrections "experts" claim strip and cavity searches are necessary in the name of security, the normalized violence, degradation, and trauma of the practice clearly outweigh its purported value as a method of contraband control.

Cavity searches are an abuse. They are not a standard operating practice around the world. They are not used at all in the United Kingdom, for example.

The United Nations adopted a set of standard minimum rules specifically for the treatment of women prisoners in 2010, known as *The Bangkok Rules*. They assert that if searches must be performed, they should be performed by female staff, and alternatives to cavity searches should be sought. Lay people may assume that custodial practices done "for security" have some evidence base, but that is often—even usually—not the case. In other words, many security measures do not have evidence to support their efficacy and are against humane international standards. In the case of strip searching, we know for sure that the practice has not stopped the prison underground economy.

Sometimes a jail will change a policy when there is too much public pressure, but then ensuring that the policy is enforced brings an entirely different set of problems. For example, I consulted with a county jail for women on the West Coast for nearly eighteen months when they were opening a new facility. They spent thousands of dollars on body scanners, which have been touted as a less invasive way to search women as they come and go from outside or from the visiting room. They got to say they bought the scanners, which was satisfying to those who had pushed for that reform. However, in eighteen months the scanners never got plugged in. The staff continued to do strip searches. When I found out they weren't using the scanners they'd invested in, I suggested they use them on the staff, to see what the staff were bringing into the jail. Of course, that didn't happen either. Cavity searches harm residents. They are an egregious form of humiliation, and yet they remain common practice throughout the United States.

You may recall Beatrice, mentioned earlier as the activist who took the Federal Bureau of Prisons to court and won on the issue of "cross-gender" strip searching. Because of Beatrice's work, women who have survived sexual assault can assert their right to an exemption in federal facilities.

They still get searched, but if they receive the exemption they must be searched by women on staff. Beatrice was able to create a precedent for reducing the harm of potential retraumatization by making sure that women could request to be searched by another woman.

Although this has been an enormous win for gender-responsive care, strip and cavity searches, mentioned by many of the women I spoke to, are still often used as opportunities for sexual assault and other forms of maltreatment, in addition to the basic indignity of the practice itself. There are many human rights groups working to end or at least more strictly regulate the practice, with the help of formerly incarcerated people willing to speak about their experiences.

The Revolving Door

In addition to the trauma that is difficult to speak about, conveying some of the realities of what it is like to live in custody versus on the outside is daunting for those who have been through it. It takes a great deal of energy to explain how things work to outsiders.

Some formerly incarcerated women, like my interviewee Serena, have devoted themselves to bridging this information gap. Serena's expertise in corrections comes from more than one perspective: she has lived experience as a formerly incarcerated woman, she developed her vocation upon release delivering addiction recovery services to incarcerated women, and she also runs an online support group of over five hundred justice-impacted women. It is rare for formerly incarcerated women to be allowed back onto the grounds of a secure facility. Serena was the first she knows of to be hired by the Department of Public Safety in Hawaii to provide treatment for women still inside.

Putting her mind back to her own experience of incarceration, Serena remembers her very first day in jail at the Women's Community Correctional Center on Oahu (usually referred to by its acronym WCCC, or "*W* triple-*C*"). She was in pretrial, going through intake, still in active addiction, and she was afraid. "My concept of prison was only what I saw on TV, which was a huge deterrent," she told me. No one in her family had been incarcerated before.

But when she walked in the reception area, something unfolded that she didn't expect. Because Serena was part of a smaller community on an island, where "everybody knows everybody, and you're somebody's mom, sister, aunty, uncle," she experienced a sense of community right away. "I realized all the women in there were people I either used with, sold drugs to, or had a preexisting relationship with," she said. This included the prison staff. Unlike most women, who experience their first days in jail with a large population of strangers, Serena found that she was surrounded by friends who were already taking care of each other.

Although Serena's arrival into an incarcerated group she already recognized as community isn't the norm (except for jails in small communities), her story highlights how important community is for incarcerated women. Another poignant example arose in Robin Cullen's story. Robin is one of the few formerly incarcerated women included in this book who has told her story publicly many times in an effort to raise awareness about both the consequences of drunk driving and the issues facing incarcerated women. She has shoulder-length, red, curly hair and bright eyes that reach people in the back of an auditorium. When I asked what she wanted to share with me, she dove right in.

In 1996 Robin had been drinking with her girlfriend at a friend's wedding. While driving home, Robin made an error in judgment about the road ahead, her truck flipped, and her girlfriend died in the crash. "That was my last drink that night," Robin told me. "It became very clear to me that if we removed the alcohol, none of that would have happened." Alcohol had been a problem of Robin's for years, but she had never had to face serious consequences until that night.

She went to prison after being convicted of manslaughter and realized that many of the women she met there had substance use disorders that had led to their arrests. "It's such a network of women who are watching each other both inside and outside," she said. "They knew each other, and they would see each other get cleaned up for a minute, regroup, and then often go back out in the same game."

Robin had come from a white middle-class family with a history of alcoholism, but not a history of justice involvement. She was confronted with how different her experience was from women who were experiencing the pressures of poverty and racism, and at the same time, how much they had in common through the consequences of their substance use disorders.

Robin described riding in the "ice cream truck," the name for the vehicle used to transport women to and from the courthouse. She said she "noticed right away that the women I was in transit with all seemed to know each other." Robin felt surprised at this, and isolated, because she wasn't part of the scene. "I didn't realize it was a bigger system," she told me. "I hadn't put thought into the revolving door. I thought it was a coincidence that all the people we were picking up knew each other!"

Later, upon reflection, Robin realized that this was no coincidence. This was the way the system had been designed to work: to keep picking up the same people. She noticed that not only did the women on the truck know each other, their conversations were very caring. "It was a network," she told me. "They were asking each other about how they were doing and how long they'd had out."

Learning the Rules

For many women entering jail and then prison for the first time, the rules and practices of the institution are only half of what they must learn. The rest involve social norms and rules that govern interactions among the residents. These rules are very important to know for individual safety, they vary regionally, and they often both replicate and exaggerate the kinds of prejudice, segregation, and social hierarchy we experience on the outside.

One of my interviewees, Lisa, offered an example, beginning with her feeling isolated because she was a white woman who had been dating a Black man before being incarcerated. She described the segregation in the prison as "horrifying" and said that even though normally "whites stick with whites," she was unwelcome anywhere because of her relationship. She had entered jail and then prison *indigent*, meaning she had no resources coming in, so she had no way to barter her way back into social safety.

One night Lisa came back to her bunk and found a pillow, a chunk of soap, a piece of chocolate, and a Bible. She had no idea who had brought her the gifts. Eventually she figured out it was a woman named Ruthie, who became her friend and protector. This was a very risky move for them both because Ruthie was Black.

Lisa told me, "Ruthie was one of the nicest people I'd ever met in my life, and she walked me to and from my programming every day so I wouldn't get hurt." Lisa described Ruthie's kindness and friendship as important sustenance in an environment where she was getting regularly threatened with violence from white women seeking to maintain a racialized social order. Their friendship endured for years, including after they were both released into treatment. For those who have not experienced the pressures of racial politics in a custodial setting, it will be difficult to fully understand the risk Ruthie took in befriending Lisa.

According to the women I interviewed, when they were offered help in their first few days inside a prison, it was often material: a shared snack from commissary, a cup of tea, a bit of advice about who to avoid. They received small acts of decency and care while they settled in and figured out with whom they wanted to align.The stereotype that incarcerated women often steal from one another is far less often true, in my experience, than its opposite: that women who live in tight, confined spaces together for years at a time figure out how to share their resources and make do with what is available.

The first few days in custody and after transfer to a new facility are a very vulnerable time for anyone. Some people are detoxing from a substance they've been using on the outside or had access to at the facility they were living in before. Some people are still in shock from the traumatic event that brought them into custody. Some are in shock from the trauma of the arrest and detainment experience. All are overwhelmed with new information as they adjust to a new institutional environment.

The very first days in custody at a county jail are when people begin the process of understanding what they face in court. The first days in prison, after a transfer from a jail, are when people begin the process of facing the reality of being locked up in this environment for years or decades. Any kindness that feels genuine during this time, whether from another resident or staff, is a memorable experience.

PART TWO:
Living Inside

In the course of my work consulting with administrators, providing programming to residents, and training staff inside prisons, I've asked myself these questions many times: How would I do living in here? How would I fare as a long-term prisoner?

I don't have an answer, because I don't think anyone can truly know how they would handle living inside a prison until they do it. I've seen incredible amounts of resilience, ingenuity, creativity, and inner strength in the women I have met inside. I have been amazed at what can only be called the resilience of the human spirit—that against all odds, they struggle to survive.

Life inside a prison is rife with contradictions. On the one hand, women are constantly taking actions to support themselves and each other, while on the other hand, they are dependent on the facility to provide for their basic needs. Daily routines in prison can be described as dull, tedious, and monotonous. However, living inside is also traumatic, confusing, and sometimes outright dangerous. There are many rules, but they don't always make sense or remain consistent. If you don't follow them, you get punished. There is a sense of terrible emotional deprivation, and at the same time you are living in very close quarters with people you may end up developing deep relationships with, or might intensely dislike. The strange extremes and contradictions are part of what makes living inside a prison so difficult to describe to people who have never been there.

At this stage of the journey, a justice-impacted woman has received her sentence and been transferred to the prison where, unless she is transferred again, she will live until she is released. Now she must discover her own way through. We will take a look at how prisons are designed and run by staff, what medical and mental health care look like for prison residents, how they work and engage with programming, and more. The following discussion is a detailed, personal look at how the system is set up to separate and punish people, and how women create support networks and cultures of care within it.

Culture and Environment

I always say I wouldn't wish prison on my worst enemy, because you are so disconnected from everything. If you've never been there, it's scary. It's gray walls, and it just smells like doom.

—**Sarah**, *personal interview*

THROUGH MY YEARS of programming and consulting work, I have visited women's facilities all over the United States and in several other countries. This puts me in a rare position, because most people who work in the field can offer deep regional expertise, but they do not often visit facilities far away from their own.

Contrary to what outsiders may expect, every prison consists of its own physical plant design and its own culture. There are so many factors that affect how a facility *feels*: the level of upkeep or disrepair, whether there are trees and grass visible, how much razor wire is up, and so on. How the prison looks makes a difference—but, of course, not the only difference. The culture of a facility is deeply impacted by the intentions of the administration and staff. This is why it is important to talk about the physical environment and the culture at the same time.

Let's start with the basics: what you'll find at any women's prison. In the United States women can be housed together in cells with two to eight people or in dormitories with up to a hundred. They are often sleeping in bunk beds. Most prisons have a community space in the building, sometimes called a *dayroom* or *common room*. The bathrooms have a series of stalls and showers. Often there are toilets in the cells.

Most facilities have a cafeteria or a dining room area, although some deliver food on trays to women in their cells. The prison will have an administrative building or office, a space designated for the chapel, a medical office, a visiting room, and group rooms for programming and classes. There will be an outdoor recreational yard of some sort, although it may just be fenced-in blacktop. Upon entering and exiting, you pass through a perimeter fence of some kind and a sally port that has two doors: one locks behind you before the next opens. These are the bare bones.

Although all prisons are mandated to include certain facilities as part of their plant, there are major differences between prisons, even within the same state. Larger prisons are more likely to have medical beds for minor health issues, rather than just a nurse's office. Sometimes a visiting room is painted with colorful murals, or there is a garden. In multistory buildings, movement among the tiers is more intimidating and constricting than movement within a single story. A prison with a tall perimeter fence, layers of razor wire, and a visible gun tower feels very different from a prison without such threatening reminders of where you are.

There is not a lot of new prison construction for women. This is good news in that the people working to stop the construction of new jails and prisons, reduce recidivism, and reduce the overall prison population are having an effect. The bad news is that women who are incarcerated right now are often living in aging, dilapidated spaces.

Because most states do not have large numbers of incarcerated women, they do not have many facilities for women. As mentioned previously, many states have only one facility. Often it is a facility that was originally built as a men's prison and then converted. If a woman is incarcerated through the federal system, she may be sent off to another state, farther from her community and family, because there isn't a federal facility closer to her home. Women's facilities are often in rural areas, where a majority of the residents are from urban areas.

Even if a physical plant weren't particularly wonderful but the staff and administration wanted to support and work with the residents—rather than neglect, intimidate, humiliate, or antagonize them—that would make a huge difference. I have rarely seen a facility that had a widespread culture of supportive interactions. Often, incarcerated women prefer staff who leave them alone, because at least then they aren't being directly harassed, degraded, or subjected to unpredictable punishments.

When I visit, I expect that I'm seeing what corrections staff would consider their own "best behavior," yet still I've witnessed degrading language like "move along, hoes," or "you can't trust inmates, they all lie." My colleague Barbara Owen has also experienced this kind of insulting language coming from staff to the residents.

Owen, who has conducted extensive ethnographic research inside women's prisons and advocated for policy change, has witnessed countless hours of interactions among staff and residents and tells a story to her training groups about an interaction she had early in her career. She was visiting an East Coast prison for the first time and was dressed professionally for the occasion. A male corrections officer approached her with the usual questions: Why are you here; what are you doing? She says, "For all he knew I could have been the attorney general of the state." When she informed him that the purpose of her visit was to do research on how the women living there were faring, he said, "Why do you care? They're just a bunch of dope-fiend hookers."

If corrections staff feel comfortable speaking this way in front of me and my colleagues, I imagine they are saying much worse in the residents' daily lives. My interviewees corroborated that it happens so regularly it isn't even seen as abnormal. This kind of verbal abuse stems from the belief that an incarcerated woman is an inferior person, a belief that permeates nearly every facility I've encountered. It is one of the reasons why I now say the system itself cannot be reformed. If you're remodeling a house and the foundation isn't any good, slapping a coat of paint on the outside doesn't fix the house.

Still, I and many others are working to improve the conditions for women who are currently incarcerated, because the fact is they are living in these facilities right now, today. And sometimes a coat of paint or a bit of respectful language would go a long way! But in an environment where some people have total control over the lives of others, if those people do not respect the dignity or understand the trauma of those in their charge, difficulties will continue. The fact is, in this country most of the environments prison residents live in contribute substantially more to their suffering than to their rehabilitation.

Every facility could make changes to improve living conditions, but some are forced to do so. My colleague Dawn, a retired prison warden, told me she is now a prison abolitionist. Some years ago she got a call from the prison where she had formerly been a warden, where for many years she had worked to create an environment where women could have a better chance to recover, rehabilitate, and prepare for reentry.

When she retired, leadership at that facility stopped many of the programs she had brought in. The staff culture became more punitive, more adversarial. They restricted residents' use of common areas, so residents weren't allowed to network and offer each other help in the ways they needed. A large number of them were placed in segregated housing for behavior modification, then left there for months without programming or access to religious services, which is their constitutional right. The entire environment became more threatening to everyone, and there was a spike in destructive behavior and resident suicides.

When the number of suicides hit a record high, Dawn was called back as a consultant to help turn the situation around. "First off, when I got there, I couldn't believe it was the same facility I had left," she told me. "The grounds used to be green, with beautiful flowers and trees. When I walked in there again, I looked around and I said, 'Oh my God, it's like the apocalypse has hit this place.' Everything was dead. There was trash all over the place. Right away that gave me a picture of what the current leadership at the facility cared about."

She told the administration that they had to let her do things her way. The high number of suicides at the facility had been kept out of the news, but the losses impacted many lives—residents', families', corrections officers'—before the administration took action. Things were so bad they gave Dawn unprecedented leeway to make changes. She launched new programs, retrained staff, and slowly began to ameliorate some of the harms that had come to the women at that facility.

Dawn's hands-on work is a departure from the way policy changes are often implemented. In my experience, when a new policy goes into effect in a prison, it is sometimes just written on a sheet of copy paper and posted on a board with *policy change* written at the top. If that is your notice of a policy change for staff, you can guess how easy it is for them to ignore it.

For some policy changes, like where to put trash cans for pickup, it might not make much difference in the lives of the residents. But if the policy bears on matters of human decency—new restrictions on the disciplinary use of restrictive housing, for instance, or how and when human beings can be shackled—everyone in the facility needs to be alerted to the change, with the expectation that it will be understood and implemented. Even when we achieve successful policy changes, we still must work very hard to get behavior to change at the facility level. That disconnection cannot be overstated.

Visitation

Although residents are the most impacted by the culture and environment at the prison, it's important to remember that visitors, especially children, also experience the tension in these environments. Everywhere, visitors are searched. There may be a brief pat-down or a metal detector; belongings are searched at the very least. People visiting a prison usually walk through at least one door that locks behind them after they pass. They are asked for ID multiple times. They may have to sign a liability release form.

Staff interactions with visitors vary, from kind to indifferent to intimidating to outright antagonistic. There is a certain arbitrariness with which rules are enforced. Generally, visitors must adhere to dress codes that usually prohibit anything resembling residents' uniforms, often denim or khaki. For women there are to be no underwire bras, no tight pants, no open-toed shoes, no short skirts. There are rules about physical contact, even with children.

However, the severity of consequences for breaking the rules has everything to do with where you are, who you are, and who is on duty. Some visiting rooms have natural light, an outside area, working vending machines and microwaves, and places for children to play. Others are dark and dirty, with hard chairs and tables, moldy bathrooms with doors that don't lock, and nothing for children to do but try to keep still.

The Impact of Improved Facilities

The culture and the physical environment of every facility are always informing each other and can change over time due to budgets, changes in staffing, new policies or political climates, and the power of the union representatives. Incarcerated women have to adapt to the stressors of these unpredictable and complex environments.

I remember touring one facility on the East Coast that was a converted university campus. It housed around six hundred women. The physical plant was nicer than many prisons: it was designed for students and faculty, so there were pleasant building materials instead of the usual concrete blocks, and there were more trees. However, the facility was located in a small, rural, conservative, predominantly white community. All the corrections officers and most of the staff came from that community, but nearly all the residents inside the prison were women of color from metropolitan areas hundreds of miles away. As a result, the culture inside that prison was rife with racism and class prejudice coming from staff. It was a nicer facility from a distance, but terrible for the residents up close.

Although we do need cleaner, brighter, and safer environments for residents and staff, renovation rarely does the job on its own. Where unhealthy cultural norms persist, it doesn't matter if the physical plant is updated or not.

One West Coast jail I consulted with went through an incredible rebuilding process, with gender-responsive principles and guidelines informing it, and wound up looking more like a community college than a jail—a significant improvement. It's clean, it's maintained, and this makes a positive impact. Although there is still a perimeter fence, it is not the first thing you notice as you approach. The yard is much larger than

This is the entrance into the Las Colinas Detention and Reentry Facility.

Source: San Diego County Sheriff's Department.

This is the yard at the Las Colinas Detention and Reentry Facility.

Source: San Diego County Sheriff's Department.

many other facilities and there are a number of buildings, so the women living there can potentially move around more.

However, a lot of the same people who had worked at the old jail came into this new environment with their old policies and practices, and it has been very difficult to make change. For instance, this facility enforced a strange practice they called "hands in the pants"—the expectation that residents must turn sideways and put their hands in the front of their pants whenever they encountered a group of visitors or staff coming toward them.

As I had never seen this before, at any women's facility anywhere in the world, I asked the staff about the practice and was told it was "for security." I worked to get that policy and practice changed, because of course it did nothing for security. The facility itself had been much improved, but the demeaning practices of the staff still affected how residents felt living there.

In California, two prisons in the middle of the state are architectural mirror images of each other. One of them no longer houses women, but when it did, you would think the two facilities would be exactly the same. They were identical buildings facing each other, each governed by the same laws and policies. However, very different cultural environments prevailed within them, and everyone who passed through those facilities could feel it. One was calmer, quieter, cleaner, and less stressful for the residents, due in part to the more respectful way the staff operated. The other was staffed by corrections officers whose union was constantly filing grievances against the warden, making it a much more stressful place to be.

Lisa, the interviewee mentioned before who entered prison later in her life than most, recalled another West Coast facility where she lived in the early 2000s "that should have been condemned long ago."

"There were sinks hanging off the wall," she told me. "For a dorm of a hundred women there were only four toilet stalls, and two of them were always broken. Only one of them had a door. The showers were disgusting, filthy with mold, and only two had shower curtains, which were half torn down." How did the women help each other deal with this situation? Lisa said, "You would have your friend stand at the door while you showered, so you weren't on display."

Sexual Harassment, Assault, and the Prison Rape Elimination Act

Lisa's concern about being "on display" in the shower was more about being seen by staff than by other residents. Although staff may receive training on how to maintain "professional distance" with prison residents, we know that sexual harassment is a widespread feature of life in women's prisons.

Violent sexual assault and rape are unacceptably prevalent. There are the cases that make the news, in which a corrections officer attempts to profit from the sex workers he meets at work, or an officer impregnates an incarcerated woman, or a facility employs a group of officers who systematically rape residents and then cover for each other (1).

But the fact is, a culture of harassment affects everyone. In my experience, every facility has officers (female as well as male) whom the women try to avoid because of the sexually predatory way they engage with residents. Most of the formerly incarcerated women I interviewed had experienced at least harassment at the hands of corrections, and sometimes more egregious offenses that weren't easily reportable because they were technically legal—an extremely rough gynecological exam, a cavity search just after giving birth, and so on.

The 2003 Prison Rape Elimination Act (PREA) made sex between officers and the incarcerated explicitly illegal. Originally conceived mostly to address resident-on-resident rape in men's prisons, PREA has now become an important part of shifting the culture in women's prisons to protect women from predatory corrections officers. Although there is occasionally sexual assault between incarcerated women, it is much less common than assault by officers. Advocates are currently working at the state level to close a loophole left by PREA that doesn't cover sexual contact between police and detainees in jail who haven't been convicted of a crime (2).

Unfortunately, as we will see many times throughout this journey, a change in policy is not enough. In 2022, a former warden of a federal prison in California was found guilty of eight counts of sexually abusing women in his custody. His facility was so violent with abuse perpetrated by so many officers, incarcerated women started calling the facility the "rape club." The former warden was promoted in rank during the years in which he was taking nude photos of incarcerated women, forcing them into sexual acts in areas of the prison where he knew there were no surveillance cameras, and promising women better treatment or early release for their compliance (3).

At the time of this publication, a former corrections officer at a California state prison is under investigation for sexual misconduct, with at least twenty-two victims already identified (4). We on the outside simply do not know how widespread this level of abuse truly is, because both prison residents and staff are afraid of retaliation for reporting. However, the people living and working inside prisons do know. When abuse like this happens in a closed space, even if there is only one perpetrator, other people know about it.

The main premise of PREA is that incarcerated individuals cannot meaningfully consent to sex with someone who has power over their life the way a corrections officer does. Although this makes sense logically, women living inside prisons are dealing with multiple pressures and priorities, and their lived reality is often more complex than policymakers can imagine. Sometimes women describe situations in which they may trade sex with a corrections officer (CO) for something of value, such as more phone time. In prison, sexual relationships can form between COs and residents that aren't physically violent, although they do exist in the obvious extreme power imbalance and are still against federal law.

When I interviewed Serena, who has built her career serving the needs of formerly incarcerated women, she made an important point about how these relationships can form. There was a major investigation at the prison where Serena was housed because a corrections officer there was involved in sex and drug trafficking with women in the facility. Ongoing conversations with the residents revealed a large amount of sexual contact among officers and residents. Serena was part of a group interviewed by internal affairs. "They asked us, How did we get to the point where the COs are sleeping with the inmates? And a lot of the women had answers to that. But I thought there was a big contributing factor we hadn't discussed."

In that jurisdiction, Serena explained, the COs could be subject to *mandatory holdbacks*, in which an eight-hour shift became a sixteen-hour shift, with no option to say no. They were often short staffed, and the mandatory holdbacks were common. "Think about this person," Serena said, "a human being, who has sixteen hours at the facility, and only eight hours at home with their family, guess what happens? They have zero interaction at home, and they start to see us as their family, their friend, but we're not. We're their inmates. And a lot of the women would do what they needed to do to get what they needed."

From Serena's point of view, a major contributing factor to the issue of sexual relationships among residents and COs was the lack of foresight at the top. She saw the COs as accountable for their own behavior, of course, and she also saw how mandatory holdbacks encouraged them to behave inappropriately.

If a resident experiences inappropriate behavior from staff and wants to report it, the culture at her facility will determine how difficult the process is. She must navigate the politics of favoritism, seniority, and bureaucracy, in addition to the way sexism and misogyny impact whether or not her story will be believed. A woman who reports staff misconduct risks retaliation, from which she cannot escape. She will need help, most likely from another resident who knows how to navigate the paperwork. Beatrice, the formerly incarcerated woman who became a forceful lifelong activist, used to do just that. "I wrote a lot of administrative remedies," she recalled. "We were going after the harassment. I was not a favorite of the staff," she smiled.

Restrictive Housing

Another important feature of prison that affects the overall culture inside is how the staff implement restrictive housing. Restrictive housing units go by different names—*administrative segregation* (*ad-seg*), *secure housing units* (*SHU*), *short-term restricted housing* (*STRH*), *solitary*, and *isolation*—but all exist to isolate individuals. Even short of the most notorious solitary confinements such as the infamous Hole at Alcatraz or Southeast Asian "dark cells," restrictive housing serves not just to isolate, but to humiliate. "It means I'm in a prison inside of a prison," one woman told me. "There's nothing lower."

Women are sent to isolation not because of their original sentence but because of something that happens on the inside. There may have been a fight, or an incident where a resident did something that an officer felt was dangerous to staff or another resident. In some cases, the isolation units do double duty as suicide watch or housing for transgender individuals who are deemed unsafe in the general population.

Restrictive housing units often do not offer programming. I had the opportunity to try to bring a program into one, and I remember feeling a sense of doom from the moment I saw this building inside the prison with its additional internal perimeter fence, its layers of razor wire, its many doors to be buzzed through, and then a sign that read *no warning shots fired.* I realized there was a person on the upper tier, watching the main space in the unit. If anyone misbehaved, they could be shot without a warning.

If the women housed in the isolation unit there were allowed outside, they were sent into a small area with fencing on all sides and overhead, reminiscent of a dog run. To be moved outside her cell, a woman was going to be put in a belly chain, hands cuffed to her waist, with shackles around her ankles. How she might do anything truly dangerous, warranting the threat of being shot, was beyond me.

If a woman in this area was going to have a visit from an attorney or counselor, she would be put into something that looks like a wire phone booth or a dog cage. This is inappropriately named a *therapeutic holding module.*

This is a therapeutic holding module in a secure housing unit for women.

Source: California Department of Corrections and Rehabilitation.

She is locked into that cage with the belly chain and all her restraints. When I wanted to get programming in for the women in secure housing, I refused to do it with the women in cages. We were able, eventually, to get special desks with plexiglass partitions, place them in a semicircle with soundproofing screens, and run the groups that way. It was a challenge, but the women have been very appreciative of these changes as the prison became more trauma informed.

This is how the space for the trauma-focused group was reconfigured in the secure housing unit. It is much more "trauma informed" and the therapeutic holding modules are not used with our groups.

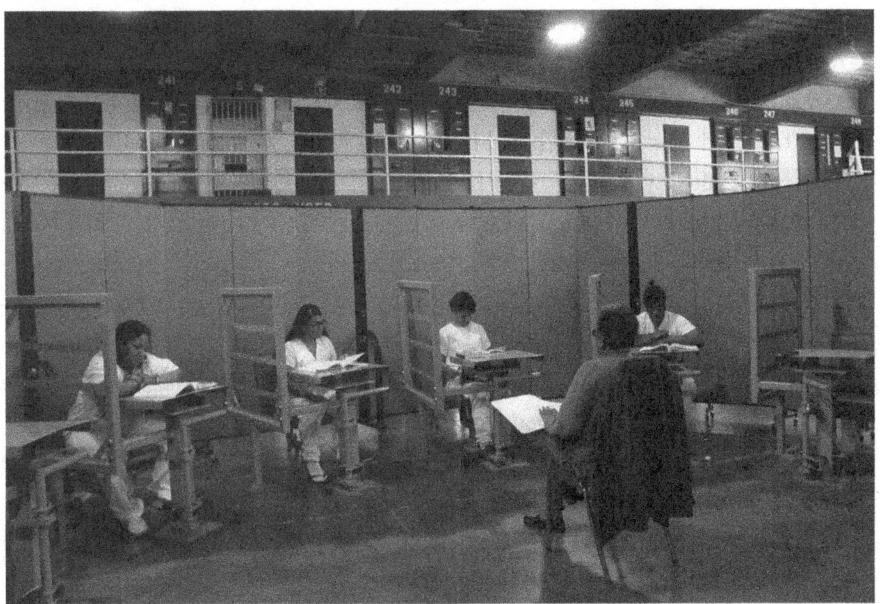

Source: California Department of Corrections and Rehabilitation.

I have been inside many women's prisons, but I haven't seen everything. Prisons are secretive places, especially when it comes to practices like restrictive housing or solitary confinement.

A documentary that came out in 1990, *Through the Wire,* was produced in conjunction with Amnesty International, directed by Nina Rosenblum, and narrated by Susan Sarandon. It told the story of a high-security isolation unit from the late 1980s in Lexington, Kentucky, where women prisoners were held in a basement in extreme deprivation. Lights were on 24/7. Everything was painted white, with no natural light.

The women were not allowed outside. They ate alone in their rooms. They were videotaped at all times, even in the shower. The women there, never more than seven at a time, were self-identified political prisoners. Although officials denied that the unit was either a secret political prison or an experiment in small-group isolation and sensory deprivation, the extreme circumstances got the attention of antiprison activists and human rights groups. The unit was closed in 1988.

When I saw the documentary, I was stunned. I sent a copy to a man named Jasper Clay Jr., who was a member of the Federal Parole Commission and someone with whom I had some professional affinity. He said he'd never heard of the unit. He asked me if I wanted to try and see it, and I agreed that we should. Jasper made arrangements with the federal prison in Lexington, Kentucky, and told them we would want to see the high-security unit. I traveled from California. He traveled from Washington, DC.

We spent all day at the main facility, following regular procedure. We visited the warden's office. We got a tour. I gave talks to both the residents and the officers. All day we got excuses for why we couldn't see the high-security unit in the basement. They told us it had been closed down. Yes, we said, we knew that. We still wanted to see the unit. Each time we brought it up, there was a reason we couldn't see it: *It's too close to the time Dr. Covington is speaking, there's nothing to see, it is too close to count time, we just use it for storage, there're file cabinets at the entrance and you can't really get in*, and so on.

If I had been there by myself, I would have presumed I was treated this way because I held no real authority in the system. But Jasper was a high-ranking federal official, and even he could not get in to see the unit, which truly surprised us both. Of course, I was aware that prisons and jails often used various forms of restrictive housing. Judging from what the documentary revealed, the Lexington unit took these already destructive practices and amplified them. The fact that we had something like that in this country, and that it was still kept so secret even after it had been shut down, taught me some very important lessons about the power prison facilities have to self-govern, to operate independently of any policy or legal procedure.

To put this story in perspective, the previously mentioned United Nations *Bangkok Rules* featured a set of rules limiting searches, discipline, and restraint. These were followed by additional UN rules (known as *The*

Mandela Rules) in 2015. Based on years of research and international testimony, Rule 43 prohibits both indefinite and prolonged solitary confinement. As defined by this rule, *prolonged* refers to solitary confinement in excess of fifteen days. Although there have been some important reforms since the days of the Lexington high-security unit, both indefinite and prolonged solitary confinement are still practiced across the United States.

We have known for years that isolation brings serious psychological and physical consequences. It is not safe. But a consistent body of research from the Vera Institute of Justice reveals that it is also not effective: widespread use of restrictive housing has never conclusively been shown to increase safety for residents or staff.

Furthermore, the systemic injustices that permeate the system are visible in who goes into restrictive housing. According to the institute's report *Rethinking Restrictive Housing*, "Just as systems have come to rely too heavily on incarceration, departments of corrections now rely too much on restrictive housing. And, as in other parts of the justice system, restrictive housing often affects disproportionate numbers of young people, people living with mental illness, and people of color" (5). The institute found that women who were in restrictive housing were much more likely to have severe mental health issues. When women are living in a prison or jail that uses restrictive housing as an answer to mental health difficulty, low-level infractions, or social conflict, they are living under a very high sense of threat and stress.

Serena, who was mentioned earlier and now runs large online support groups for formerly incarcerated women, told me a few details about her experience in solitary. "There's a buzzer," she recalled. "And you can press it all day long, but they don't answer if they don't want to. So I was really trapped."

She had been moved from a facility where she was allowed to interact with her fellow residents, even on lockdown. In the new facility, lockdown meant true solitary confinement. Interestingly, she told me, the old facility saw zero incidents of escape. "When they moved us over, within the first year, six women tried to climb that barbed wire to get out," Serena recalled. "I mean, they weren't going to get out of that barbed wire, but they were so disempowered, so trapped, they were driven to try to get out. All we did was change buildings, but the structure and the nature of the environment was enough to drive them to risk adding five years."

A Different Kind of Space

We must continue to ask the question: How do we envision something other than a prison as an answer to harm in a community? Until the major societal shift that will be required for us to implement true alternatives, there are many of us working to improve conditions for people who are incarcerated today. Although there are definitely those who simply want to see a "kinder, gentler" prison and aren't questioning the functionality of incarceration as a foundational principle, I count myself among those who believe we should be working *both* to better support incarcerated people today *and* to dismantle and completely rethink the system for the future. This includes taking a serious look at the spaces in which we house people sentenced to prison and the cultures that are cultivated there.

In a 2019 article for the *International Journal of Environmental Research and Public Health*, researcher Yvonne Jewkes and her colleagues argue that introducing trauma-informed practice into dilapidated institutions serves as mere "window dressing" and that the facilities need to be holistically restructured. Taking their cues from incarcerated people, the researchers list the "basic environmental elements that are near-universally desired by people in prison." These were "not expressed as mere preferences, but were framed as matters of ontological security"—that is, the most primal human needs relating to their very being and existence—"which if not present, are apt to trigger mental instability and trauma."

These needs include privacy, socialization, warmth when it is cold and effective ventilation when it is hot, some freedom of movement outside as well as inside, regular and high-quality family visits, meaningful and appropriately paid work/education/activities (including essential transferable skills, e.g., use of digital technologies), the ability to undertake a pastime or hobby beyond those traditionally permitted within custodial settings, facilities to occasionally cook one's own food, interaction with nature, and—crucially—a high degree of choice, autonomy, and control over all these fundamental actions (6). A facility that could support these needs would be very different from what is currently operating in the United States.

In fact, a facility that truly supported the needs of the currently incarcerated would look different in nearly every country. Sometimes I say, "All prisons are bad, some are just worse than others." However, I'm hopeful that with a large-scale movement to understand trauma as the foundation of much of the harm that is caused by women, a movement to create safer spaces with respectful environments and cultures of recovery may not be far behind.

For example, when I visited Scotland there was only one women's prison, and it was in an older building. Based on my experience, in the United States this building would have been considered just fine for the purpose of imprisoning people, but in Scotland it was considered too rundown. Two women were appointed to work with an architect to envision a new facility. The women thought there should be a large outdoor space. The rooms should feel like those in homes, and there should be a beautiful mother–child space. Everything was thought out in terms of a sense of safety and serenity.

When they described what they wanted, the architect said, "Oh, you don't want a prison at all, you want a wellness center with a focus on healing." They said, "Yes, that's exactly what we want." Unfortunately, with a change in administration, the facility was not built, but the concept had finally been acknowledged: perhaps the design of the prison itself is causing people an excess of harm.

This is the entry into the proposed but unbuilt women's prison in Scotland.

Source: Scottish Prison Service.

This is the interior of one of the housing units. This is what is often called "the day room."

Source: Scottish Prison Service.

This is the design for a woman's living space. Note the use of doors, privacy for the toilet area, space for movement, and size of windows. Color is also used.

Source: Scottish Prison Service.

WORKING INSIDE THE CULTURE OF CORRECTIONS

By now I am sure it is clear that incarcerated women endure innumerable experiences of ongoing humiliation and abuse. In the midst of this, it is also important to acknowledge that there are staff who care.

The two most common acts of kindness formerly incarcerated interviewees mentioned were when staff made sure they got their telephone time to talk to their family, and when staff helped them get the right amount of feminine hygiene products for their needs. But although many of my interviewees remembered one or two corrections officers or staff members who treated them with dignity, they were generally the exception that proved the rule. Staff who are kind to prison residents—working against the broader culture of corrections—often feel they must hide their actions, so they find themselves isolated from their peers.

In my experience about 25 percent of those who work in corrections are sincerely helpful and believe in rehabilitation, and even represent some of the hidden healers I refer to. But 75 percent of staff create barriers and are challenging to be around as a visitor, let alone as a resident. A significant number of people in that 75 percent are actively abusive and violent toward prison residents. We don't truly know how many from the outside, but it is definitely more than make the news.

This suggests the extent to which prisoners aren't the only ones harmed by toxic prison culture. I interviewed Velda, Rochelle, and Dawn, three former high-ranking prison officials who were moved to advocate for incarcerated women both during and after their formal prison careers. They understood that the system overall was damaging to everyone.

The numbers tell the story. Thirty-four percent of corrections officers suffer from post-traumatic stress disorder (PTSD). This compares to 14 percent of military veterans (7). Corrections officers are more likely than vets to experience violence, stress, burnout, PTSD, mental health challenges, divorce, and other negative outcomes. We also know that they have high suicide rates and many studies show they have a shorter life expectancy than the general population (8).

Finding Your Program

This is where we are, so what are we gonna do with our lives? I have to have meaning when I wake up, so what does that look like for me? Every day I asked that question. That's how I did my time.

—**Geri**, *personal interview*

I MET STAR through a mutual friend and colleague who knew her when they were both incarcerated in California. A calm, smiling woman now in her early forties, Star was incarcerated at twenty-two with a fifteen-to-life sentence. She served seventeen years. She went before the parole board three times before she was eligible and has been home since 2017. Since then she has had a baby, a son, who turned two in 2022.

Star is now a community health worker for a nonprofit, helping people coming home from prison with their reentry needs. However, early in her prison time, Star told me she got in "a lot of trouble." She said, "I fought because I was too afraid to speak." In her first facility there weren't enough programs for her to participate in. "If you go into a house, and everybody is negative, and nobody has anything good to say, and there's no productive outlets for you, what are you going to do?"

Eventually she was moved to a prison where there were more opportunities and a more sympathetic warden who supported rehabilitation and self-help. She took advantage of prison programs, receiving certifications in conflict mediation and dog training, and becoming a facilitator of *Beyond Violence*. Star told me that once she found her own focus, she would try to help other women struggling with the pressures of living in prison. "If someone was wavering, starting down the wrong path, you have to try to bring them in, because everybody needs to participate in making the unit a good, clean place to be."

Star believes that change is possible, and she told me she had seen "the worst people make changes and become a completely new person." However, she cautioned, any kind of person is vulnerable to the effects of incarceration. "Fundamentally, change has got to start with what the system has set in place for you," she said. "It's up to the individual to take advantage of opportunities, but the opportunities have to be there, or you're just gonna fall through the cracks."

The Federal Bureau of Prisons and each of the states' corrections departments provide different programs inside prisons: educational, vocational, drug rehab, parenting, and others. Programs run a huge gamut in terms of content, quality, and availability. Some are facilitated by prison staff to the residents. Some are outside programs, for which the prison contracts with a community provider like me.

Those programs are overseen by people who are not employed directly by the prison and in some cases are facilitated by peers inside. Many outside programs are run by volunteers in the community—college students, people with loved ones who have been incarcerated, activists, and others. A few programs are affiliated with academic researchers gathering data for publication. Some states also maintain research departments within their department of corrections, of varying degrees of usefulness, and some of these are designed to evaluate programs.

Programs are always considered a privilege and can be revoked at any time, so they are used as an incentive. During the 2020–2022 lockdowns associated with the coronavirus, many programs were simply canceled until further notice. Immediately upon learning of the lockdowns, my team created and delivered in-cell programming. We didn't wait to be asked because we know how important programming is. It took one state system six months to ask outside programs if we had anything we could provide for the women who had been meeting in our program groups prior to the pandemic. They didn't even know we had already rolled it out. Despite the fact that the only way COVID-19 was now entering the prison was through staff, it was the prison residents who were locked down in their cells and given nothing productive to do.

According to all the women I spoke to for this book, programming is a way to do more productive time, despite the wide range of quality in the programs. As Star put it, "Either I'll like it, or I won't. If I don't, I don't have to do it anymore. If I do, then this is the doorway that I need to go through to get me into this new world."

In addition to the personal benefit of feeling engaged with something that offers a window to life outside the prison, incarcerated women may be able to earn "good time" (a reduced sentence) with certain programs and are more likely to be deemed "suitable" by a parole board (if their sentence allows it and they are incarcerated in a system that has the option for parole).

In some cases, prison residents are even required to complete certain programs in order to obtain their release. This means that the revocation of a program can not only harm residents in the present moment, but it can also postpone their release date. Prisons run on the labor of the people living there, so a woman's program schedule has to fit in around her prison job, for which she is lucky if she gets a few cents an hour. For these reasons a prison resident faces many considerations when selecting a program: what might be of value to me now, what might serve me after I am released, what will have value to the parole board, and what fits in with my schedule.

In some places programs don't become available until shortly before an incarcerated person's release. This means a woman could spend years inside without access to programming. Correctional logic holds that women who are not leaving the prison (condemned women and women with life sentences, especially life without parole) do not need programming, and in many places they do not have the option.

As mentioned earlier, I have worked to make programming available to condemned women. Because I believe that programming is a big part of what helps people stay sane in our current system, I see withholding it as a human rights issue. At the very least, programming gives women in difficult living environments something to focus on. At its best, programming offers women opportunities to connect with each other, to build important emotional and practical skills in a community—even, for some women, to begin a healing process.

That said, not all programming is created equal, and bad programs can block programs of value from being implemented. I once visited a women's prison where I was asked to weigh in on a new therapeutic program for recovery and sobriety. What I saw was a collection of unrelated activities that seemed purposeless at best, and sometimes deliberately humiliating. In the evening the program director led a large group of women in an exercise called "barnyard," where women played farm animals. Some were chickens, and they would flap their wings and cluck. Some were pigs, oinking. Others were cows. I was horrified. The corrections officers were laughing. Some of the women wouldn't get up and do it, more power to them. This was humiliation, not a program.

Speaking very generally, the most successful programs respond directly to what incarcerated women say they need and want. Former chief deputy warden Velda, who oversees *Beyond Violence* and *Healing Trauma* programs, has launched numerous other groups at the facility where she serves, many at the request of the residents.

She is committed to providing programs that are peer led. "I listen carefully to their conversations about what they want to do, so we created 'Felons Against Distracted and Drunk Driving' and a program about emotional neglect and abuse called the 'Breakthrough Parenting' program," she told me. "We did one called 'Lord Deliver Me from Me' ... all in addition to the work I was originally in there to do. Different women brought the projects to me, and then we just took them and gave them life."

Many who work in corrections do not believe that women living inside a prison know what they need. However, former warden Dawn shares Velda's conviction that the women themselves need to guide their programming. She told me that during her tenure at a large West Coast women's prison, "the women were given the respect, the acknowledgment that they knew what was best for themselves. Because of that respect, we were able to help get them what they needed. Then they were able to help each other."

This manifested in multiple ways. "We had a mentor program that helped the women know their rights under the Prison Rape Elimination Act (PREA) and trained them to be mentors," Dawn told me. "So when women came in that were new to the institution, they would see a mentor who would share information on what they could do if there was a sexual assault. It was much better for the women to hear this from each other instead of hearing it from staff."

The way staff interact with programming also varies widely, and it directly affects the experience of incarcerated women. When staff are supportive of programming, women can concentrate on the content, know they will be let into the program space on time, and trust that the hours they put into the program will be recorded properly. However, sometimes staff are not only unsupportive, they may passively or actively sabotage women trying to participate.

Robin, the prison resident who went on to deliver programming inside, told me she witnessed what felt like a "civil war" inside the East Coast prison where she spent three years. "The corrections officers are one team, and then there's the counselors and the teachers, and very often we'd see the rivalry. Officers would say, 'Those women don't need to know how to read, they don't deserve this, they shouldn't have a better education than my kids do. They don't need to go to that group, they're just coming back here, they won't amount to anything.'"

In the twenty-two years since she left prison, Robin has devoted her life to service, and I have known her for over a decade in that capacity. Although her focus is women's recovery from substance use disorders in the community, she also works with incarcerated women and young people in the juvenile system. During her incarceration, Robin took a writing class with bestselling author Wally Lamb. Her work was featured in *Couldn't Keep It to Myself: Wally Lamb and the Women of York Correctional Institution*, and she has continued to work on getting creative programs running inside ever since.

Robin facilitates programs that use art to encourage healing and growth and faces a steady stream of obstacles built into the systems. When she first began working with incarcerated women to create original dance performances through the Justice Dance Performance Project, she said, "It took seven or eight years of doing the program to get juice and cookies at our performances. Then it took another five years to offer lunch. Then it took a while more to have a visitors' weekend. Finally, we've been able to invite everyone inside—children, families, people from the community, even the mayor. They all come see the women perform and spend time together."

Robin has devoted her life to supporting incarcerated and formerly incarcerated women through creative programming, because a writing group she participated in while she was inside made a huge difference in her life. She had to tune out messages from unsupportive staff and stay focused on the programs, and now she advocates for other women to have a chance to do the same.

Barriers to Effective Programs

Corrections is a culture of control, and programming is a culture of change. This is a serious culture clash. Even those who are not incarcerated can see the way some staff resist high-quality programming. There are many people working on the inside who don't want the residents to get anything "for free" that they themselves might have to pay for in the free world. I remember one administrator who complained to me that the prison residents were getting "free education and training" while her kids had to pay to learn a skill in a trade school. She was furious. That attitude, which given the complex socioeconomic realities is not hard to understand, does not make for a good working relationship with incarcerated women who are trying to productively program.

Rochelle, a former captain in the California correctional system, remembers what it was like to return to a women's facility as a program coordinator and encounter resistance from staff. "A lot of the staff did not like that I was advocating for the women," she told me. "They were used to me dispensing rules and regulations, and then when I came in to advocate and oversee programming, it showed some of my disdain for the punishment system. They thought of me as a traitor. They were really resentful when we started the [*Beyond Violence*] program." Rochelle described this resentment also as jealousy, and I have witnessed the same countless times.

Rochelle would respond to staff concerns with practical realities: "My reply was, these ladies are going to be leaving one day, and may be living next door to you. So would you rather them come out and be equipped with skills and tools? Or would you rather they come out just like they came in?"

Still, staff would sabotage the program. This happened through small acts of passive aggression, like walking through a group jangling their keys, disrupting a moment of emotional processing; discouraging Rochelle from accepting a particular resident into the program because she was "horrible" and "the devil" (Rochelle worked with her and she was a strong participant who eventually got released from secure housing); or keeping program participants from arriving to their group on time through various forms of interference.

The program participants admired and adored Rochelle. Years after participating in a program, Liz told me that when she met Rochelle she felt "like she could see right through me." After her years of abuse as a child and then her years in prison, Liz said it was the first time in her life someone had challenged her to really reflect on her life while treating her with kindness and respect. Rochelle stayed the course, and her facilitation has positively affected the lives of hundreds of women.

The subtleties of how a program is developed, and which beliefs or prejudices about incarcerated women guide its implementation, are very difficult to parse without being physically present to bear witness. Some facilities will look great on paper—they say they have vocational, educational, and self-help programs. However, what they actually offer for job training programs may be training in outdated technology, or in "feminine" skills like cooking and cosmetology only, because those skills are still considered appropriate ways to rehabilitate women. For education, they may offer a GED program but no higher education, because they haven't maintained a partnership with an accredited institution.

Activist Beatrice remembered that the women in the Spanish-speaking classes at the East Coast prison where she was incarcerated for fifteen years were always treated worse by staff than the women in English-speaking classes. "They weren't allowed books or pencils," she recalled.

"So a few of us helped them write a request and we advocated for them to get the supplies they needed." On paper, a facility may have a program designed for reentry that gives a few pointers on where to look for a job or apartment, but it is not common for women getting ready to go home to feel truly supported in what they learn there, an issue we will return to.

In addition to the disparity that may exist between what a prison offers on paper and in reality, some facilities will actively discourage programs that allow women to communicate with each other about changes they want to see inside the prison. Brandi, who served twenty-eight years in what she calls the "gated community," was part of a group called the Long-Termers Organization. The group was disbanded, and Brandi organized with a few other women to fight for it to be reinstated more than once.

When I asked her why the prison had canceled the program, she told me, "They said they didn't want all these LWOPs [women sentenced to life without parole] getting together in one place. They thought we were gonna take over the prison or something, because we did have a lot of power when we got together. We fought for our rights in there together, and even though we may not like each other or associate outside of the group, when it came to all of us doing something for all of us—we came together." Brandi's Long-Termers Organization worked to keep access to hobby crafts, commissary boxes, and fundraising programs, all of which could be canceled at any time by the administration of the prison.

Alcoholics Anonymous and Other Recovery Programs

It should follow from our discussion of substance use disorders in Part One that one of the most important programs for many prison residents is drug treatment. Treatment for substance use disorders and recovery groups are a critical place for many women to start a process of changing their own lives for the better, but they are not universally offered or of consistent quality throughout the United States. In prisons, substance use disorder programs vary widely in quality of leadership and impact on users. Often when a prison says they offer treatment, they actually mean drug education classes, which years of data have shown to be ineffective.

Serena, who had experienced more than one of those programs in Hawaii, finally signed up for a gender-responsive pilot treatment program offered inside the prison that sounded a little different. She told me, "The only reason I agreed to attend it is because it was the first time I heard a treatment program saying to me, 'We aren't focusing on drugs. You know everything you need to know about drugs. We are going to focus on how to keep a checkbook, how to pay your bills, how to do budgeting, how to do parenting.' It was really different."

Serena eventually developed her own nontraditional harm reduction approach to substance use disorders that she now offers to women through online groups and in-person trainings. If she had been incarcerated at one of the many facilities that only offered an Alcoholics Anonymous or religious group, she may not have found that path. Although some women are helped by a more traditional treatment approach, those who are not need other choices.

Perhaps more people in the United States are starting to understand the connection between our burgeoning prison population and the criminalization of addiction. Many, if not most, women come into their incarceration with some type of substance use disorder. An issue we have even more trouble discussing is the people who *don't* have a substance use disorder when they arrive but have one when they leave. There are people who start drinking and using on the inside as a way to manage the stress of living in prison.

What I understand, and what has been corroborated by my interviewees, is that drugs and alcohol are readily available in prison. All the security measures we've discussed, and many more we haven't, have not stopped the flow of substances into prisons. In some cases, alcohol is made inside by residents. It is a reality, and one that many courts do not acknowledge when they sentence a woman to prison claiming she will have to "clean up" there. It makes a lot of sense to me that women turn to drugs and alcohol to deal with the stress of living in a prison. As interviewee Jackie, who had spent years addicted to opioids, said, "I hate when people are like, 'Why did you use drugs?' I'm just like, duh, you know, because they *work*." And it's true that self-medication can work for a time. Then, for many people, the solution becomes its own problem.

Even for women who make the decision to become abstinent in prison, abstinence on the outside is different from abstinence on the inside. There are new life challenges when they are released, and so many triggers to relapse. Research shows that if you give women something that they feel is useful and supportive to them, they stay in substance abuse treatment (9). They leave treatment when they don't think they are getting anything of value, which just makes sense. Why stay in a program when it doesn't seem useful?

This logic applies to most programming for incarcerated people. The programs that my interviewees remembered as truly supportive and useful to them included reading and writing groups, puppy programs, gardening, addiction treatment that was focused on coping and life skills (not drug education), educational courses that helped them attain a GED or higher, and therapeutic (especially trauma-focused) groups facilitated by their peers.

To be clear, I do not believe that treatment for trauma should be mandated. The therapeutic groups that are most helpful are voluntary. Although some women have positive experiences with counselors employed by the prison, the ones I spoke to were always aware that revealing the true depths of their struggles might make them less suitable for parole. As we will discuss, mental health "care" in prison is often just medication management. So for women who are ready to do deeper psychoeducation and emotional work, voluntary peer-led groups are a real resource.

Creating Safer Spaces Inside

As a creator of programming for carceral settings, I understand that my primary job is to stay attuned to what *works*. That was my goal when I developed *Beyond Violence*, the previously mentioned program designed to help participants look at the impact of violence in their lives and to create opportunities to make changes to prevent violence in the future. Most of the interviewees who offered their stories for this book participated in this program, either peer facilitated in California or staff led in other places, and operated by a program coordinator who is affiliated with the program, not the prison.

Based on what I had observed and absorbed over years working with justice-involved women, I knew when I began this work that programming in prisons would only be as effective as its participants could be made to feel safe. I can't guarantee that a woman is going to be safe in a prison. But I can be reasonably sure that the women who participate in *Beyond Violence* can expect at least forty hours over a few months where she will be relatively safe.

This safety arrives initially through the intention of the program and coordinator, but is most meaningfully built and sustained by the group itself and the emotional environment they create together—which happens in spite of the prison. Interviewee Geri described this as the importance of "camaraderie in the sharing of the stories." She said she felt supported in her group, "and for the first time, I can just be honest and open. I realized everybody has a story. All our journeys are different, but we all have a story." The group maintained confidentiality, and Geri went on to become a trained facilitator who led groups for other women.

These are peer facilitators for the programs *Beyond Violence* and *Healing Trauma*. They meet weekly between the groups they are facilitating to plan for the following week and to support each other.

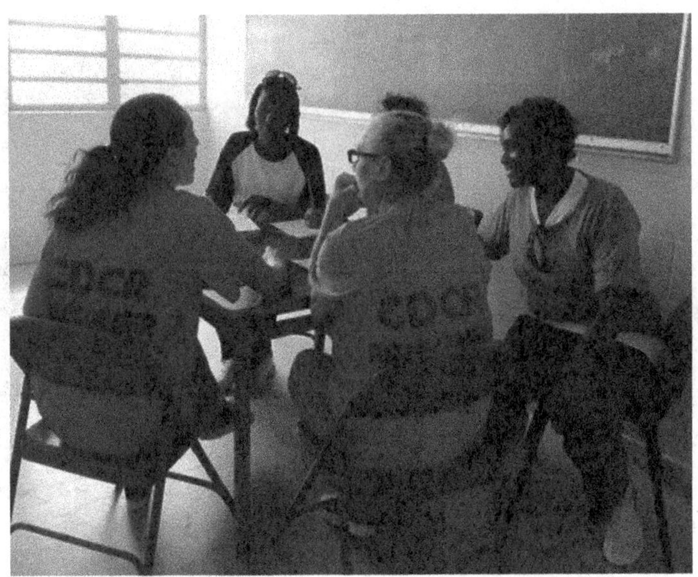

Source: California Department of Corrections and Rehabilitation.

Groups work because they're built on relationships, and relationships are the most powerful way to heal. Currently trending are evidence-based programs and programs that are manualized, which can deliver valuable consistency to participants. Indeed, in 1999 I wrote the first manualized addiction treatment program for women, now in its third edition. It was selected as the core substance use disorders program in the California Department of Corrections and Rehabilitation. Currently there has also been a turn toward digital programming in lieu of in-person groups.

There is value in these things, but it is crucial to remember that healing is not a pill or a piece of paper. How staff relate to women (with their language, intention, and level of kindness) and the way women are able to relate to each other in a group—*this* is where the magic happens. What we have learned from these peer-led programs is that when you give women materials developed for them, with their input, they take those materials and run with them. They can begin to powerfully change themselves and others.

This group of women is participating in the *Beyond Violence* program and a peer facilitator is leading them in a guided visualization.

Source: California Department of Corrections and Rehabilitation.

When a person moves from jail or a reception center into the general prison population, their opportunity to start regularly participating in ongoing programs usually opens up. Whether in traditional addiction recovery treatment, specialized trauma recovery support in a peer-led group, a writing class, or a crochet circle, that decision to find and maintain a program is one of the most important ones an incarcerated woman can make. It is where she may find community, support for her emotions, and information she needs about how the prison runs and how to navigate it. In-person programs are valuable not just for the content they deliver but also for the opportunities they provide for women to connect and create networks, mentorships, and friendships.

Food

Instant coffee comes in bags, right? And if you open the bag, it gets stale. So, someone might put the coffee in an empty peanut butter jar, and then the COs [corrections officers] would come and throw it away, saying that's contraband. Or they might not. It was whether they felt petty that day.

—**Beatrice**, *personal interview*

It cost the state fifteen cents per meal to make our food. That's not real food. It's absolutely disgusting. So people lived on commissary and got really creative. Women were outstanding with it, making great things.

—**Linda**, *personal interview*

ON THE FIRST morning of my voluntary three-day stay inside the Black Mountain women's facility in North Carolina, as I stood in line for breakfast, I noticed a few apples on a ledge above the rest of the food. I moved to take one, but the woman behind me stopped me. "You can't do that," she said. "Those are only for the staff."

Instantly, I wanted to take one anyway. That was an unfamiliar impulse for me. Somehow, knowing that apples were available to the staff and not to me as a person living with the general population of prison residents activated a deep sense of injustice and desire to rebel. I didn't do it, because I was a guest of the administration and knew it would be inappropriate to break the rules. Still, I was struck by the cruelty of it: they put the apples out where the women could see them but not have them. And why couldn't they have fresh fruit? What was stopping the prison from having enough apples for everyone?

The answer from the corrections side is predictable. The way prison residents are fed is a result of budget constraints. However, we know that food currently makes up a small percentage of the overall budget of the prison system, as low as 4 percent in Texas. The majority of states spend under $3 a day, and some much less, per person (10). It is true that there have been budget cuts or stagnant spending on food and a drastically increasing population to feed.

However, the claim that we can't change the way we feed our incarcerated population because the money isn't there is simply untrue. The money has been allocated elsewhere and could be reallocated. The priority of nourishment has fallen far below the priority of keeping costs low. It certainly doesn't keep health care costs low in the long term for prison residents and their families, as incarcerated people suffer from higher rates of diabetes and heart disease than the general public, undoubtedly exacerbated by the diet they are forced to eat (11).

There are so many ways to think and speak about food. Food is both cultural and personal. It is both practical and symbolic—a way to show care, a form of nurturing, an element of celebration. When withheld, it can become a powerful method of control. My research colleague Barbara Owen tells of a visit to one women's prison where the senior corrections officer had a candy dish at the edge of her desk, near where the women would sit. "I said something about how nice it was that she had a treat for the inmates," she told me. "She said, 'No, it's not for them. It's there so they know that if they live a law-abiding life, they can have candy in their home.'"

On an even more elemental level—food is sustenance. We need nourishing food, and access to high-quality food is a profound concern for many in this country. Food insecurity and food deserts affect tens of millions of Americans in the same communities disproportionately impacted by mass incarceration. Although food justice movements are building more city gardens, starting more farmer's markets, and doing the important work of creating better access to good food, we have not yet seen a large-scale positive change in the way prison residents are fed.

A 2020 report from Impact Justice indicates that "most prisons now rely on refined carbohydrates (e.g., white bread, biscuits, and cake) to reach the mandated calorie count, and many have turned to fortified powdered beverage mixes as the primary source of essential nutrients" (12). Not only are the selections low in nourishment, often the food is stale, spoiled, moldy, or of obviously low quality.

When I emerged from my stay at Black Mountain, the first thing my friend asked me was, "Do you want to go eat?" Of course, my answer was yes. I was ravenous because I had been avoiding the food in the cafeteria. Change needs to happen because the food in prison is still terrible, all these years later.

Low-Quality Food at Cheaper Prices

It took me time to get a sense of the larger systems involved in the way meals worked inside prisons and jails. Some years ago I joined an advisory group at Hazelden, a publishing house. Our purpose was to guide their publications used within the criminal legal system, and as part of my role I was sent to the American Correctional Association conference. This is an enormous annual gathering in a major convention center, with an exhibit hall full of vendors. Booth after booth is filled with products related to confinement, such as shackles and restraints. Periodically, there would be a booth selling food and cigarettes. These items would have no identifying brand label.

While I noticed it, I didn't think much of it at the time. I was focused on the commercial culture of punishment at the conference, like the booth with a display of a yard and a small figure running across it. Conference participants could push a button, zap the figure with electricity, and make him fall down. This cruelty was more dramatic than the more insidious ways incarceration harms people—like through low-quality food.

Later, doing some consulting work for a department of corrections on the East Coast, I was going inside prisons often. On the first day I had to eat on the inside, the staff told me to try the salad bar. Almost everything in the salad bar had come from a can. Canned beets, canned corn, and browning iceberg lettuce. I had to find another solution. I found some saltine crackers, peanut butter, and cottage cheese. I decided I could make a lunch out of that, because what could go wrong with those things?

As it turns out, a lot. You would never find these products in a regular grocery store. They are off label. They don't taste right, much less *good.* These were the products being sold so enthusiastically in vendor booths at the conference I had attended. The message to incarcerated women is clear: Your experience doesn't matter. Your health doesn't matter. You don't matter.

For women in jail, detention, and prison, food is part of the punishment. Poor-quality food leads to health problems that families struggle to support upon reentry. Food plans in women's prisons are borrowed from the high-carbohydrate plans in men's prisons. Fresh fruit and vegetables are rare. At one West Coast gathering of released women, a research colleague of mine was surprised that the veggie trays were gobbled ahead of everything else. The women told her they craved fresh vegetables because they never got them inside.

Food as Contraband

Interviewee Jackie, who is now an advocate for sex workers and women in recovery, told me that "when you are in jail, food is priceless. You wouldn't serve the cafeteria food to your dog. So when people share commissary, it is a way of uplifting each other." Commissary food is purchased by incarcerated women separately from the cafeteria food states are required to provide. Common food items available at prison commissaries include tuna, chips, candy bars, ramen noodles, and processed cheese. The commissary is also where incarcerated people can buy over-the-counter medicines, toiletries, approved clothing items, and so on.

Women are not technically allowed to buy things for each other. Gina Fedock, a researcher and colleague, explains it this way: "If you give or lend something to someone, it could be considered a form of coercion, which is a threat to security." A resident could be subject to a *shakedown* (disruptive search) of her cell, or even placed in solitary confinement, for providing nourishment to another resident—nourishment that the prison itself has refused to provide.

Still, sharing commissary food was a regular practice among the women I spoke to, and it was an important one. Finding workarounds to the tight food regulations in prison is part of the culture. Said Rose, who was incarcerated in the United Kingdom: "You always want to have a kitchen girl as a friend because they are the ones who will try and smuggle a few things out of the kitchen for you."

Linda, who now teaches somatic healing practices internationally, told me she had nearly gone to administrative segregation over an orange peel. Security concerns govern every protocol and affect how residents are able to engage with even the food they do have access to. Early in her incarceration, when Linda had "no idea about anything in jail," she realized that fresh fruit was a big deal. "Oranges were really special," she recalled. "One day I got one and decided to keep the peel in my room to freshen the smell. I put the peel on my west-facing window, where the sunshine could hit it and make my room smell like orange. I got threatened with administrative segregation, and I was so confused."

Eventually she did learn: the orange peels were contraband because they could be used to make alcohol. "I didn't know about that at all," she recalled. "I felt like I'd been doing everything right, and one day I might just accidentally end up in ad-seg. That was terrifying."

Food as a Method for Rehabilitation

A human being nearly getting sent into isolation for possession of an orange peel should signal something to us about how broken our policies are. I know there is another way to engage with food in a carceral setting, because I've seen it done.

In 2005 I spoke at an international conference where I met a warden of a women's prison in Dublin, Ireland. Listening to him discuss its release policies, I quickly determined that this warden was interested in actual rehabilitation and seemed to be trying his best to advance prison residents' health and dignity.

The facility he managed allows incarcerated women who are nearing the end of their sentences to go home for an overnight, or even a few days, to begin their transition. They offer a graduated release program that gives women a chance to live in an on-site apartment, go to work, and check back in before they are fully released—not as time added, but as the way they do the last few months of a longer sentence to make reentry smoother.

But he didn't stop there. He noticed one day that a person he called Miss Jones was getting escorted off the premises for a doctor's appointment. Miss Jones had just returned from a weekend at home but was shackled for her trip to the doctor. The warden began to push for a change in practice so that wouldn't happen. I was taken by this because it is unfortunately quite rare for people so deeply embedded in the system to see how ridiculous and dehumanizing the practices actually are, much less share the problems of their facility with an international audience. When he invited me to come visit the prison in Dublin, I eagerly accepted.

About a week later I was on my way to Ireland, and we spoke to confirm the plans. He offered to send a car to pick me up around eleven o'clock in the morning, but realizing that would mean I would have to eat lunch at the prison, I asked if I could come later. When he said that wouldn't work, I figured, *I can eat at the prison for one day.*

I got picked up, took the tour, and at the end they led me to a dining room.

"Is this where the staff eat?" I asked.

"No, this is where the residents eat," the warden told me.

We sat at a table with a white tablecloth and a small bouquet of flowers. I laughed to myself, convinced that this was all a big show. Out came lunch, which was salmon. There were oven-roasted potatoes and other vegetables. It was a delicious meal, complete with homemade ice cream for dessert. I must have sounded quite sarcastic when I asked what the women in the prison had eaten that day.

"They ate the same thing," the warden told me. "They finished just before you came in."

At my look of shock, he finally seemed to understand me. "Didn't I tell you we run our kitchen as a culinary training program?" He started to laugh. "*That's* why you wanted to come after lunch!"

He explained that this prison runs a complete culinary training program to train incarcerated women in restaurant work for after their release. A Dublin restaurant contest they enter every year reliably returns high scores for not only food but also preparation, presentation, and cleanliness.

"One year we won!" he added proudly. Some local restaurants had even visited the dining room to learn more about how to feed large numbers of diners as well as they did.

The task is always to feed a large number of people, but in nearly every American prison the priority has been cutting costs and doing the bare minimum to keep incarcerated people alive. Not *healthy* but *alive*, per state and federal minimum guidelines. It was a revelation for me to experience eating in the Dublin facility, where actual job training, nourishing and delicious food, and a calm atmosphere were not just dreams but reality for the residents.

In England there is a program that establishes restaurants inside the prison. They are called the Clink Restaurants. Prison residents learn to prepare and cook food, set up and serve tables, and make cappuccinos and lattes, similar to the Dublin prison. In addition, they can learn skills like resume development and job interview preparation.

What really distinguishes the program, however, is that it brings community residents into contact with justice-involved people. In these prisons (men's and women's), people who live outside the walls can make a reservation for breakfast or lunch. The food and service are exceptional, and the Clink restaurants in London is rated five stars and #62 out of 15,607 by Tripadvisor.

This is a photograph of the Clink restaurant established in one of the women's prisons in England.

Source: One Small Thing.

When I have discussed this program here in the United States, the various state departments of corrections are incredulous. When I share the details, they have a difficult time believing me. This is because the US prison system presents such a starkly different reality, which it does its best to hide from the public.

Creative Solutions

People incarcerated in American prisons are simultaneously disgusted by the food they are served and unable to get enough food. Nearly everyone surveyed by the prison reform nonprofit Impact Justice for its 2020 report *Eating Behind Bars*—a full 94 percent—reported that they did not have enough food to feel full (13). In both men's and women's prisons, people must adapt to survive.

With a few pieces of kitchen contraband, some commissary items, and a lot of creativity, incarcerated women make their own food in their cells.

Impact Justice reports that 71 percent of its survey respondents had to do things that were against policy to get access to more food (14). Often residents will barter and trade for commissary; most anything becomes currency inside the facilities. Geri traded her skill at braiding hair for ten dollars' worth of commissary goods. She also recalled how the women in her unit would pool their resources to celebrate holidays and birthdays. She said, "We stayed connected with life on the outside through creating our little celebrations, and that's how the ladies made the best of the situation."

When I told Geri I was always amazed at how the women I'd met could make something taste good from the ingredients available in a prison, she smiled. As with many formerly incarcerated women, memories of shared meals were some of the few that could bring a smile to her face when talking about her time being locked up.

Her favorite "home-cooked" meals were tamales and cheesecake. A friend she met had taught her how to break down corn chips into a fine powder, then cook them in a plastic bag with a *stinger*—a metal element connected to an electrical wire used to boil water. For cheesecake, she told me, "You need two creamers, some milk from the kitchen, and the patience to mix it up until it gets really super thick. Then you put it in the window and let it stand and get cold. If you're lucky enough to know someone from the kitchen, they'll give you some ice. You break up graham crackers that you get in your commissary box. You use some of the butter from your breakfast to get the graham crackers to stick, and then pour the cold, creamy top on." Geri said that making food together was one of the ways she was able to connect with others while incarcerated and also how she kept a sense of meaning in her life.

Star, who now works in community health and specializes in reentry needs, echoed Geri's wisdom about using food to help create meaning. She remembered how her unit would regularly hold potlucks in their dayroom, where they could gather together and share versions of the foods they loved to make at home. "We made our own decorations, and everybody made their own dish," she recalled. "It was very important for us to still be able to participate in life that way, to keep us from getting too depressed and disconnected. It helped us maintain a semblance of the person we wanted to be. Sharing foods, experiencing the diversity of the meals, was a learning experience for all of us, and we were able to connect that way."

Cakes for special occasions were a common theme in my conversations with formerly incarcerated women. Beth and Kirsty, who met while incarcerated and have remained dear friends for years on the outside, remembered the importance of making birthday cakes for "clean time," celebrating important markers in their sobriety.

One young woman I met told me that the birthday cake her community made for her was the first one she'd ever had. She was twenty-two. Jackie also remembered a birthday celebration that was a rare bright spot. "We had a staff person on that night who was more compassionate than the rest. We were able to have fun. We played cards, talked, bonded; no drugs, no drama, no chaos. Just women truly enjoying each other's company. A few of us said we couldn't remember the last time we laughed like that, because there's no laughing when you're out there on the street dealing with addiction. We ate cake someone had been able to make using a plastic bag and a blow-dryer. We made confetti out of construction paper. We had an amazing time together that night."

Incarcerated women find ways to nourish each other through sharing food in an environment that expressly forbids them to do so. They cook as a way to connect with each other and to connect with their own cultures and histories. They are resourceful, creative, and generous, despite being deprived of nourishing ingredients, safe environments, and basic respect for their health. They survive by helping each other.

Mothering from Inside

As mothers, yes, we suffer, but our children are paying the true price.

—**Patricia**, *personal interview*

THE MAJORITY OF incarcerated women are parents of children under the age of eighteen. Some estimates say over two-thirds of incarcerated women have children, and some say 80 percent. The myth most often repeated about incarcerated mothers is "if they really cared about their children they wouldn't have done whatever they did and gone to prison." Somehow people truly believe that justice-impacted women consciously choose to be separated from their children, which is preposterous. For many incarcerated mothers, the crime that led to their arrest involved trying to provide for their family or trying to protect themselves or their children from someone. Sometimes the strategy they adopt to cope with trauma, like drug use, harms someone else. None of these situations has anything to do with how much a woman loves her children.

Although the word *mother* holds as many meanings as there are people born, it also points to something important about the experience of incarcerated women. Many are the primary caregivers of children at the time of arrest. This isn't as often true for men, by a large margin.

So when a woman with children is arrested and incarcerated, we are actually incarcerating a family. That family is going to experience the loss of their mother, but also probably the loss of income and, ultimately, the loss of their home. If there are siblings, they may be divided up in the foster care system. They may or may not go to other family members. Often, if there is a family member willing to take in children, they are willing to take only one child. From a public health perspective, the destructiveness of family separation based on the incarceration of women is shocking.

In one poignant story, Rose recalled a woman she befriended in the UK prison where they were both housed many years ago. "I used to go talk to her all the time because she was clearly not well," Rose remembered. "She had no criminal record. She lived in social housing flats with her child. A guy down the balcony abused her child, and when the child came home distressed, she ran out and confronted him and attacked him." There was no loss of life, and the woman's sentence wasn't long. But she was not adjusting.

Rose thought of the woman as needing much more help than she was getting. "She had to be taken out of the general population because she was breaking down after the trauma of this one extremely distressing incident. She shouldn't have been in prison; she needed much greater care." Rose saw this woman's experience in the context of a traumatized mother protecting her traumatized child, who needed services and care. Instead, the mother and child were separated.

Justice-impacted mothers express their love for their children in many different ways. In studies on contingency management, a method used to increase behavioral change, researchers looked for the rewards that would be most meaningful to incarcerated people. When asked to provide a list of desired items, in general, researchers have found that men are more likely to list personal needs, like an extra pair of socks or a new comb. Women are more likely to list items they can give to their children, like an inexpensive book or a small toy. This is even more poignant in light of the fact that women are generally more likely to enter prison indigent and less likely to receive financial support from the outside.

I do use *mother* here to refer primarily to people who identify as women who have given birth, and/or who raised children they may not have birthed themselves. Transgender, gender nonconforming, queer, and nonbinary parents often build families and kinship networks outside of biological relation. As with the term *woman*, the word *mother* here is meant to acknowledge the words justice-impacted women I've worked with have used most often for themselves. Queer families especially struggle to navigate systems that were built only to recognize binary gender norms, biologically related family members, and a heteronormative understanding of *mother* and *father*.

That our country recognizes marriage between two men or two women does not mean all of the systems associated with state governance have caught up in their practices, much less worked out how to recognize nonbinary individuals who do not identify either as men or women, children who live in complex family structures, or families that do not have paperwork proving their bonds. The complexity of family bonds and the difficulty incarcerated people face in maintaining them are enormous.

Generational Trauma

One thing I rarely see discussed in the literature but know to be a real issue for many incarcerated women is the safety of their children once they are incarcerated. So many incarcerated women have been physically and sexually abused in their childhood, often in their family of origin. When they go to prison, their children are oftentimes then raised in that same family system. What we see on paper is that the child is not going into the foster system, and that seems good. However, they may be living with a family that wasn't safe for their mother and is often still not safe for them. A family already dealing with the effects of incarceration is not likely to be receiving help and support for generational traumas and cycles of abuse.

I remember meeting a young woman who wrote to her incarcerated mother: "I think I'll commit a crime so I can be in there with you." Many incarcerated mothers do have children in juvenile facilities. It is very common to hear mothers talking about their young sons or daughters who are in the criminal system. We see significant impact across generations when parents, especially primary caregivers, are incarcerated.

Patricia, who worked as a peer facilitator of the *Beyond Violence* program while she was incarcerated, told me, "The women I connected with had stories of great pain for the children that are displaced outside of prison walls. There is such injustice around the children who cannot hug their mothers for years while their mother is fighting for her freedom. As mothers, yes, we suffer, but our children are paying the true price, and then the pain is moving intergenerationally. The children are now trauma survivors. They have done the time while we did it ourselves."

In 1993 my colleague, criminologist Dr. Barbara Bloom, published a book titled *Why Punish the Children? A Reappraisal of the Children of Incarcerated Mothers in America.* The issues she raised thirty years ago are still relevant today: our reliance on the foster care system isn't safe overall for children, mothers often lose contact with their children in foster care with no way to find them upon release, and the incredible burden of meeting legal post-release requirements plus the practical aspects of bringing children home create insurmountable difficulties for mothers.

Sometimes families will hide the fact of a mother's incarceration from children. They may tell a child that their mother is on a trip, or their mother is in the hospital. Families may invent an illness because they believe it's better to think about the mother dying than going into the criminal legal system.

I've worked with incarcerated women who were the children of incarcerated mothers. Children can feel so much shame when their mothers are incarcerated. They would talk about how long they tried to go without anybody knowing their mother was in prison, trying to cover it up by making sure their siblings got off to school, and the difficulty of being suddenly thrust into the position of an adult when they were still children themselves. What they found was that it was incredibly difficult to manage and eventually they couldn't, because they had no means of support.

Not all children will handle the stress of having a parent incarcerated the same way. Geri was incarcerated later in her life than many women are. Her children were already out of their early childhood years when she received a life sentence. She recalled that her middle child would receive her calls every Sunday and make sure she was getting the extra food the prison had for sale. "My middle daughter made sure I shopped my canteen once a month, plus receiving my quarterly box," Geri recalled with gratitude. "She did that until I paroled."

Geri's other two children "just did the best that they could to cope with the fact that their mother may die in prison because of her sentence." Although it was painful, Geri understood that her other two children were coping in a different way by stopping all contact. "They were raising their own kids," she said with love. "They were just doing the best that they could."

Staying Connected to Children

My colleague Gina Fedock researches trauma-informed best practices for improving outcomes for justice-impacted women. After conducting a series of interviews with incarcerated mothers in a midwestern prison, she was surprised to discover the myriad ways women helped each other to navigate the difficulties of staying connected to children on the outside.

"In one of our first interviews a mother described how she and other mothers meet to talk and support each other," she told me. "These mothers have helped their children connect [with each other] on the outside. They've found a way to create space for the children to talk to each other about what it's like to have a mother on the inside." It is not common for children of incarcerated mothers to have peer support organized for them in this way.

Other mothers may find connection too painful or difficult to bear and seek support within their communities on the inside. Gina met women who had taken down pictures of their children because it was too painful to look at them every day, or because their child had been adopted and the loss was overwhelming. "They handled this by finding other mothers who understood, who had similar experiences, who weren't going to judge them, who could provide the empathy they weren't receiving elsewhere." These informal peer-support networks arise in the absence of any institutional support.

For mothers trying to stay connected to children on the outside, instead of support they find plenty of barriers. There may be a scarcity of stamps if they want to write. Phone calls are controlled and limited. Sometimes there will be just a few phones for a large group of residents. Often each resident is assigned a specific time to use the phone. If a mother is assigned 10:00 a.m. as her phone time but her children are in school, there may be issues for her trying to trade her time, which of course is not allowed by the facility.

If a mother asks staff for help with communicating with her children, it may be used against her. Gina's interview respondents told her that "staff might say things like, 'Well, if you really cared about your children, you wouldn't be here.'" In an egregious violation of ethics, one counselor at that prison was found to be requiring the women in custody to engage in sexual acts in order to contact their children.

Gina found that, in her groups, mothers would take on responsibilities for each other if needed. "When a mom goes to segregation," she recalled, "she may not be getting her phone calls or letters. A lot of times the other moms would make sure to get those updates, or even allow her children to come visit them, so they could then communicate news to the mom who was segregated. These networks of communication have been really essential, especially when the mothers were cut off by the prison itself." Informal networks of communication are the way many incarcerated mothers stay connected, because the formal means provided by the prison are often not designed to support their families.

When Children Visit the Prison

The issue of visitation is very complicated for mothers and children. I have witnessed and heard stories of incredibly touching moments between incarcerated mothers and their children. I've seen little ones run to their mothers, arms raised in the air, yelling, "Mommy, Mommy!" with utter excitement and joy. I have seen countless pictures drawn by children, brought into the visiting room, to share with their parents. I remember one child who drew a picture of the family dog for his mother, "since you can't see him." However, every beautiful, sweet moment of a visit is pierced through with the grief of separation.

Let's say an incarcerated mother has been able to leave her children in the care of her own mom, the children's grandmother. Let's imagine she has a supportive mom who is willing to take the kids. But over time, the grandmother may become resentful. She's at a point in her life where she doesn't want to be raising children. She's angry with the mother for getting everyone into this situation. She's the one responsible for getting the children bundled up in the car and driven a long way, because most women's prisons are not near any form of public transportation. The grandmother has to have enough financial resources in case she needs to spend the night and buy food on the trip. By the time the grandmother and the children arrive for a visit, emotions can run high and the situation can get very complicated for everyone.

This illustrates a painfully regular issue I see with visitation: the pain of reality versus fantasy. A woman may get very excited to see her children at a visit. She thinks, *Oh, this is wonderful! I'm going to see my children.* And it may be wonderful for a period of time, but often there are tensions and unspoken pieces of business that impact the visitation.

Normally in the United States, there is nothing in the setup of the prison to facilitate this visitation, especially not for younger children. Usually, a prison visiting room just has a lot of chairs, sometimes a table and chairs, with rough surfaces like concrete, and the room is noisy, with vending machines and grates on the windows. There is nothing for kids to do except what they bring with them, and many facilities will not allow children to bring toys or coloring books. Both the children and the mother have to go through a screening before the visit, which can put the children on edge.

Given the constraints, the visits often do not go as well as the mother had hoped. When she goes back to her cell, she is devastated. She thinks, *My kids don't love me. I don't know how to be around them. I'm going to lose them.* And the kids leave thinking, *Seeing Mom is awful, I hate her.* All of which has very little to do with how much families actually love each other. It is a consequence of the separation and a terrible, unsupportive setup for visits.

When an incarcerated parent does not see their children often, they feel the separation as "lost time." I've often heard things like, "I lost the years from ten to sixteen," and "I don't know what my kids are into, what kind of activities they like. I don't know what they're doing." There is a lot of concern for the kids' safety, education, and general well-being. Are they well supervised? Are they doing alright in school?

I spoke with a warden who had visited her own mother inside a prison. Mary told me that her career path was largely influenced by circumstances involving her mother, who had been incarcerated several times in different states. Although as a teenager Mary struggled with feeling hurt and angry at her mother, her perspective shifted when she learned more about her mother's trauma. Mary shared that her mother was a sexual assault survivor who began using drugs as a means to cope. "When I learned what my mother had been through," Mary explained, "the lens through which I viewed her addiction and involvement with the criminal justice system changed. That lens brought her trauma into a sharp focus for me, and it became a powerful agent of change in my own life."

Still, though she knew her mother loved her, it was very difficult for Mary to deal with the absence of a mother. She could easily recall the fear, shock, and anxiety she felt visiting her mother as a child. The officers would bring her out in restraints. "For a kid, to see your mother with two large, uniformed officers flanking each side of her, and her in full restraints, was just shocking."

Mary entered corrections with a vision for improving the visitation experience for children. "Many [children] already have trauma with law enforcement. They see razor wire and fencing, they sit across from their parent and can't hug them, and the tables and chairs sometimes have big dividers in them. I wanted to change all that."

The first facility where Mary was able to effect change was a men's prison. She brought in new furniture that facilitated fathers holding their children. They went from a collection of ratty books that were falling apart to a TV playing a kids' movie, a large chalkboard painted on the wall, and more toys than Mary thought they'd ever use. Mary plans to drive similar changes in the women's prison where she now works.

As a child Mary worried that her mother wasn't safe on the inside. Now, as a warden, she tries her best to facilitate positive interactions among residents and staff, especially when children are visiting. She remembered one visit where her mother entered with an officer and told them, "Hey, this is my daughter, the one I was telling you about!" The officer was polite, caring, and kind to Mary and her mom, which had a huge impact on Mary. "I just don't think we put enough emphasis on how kindness can change the trajectory of someone's life," Mary said. "Whether either of them knew it or not, one of the takeaways for me was that seeing a positive interaction between my mother and a corrections staff member was important for me. I don't see that discussed often."

It became something Mary took forward into her career. When Mary was running a program that invited families to come in and visit, she told the residents she was willing to wear plainclothes on the visitation day, thinking it would make the children more comfortable. "The residents unanimously told me to wear my uniform on that day," she recalls. "It was important, they told me, for their families to see a positive interaction with correctional staff, so that they could know their loved one was safe."

Creating more safety in visiting environments for children can go a long way to help incarcerated mothers connect with their kids. It's also about being creative and thoughtful. A number of years ago I visited a women's prison outside of Honolulu, Hawaii. There, they would arrange for kids to come on weekends and experience wonderful, culturally relevant activities with their mothers. The residents worked to help organize music, dancing, and other ways the children could interact positively with their mothers and their culture.

There are other hopeful examples. When San Diego built its new jail for women, they created one of the best visiting rooms I've seen.

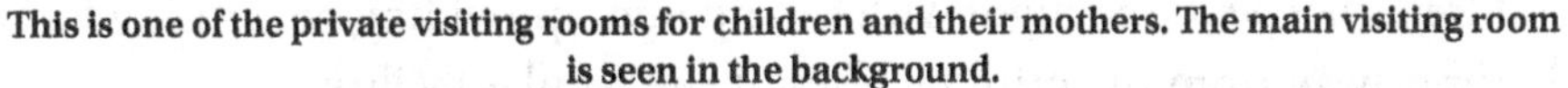
This is one of the private visiting rooms for children and their mothers. The main visiting room is seen in the background.

Source: Las Colinas Detention and Reentry Facility/San Diego County Sheriff's Department.

The visiting rooms have bright colors and are furnished with chairs and toys.

Source: Las Colinas Detention and Reentry Facility/San Diego County Sheriff's Department.

The room is child friendly in terms of the colors, textures, access to toys, and even small rooms where a family can grab some semiprivate time. Another facility in a southern state offers a visiting cottage where children can spend the night with their parent, providing nourishing family time away from the grim realities of the regular facility.

Changing visitation to create more supportive, positive experiences for families is something that could happen in any facility—but most often doesn't. Even prisons in the same state with the same policies and regulations will do things differently because visitation experiences are up to each warden. The whole experience comes down to how much risk the warden is willing to take on.

Pregnancy and Birth

Unbelievably, shackling people giving birth in prison is still the norm in most of the United States. Activists have been working hard to ban the practice since the 1990s, but although it is no longer legal in the federal system to shackle a woman in labor during transport to a hospital or during the birthing process (unless a corrections officer perceives a "serious risk of harm or escape"), the state systems have not all caught up.

According to Alexa Richardson at Harvard Law's blog *Bill of Health*, "Thirty-two states have some form of restriction on pregnant shackling, but only thirteen ban it broadly throughout pregnancy, labor, postpartum, and during transport; only nine states cover juveniles; only twenty states allow the physician to immediately remove the restraints if necessary; and only nine require that correctional staff stand outside [not inside] the room for privacy considerations during childbirth" (15).

The majority of people who give birth while incarcerated in the United States do it without a family member or advocate in the room. Residents file complaints when they are subjected to cavity searches upon returning to a facility after giving birth, but the practice does not change. Years ago, New York had the only women's prison with a baby nursery in the entire United States; now eight states have nurseries. As long as we have prisons housing pregnant, birthing, and postpartum people, we need extra support in all fifty states, but this is how slow reform can be in corrections. Even in states where it is no longer legal to shackle a pregnant resident to the bed, it still happens because there is such a large gap between policy change and implementation.

A colleague and I worked for two years to get legislation changed regarding the shackling of women during pregnancy, birth, and postpartum in a midwestern state. Although we were glad to finally win better laws, what we found was that the practice persisted. No one had required the officers to stop it. We went inside a county jail, saw firsthand that the shackling was still happening, and tried to intervene. We told the officers what they were doing was illegal. They had no idea if this was true, even when we showed them the paperwork, and they continued to do what they always did. We went up the chain of command to an administrator who was aware that the law had been changed. I told her that once a policy was changed, you have to train and inform your employees. I couldn't believe I had to say that, but clearly it needed to be said.

What rightfully angers advocates is that changes *can* happen quickly, as they tend to do after an especially dramatic and newsworthy incident, as when a woman gave birth alone in her cell in a US jail in 2019. Suddenly, all the pregnant people who show signs of labor in that particular jail system will be transported to the hospital for care regardless of the stage of labor they are in (16). This happens after years of advocacy, research, and attempts at policy change. In other words, data don't affect prison practices nearly as much as bad public relations does.

When I interviewed Jackie, who is now an addiction counselor and a community organizer for sex workers' rights, her son was sleeping in the room next door. Although she now feels "blessed" to be reunited with him, she described giving birth while incarcerated in an East Coast prison as "one of the most traumatizing things I've ever been through."

Jackie was shackled to a hospital bed, and a male corrections officer was assigned to be in the room with her. Her mother was on an approved visitation list but was not allowed to be in the room with Jackie while she gave birth for the first time, just two months after she was incarcerated. Jackie was allowed forty-eight hours with her baby before she was separated from him and sent back to prison. She remembers "crying hysterically, knowing I was leaving him in the hospital."

When she returned to prison, she describes the kindness of her community inside as the way she made it through the pain. "They were there for me. They taught me lessons I'd never learned before, like how to put cabbage on my breasts to help soak up the milk. They bought extra menstrual pads for me, because I needed them and couldn't get help from any COs [corrections officers] to buy more. They always asked to see pictures of my son when I got new ones." Jackie told me that the women who supported her through her postpartum period "saw me at my literal worst, stripped down of everything, and we survived together. My bond with them was stronger than it is with people I've known for twenty years."

It is important to acknowledge that women who are pregnant and come into custodial settings have special needs.

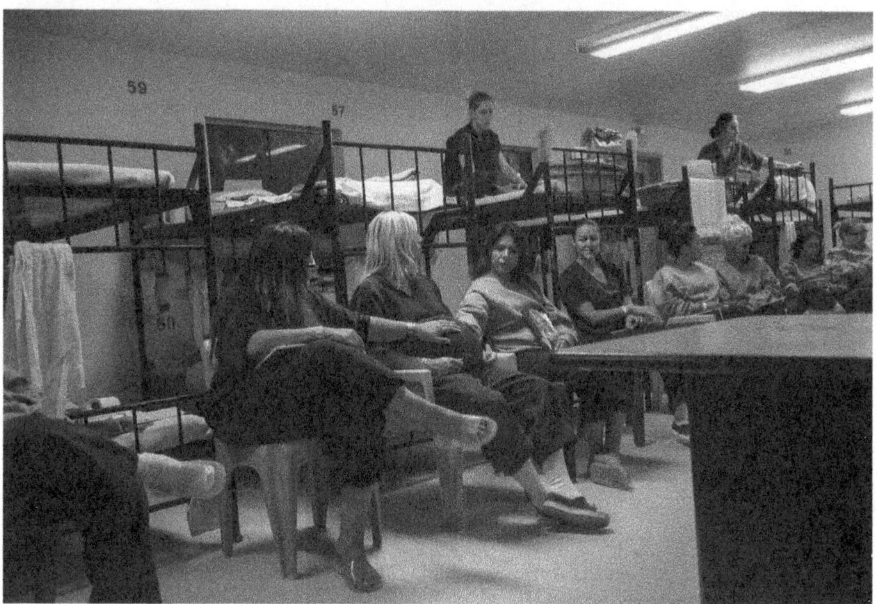

Source: Michele Zousmer.

In some countries in Europe, incarcerated women who give birth inside and have longer sentences can stay with their children until they are school age. Women's prisons in most of Europe are built with a nursery without debate. It's as necessary as the cafeteria. Women who have just given birth are placed in a part of the facility where the children are not seeing bars or razor wire. In Switzerland and the Czech Republic, there are mother-child units that encourage bonding during the crucial early months and years of children's lives. There is a different level of consideration for parenting.

This is a photo of a room for a mother and her child in a special family unit inside a women's prison in the Czech Republic.

Source: Gabriela Slováková.

This is the hallway in the mother-child unit with colorful art on the walls.

Source: Gabriela Slováková.

In the United States we have a few hopeful options emerging. A facility on the East Coast started a mother-baby unit many years ago. The warden at the time was one of the few who designed programming based on what the residents had been asking for. The residents mostly ran the mother-baby unit. They were helping each other to create a microenvironment of support and nurturing.

In the Midwest, a nonprofit called the Ostara Initiative has been working to improve the birth experience for incarcerated women through a prison doula project. They have seen significantly improved outcomes for participants in the project and have overcome years of institutional hurdles to create more space for education and nutritional support during pregnancy, presence and advocacy during the birth process, and postpartum support.

Connecting with Children after Release

Incarcerated parents grieve. They grieve what couldn't happen with their children, what didn't happen, what they missed. They confront some of this grief while separated and much of it when they are going home. At that point they must confront what they thought it was going to be like versus what it actually is.

Some mothers do not want to be reunited with their kids immediately upon release. Part of the problem may be that they don't feel capable. They haven't been acting as mother for enough years that the role has been taken on by somebody else. They may feel deeply overwhelmed, after years in prison, to suddenly be in charge of children they don't know very well. A recently released woman often has no job, no housing, and is expected to reconnect with children without any of the structures in place that families need. People in our field often call the difficulties of reentry the *unspoken sentences*: financial instability, lack of support, and stigma, all of which make rebuilding a stable family home extremely difficult. We will return to these issues in Part Three.

Many of the women I've spoken with described a slow process of reconnecting with their children after release, especially if their children were a bit older. Interviewee Patricia's connection with her daughter is a "work in progress," she told me. While incarcerated, Patricia sought help from a counselor to work on her relationship with her daughter. After her release, during a stay-at-home order with her daughter due to COVID-19, Patricia taught her how to play chess. "My love of chess came from playing with friends in prison, and now I've passed it on to my daughter," Patricia said. "Our attachment was severed by prison. Now we are working through it."

Grief and Loss

Grief wasn't necessarily a component of the [Beyond Violence] program, but it always came up. I saw it over and over again, that people hadn't been able to grieve their losses.

—**Angela**, *personal interview*

LOSS IS A dominant theme in the lives of women who are imprisoned. Incarcerated mothers experience grief about their families and children. Incarcerated women lose jobs and careers, relationships, community, and physical health in addition to their freedom. If they suffered childhood trauma, they've lost much of their childhood. They may lose a belief in the possibility of a good family, a family that cares for them. After twenty years in prison, one of the paroled women I interviewed did not attempt to reconnect with her nearby family, who did not support her while she was incarcerated. The chasm is too large to cross now. She grieves this loss still, as she has for twenty years.

Like Angela said when I brought up the topic, "Grief is not just about the death of a loved one." Angela was a peer facilitator of the *Beyond Violence* program during her incarceration; she now works as a counselor at a treatment facility and runs a life coaching business. She listed some of the many ways incarcerated women experience grief and loss. "Grief can be triggered by the loss of innocence," she said. "We grieve the loss of what we'd hoped our lives might be. We grieve those things we can't do now that we've caught a felony." Angela's understanding of grief as an integral part of a healing process has served many women she has worked with over the years.

Velda, whose work creating programs with residents' input was mentioned earlier, was one of the few women I spoke with who came from the corrections side. She is a retired chief deputy warden and now a program coordinator for incarcerated women. She observed that a deep grief she sees in the women she works with is tied to motherhood and family. "I do believe that when women start healing, it comes from their grieving," she said. "Some grieve the mother they never had, the mother they never were, and the mother that they may never be. Some came in too young to have a child and will miss out on the chance."

As they get older, incarcerated women may grieve their old aspirations, the feeling of competence. One woman I worked with told me she was on a good path and could see where her life was going in high school. Then she was raped, and all of a sudden her path changed. She said, "I felt terrible about myself. I lost my ability to concentrate in school, my aspirations for the future, my sense of safety around people, my whole social life." Trauma can change the trajectory of a life, and there are so many losses that come along with it.

Grieving is the normal response to loss. Grieving and depression are different things, although they can look and feel similar. When there is a loss, grief is an appropriate reaction, and there is no set timeline for grief. One person may have a profound sense of loss and grief that lasts months; another may experience grief for years, or even throughout the rest of their life. When they are coming face to face with their losses, incarcerated women lean on each other for support. Especially now that we have a large number of women incarcerated with very long sentences, the inevitable loss of a loved one on the outside is part of the prison experience.

The Death of a Loved One

Although many women told me stories of how they were able to physically support each other during times of grief, it was always at some risk. In almost all jurisdictions, comforting touch among prison residents is not allowed.

Beatrice remembered a particular instance at the East Coast prison where she was incarcerated that still hurts to recall. She knew that getting called to the chaplain's office usually meant bad news, so she and other residents would make sure to walk with the person who was going. She remembered walking with a woman who was informed that her mother had died. "We put our arms around her," Beatrice told me. "The officer who saw us said he was going to give us a ticket. You're not supposed to touch another person. We were like, 'What is *wrong* with you? We need to comfort her.'"

What may seem obvious to people outside the system—that we may be moved to comfort someone in distress—is not a given on the inside. When the rule is no touching, incarcerated women must choose between following their very human, very compassionate instinct to reach out and support another person who is suffering—thus risking punitive consequences—or suppressing their humanity for an institution that seems bent on taking every last shred of it away.

What I heard most often in my interviews was that prison residents would choose to help each other in the case of grief and loss, even though it put them at risk of disciplinary actions. Providing physical comfort, such as a hug, was one of the ways to connect with each other that was meaningful and important. The women I spoke to who worked inside the prisons also observed this. Rochelle, the previously mentioned retired captain who reentered women's facilities to be a program coordinator, told me it was an unspoken rule beneath the official policy that "when someone had a family member pass, the women she knew would rally around her and be very comforting."

As mentioned earlier, Jackie gave birth while incarcerated and then had to give her baby to her mother after forty-eight hours. When Jackie's mother died, Jackie was still incarcerated. She was grateful to know her son would be safe with her stepfather, but she was unable to be with her family to grieve. Her mother's death came just six months after her best friend had also passed, and Jackie was in terrible pain.

She told me that "the women will find ways to take care of you even in a setting where you have no control over anything. They were cooking for me, writing letters for me, checking on me every day." Jackie's mother had also been her main source of financial support while incarcerated.

"Suddenly in the middle of all this pain, I didn't have money coming in for things I needed. I can tell you I never went a day without eating, without someone sharing commissary with me. My tier just took care of me."

As she worked through her grief, Jackie relied on her support network of the other residents on her floor, or tier, rather than seeking help through the institution's mental health services. One reason, she told me, was that if you were too emotional they would put you in isolation, on suicide watch. "That wasn't an option," she said. Isolation makes grieving more painful, a fact one does not need a degree in psychology to know. Jackie's support network on the inside kept her safe from segregation.

The activation of a network of care in the face of a death does not surprise Kim Carter. The founder and ambassador of the Time for Change Foundation, which supports women who need housing and other services, Kim learned from her experience of incarceration that one of the most important experiences a hurting person can have is helping someone else.

"It feeds our soul to be of service, helping people, because we've been told, 'You're nothing,' 'You're just a number,' 'You don't count.' We feel that dehumanization at all levels," she said. "So when someone gets devastating news on the inside, you feel more human if you can be your sister's shoulder to cry on. You get to make a difference in your roommate's life when she gets that letter that she lost her child to the welfare system, by all coming together like glue."

Kim's observation about the positive effect of supporting another person was echoed in Lisa's story about the death of her father. "I got a phone call from my ex-husband that my father had died," she began. "I pretty much lost it. I remember the sound coming out of me, it wasn't like any sound I'd made before. I was just frozen, making these horrible sounds at the phone. The cops came running and they tried to give me Valium. I said, 'I can't take that, I'm an addict!'" She shook her head. "I was completely grief stricken."

She stayed that way for weeks, she said. "My hair started to turn white, and I got a bald patch on the back of my head." In the midst of her pain, however, Lisa noticed that "the women in my room changed. They hadn't been very nice before, but something clicked in their humanity. They were very, very kind to me during that time. They were helpful and nurturing.

They sat on my bed, prayed with me, held my hand, and hugged me. I hadn't had human contact in such a long time; it was very emotional for me." Lisa's grief opened up a space for the women around her to step into; a space where kindness and care were clearly needed. They took the opportunity to treat her and each other well, and it was one of Lisa's most poignant memories.

In a prison setting it is very difficult for residents to know when it is safe to show any vulnerability. Women who are grieving have to navigate not only their pain but the many risks they incur by showing their pain to anyone. This is especially true for those who have taken a mentor role in their social community, like Linda, an interviewee who lost her father while incarcerated.

Linda was facilitating a peer-led women's group, and at first she was reluctant to share about her loss because she wanted to keep some boundaries and hold space for the other women in the group. "I tried not to share too much about my personal life," she told me. "But you can't always hold everything to the side." She began to grieve openly in her group. "I shared that my dad had just passed away, and I told the group that I was 'daddy's little girl,' so it was really, really tough for me."

While Linda shared, a member of the group began to color on a piece of tissue. Linda remembered the woman well. "She had gotten a life sentence at fifteen years old, which she is still fighting. She used a red crayon and made a rose out of the tissue and gave it to me at the end of the meeting. It was the sweetest, kindest thing somebody had ever done for me. I kept that rose for such a long time. Here was somebody that has nothing, who is incarcerated, and still finds a way to give."

As the years have passed and Linda has had time to reflect on that moment, she has grown increasingly grateful for the kindness of the rosemaker. That creative young woman had not been shown any compassion by a system that gave her a life sentence as a minor. Still, "she has that much compassion to offer someone else? We need more compassionate people out in the world like her," Linda said.

According to policy, residents of federal prisons have the right to apply for furlough to attend a family member's funeral (17). State prisons and county jails all have their own policies and procedures for requesting furlough. In all my years of working with grief and trauma in prisons, I have never heard of someone getting a furlough. I have never even heard of someone requesting one. I suspect that this is one of those invisible policies that is technically on the books but very rarely put in practice, because of the effort it would require from the administrative and custodial staff.

Another major barrier is that the family of the incarcerated person must pay the enormous cost of guarding and transporting the prison resident. It is likely that most women haven't heard of the option. Even if they were to put in a request, their paperwork would likely not move through the system quickly enough to matter. Therefore, in most cases, an incarcerated woman who suffers the death of a loved one will need to turn to her network on the inside for support and hope as she processes her grief.

Developing Relationships

> *They say you cannot miss what you've never had. I don't agree with that. When I started coming out of my fog in prison, family time was what I missed the most. Even though you've never had it, [that] doesn't mean that you can't miss it.*
>
> —**Star**, *personal interview*

SINCE THE 1970S people studying incarcerated women have described the importance of women's relationships on the inside. Researchers have paid the most attention to romantic/sexual partnerships and kinship/family groups, and we will discuss those important bonds here.

But my interviewees all confirmed that mentorships, friendships, and aid networks also support and protect women as they navigate incarceration. These relationships develop from a core question that Angela—the woman who became a substance abuse counselor and life coach after leaving prison—articulated: "How do you create a sense of peace and safety in that chaotic environment?"

Humans are wired to be in relationship and form connections in a variety of ways. *Relational-cultural theory* (*RCT*) identifies the relationship qualities that foster growth: connections that are mutual, empathetic, creative, energy releasing, and empowering for all participants. These are the qualities that the women I spoke with described seeking in prison. These connections are so crucial for women that women's psychological problems can be traced to disconnections or violations within them, in families and with personal acquaintances, inside prisons or in society at large.

RCT also describes the impact of disconnection, which is accompanied by diminishment of zest, empowerment, clarity, worth, and desire for connection. Disconnections happen at the sociocultural level as well, through racism, sexism, heterosexism, and classism. The issues of dominance and privilege are another aspect of relational-cultural theory. Without the relationships women form in prison, they would exist in an environment of disconnection and subordination, which, for many, is a re-creation of their relational life outside the walls (18).

In prison the system tries to limit and enforce rules about how residents experience connection. We'll say "tries" because the only way to truly contain human connection is through sustained isolation, and that is thankfully on its way out in many jurisdictions. There is no facility in the United States that allows women to be in romantic relationships with each other, and the rule for everyone is quite simply "no touching." There are usually strict limits on visitors as well: maybe a hug at the beginning and end of the visit, maybe a short kiss for married partners visiting their spouses.

Even as friends, people outside often touch each other—hugs, a pat on the back, joining arms while walking down the street. Indeed, nonsexual touch is so culturally common, a blanket "no touching" rule is going to be a problem to enforce and a huge stressor to live under. Add the very close quarters of prison, and touching each other is going to happen simply by accident some percentage of the time.

Despite these rules, justice-impacted women develop relationships, and that is how they survive. In the next few pages, I will highlight some relationships that were or are especially meaningful to the women who shared their stories with me. In so doing, I will attempt to steer clear of romanticizing. All relationships are complex. Those that form under the scrutiny of corrections—within the prison environment of scarcity and survival, among women who often have little experience with healthy relationships—are even more so. A woman may stick with whoever makes her feel physically safest, even if the relationship or group is otherwise uncomfortable for her. There are many complicated dynamics and contradictions to navigate.

One example of a contradiction that came up in most of my interviews is that a woman may feel safest when she is as invisible as possible, even as she needs to feel seen to begin her healing. Newcomers may need to rely on strangers at first, but ultimately they must find a way to settle into the culture of the place where they live, either by keeping mostly to themselves or entering the community. Each woman's experience of prison will be different, as she makes sense of the social choices before her.

Creating a Sense of Family

The length of a woman's sentence can have a strong effect on how deeply she invests in creating community for herself inside a prison. While living in close quarters for a year or two is still a life-altering experience, living inside a prison for decades is a very different thing. One effect of living inside for a long time is that a woman may feel a clearer need to create safer spaces for herself within the institution.

Many of the women I've met over the years have described forming relationships that felt like family while they were incarcerated. Angela's story stands out because of how intentional and well recognized her family group became. Angela was sentenced under an aiding and abetting law that gave her the same sentence as the person who took her abuser's life during a confrontation that became violent. A sentence of twenty-five to life came as a huge shock to her.

Eventually she was able to get into an eight-person room with women who helped her feel "a little more stable, a little more comfortable, a little more safe." With them, Angela was able to form "a familial-type unit." She wanted to be clear that it wasn't modeled strictly on a nuclear family. "It wasn't that there was a mother and a child," she told me. "It was just this nurturing environment that we created. We would cook together. If one of us maybe didn't have money to shop in the canteen or commissary that month, the other person would come in to help, or we would pool together and shop together. I think it was in that nurturing environment that we created that I found the strength and the courage to heal."

Angela and her unit called themselves "the Nest," and she remembers a sense of community that was integral to her finding a way to start healing herself. "A lot of us may have had dysfunctional families, so there was no such thing as the family table," she recalled. "But as we got better, and we began to grow, and we started our journey toward inner healing, we knew we wanted that. We said, 'Let's create that for ourselves in here.' We began to reparent ourselves. We had family dinners together every Sunday."

The eight-person room that Angela shared held six women serving life sentences and two beds that were filled by different women with shorter sentences. This meant that six women were in charge of the culture of the room. Angela remembers setting boundaries with newcomers, "and most of them were so grateful to be in that environment that they would just flow with us. What we found is that most women were just looking for that family feel. They were looking for connection."

For Angela, the Nest was a refuge from the brutal anonymity of the prison. "Human beings are created for love and belonging, and most of us did not get that when we were younger, so we turned to self-destructive behaviors, to dysfunctional relationships, to alcohol and drugs. Then we got into jail, and we lost our name. A lot of people bought into it. They became so institutionalized that they would tell me their number when I asked for their name. I'm like, No. We don't do that here. This is home for now. We don't want it to be home forever, but it is our home for now. So you are a human being, and you're going to be treated as such in here." This was such a contrast to the way people were being treated outside of the unit that Angela remembers it being a startling moment for newcomers.

Angela's group developed rituals and schedules that gave them a sense of control and normalcy. In the mornings Angela remembers the smell of bodywash. "There aren't many good smells there," she said. "Sometimes when it was my turn to wake up, it was because I smelled a person's bodywash and I knew instinctively that I was next. It was a sweet smell, and it was one of those things that mattered because in so many other ways they were stripping us of our femininity."

In addition to keeping a shower schedule that allowed everyone time and hot water, Angela remembers a morning coffee ritual that her unit would observe. They had eight cups and two stingers (heating elements available in some commissaries, but also handmade). So the person who got up first would fill all the cups with water, and then each person would take the stinger out of a hot cup and put it in the next one. She remembered that "we just started making coffee for each other this way, and it became a ritual. It was comforting."

Angela's unit took care of each other in ways she doesn't even see people doing on the outside. She got to know the women in her unit deeply, and they could all tell if someone was not feeling well, physically or emotionally. "Someone would go up to your bunk and say, 'Hey, how are you doing?'" she remembered. "You could tell them, 'Oh, I'm fine,' but they would stay and say, 'No, really, how are you doing? What's going on?'"

This level of attention and care was uncommon in Angela's life. "Even in my healthier friendships in society I didn't get that connection. I never felt that warmth in my other relationships. That's why I would trust the women in there with my grandchild; I don't care what they're in there for, I'd trust them more than people I know on the outside."

The Nest "changed the trajectory of our lives," Angela told me. "I don't know if any of us would really be free today if we hadn't connected with one another and had that woman-to-woman healthy connection."

From Angela's perspective, those connections were based on mutual respect, shared values, and care for each other. This sense of family raised her standards. When she was released, Angela poured her energy into working with women as a drug and alcohol counselor, and now she also coaches private clients, helping people to nurture their own relationships.

Romantic Bonds

About ten years ago I was facilitating a training in a midwestern prison. I had never been inside a facility so laser focused on women's romantic and sexual relationships. Every conversation, every hour, every staff interaction was about keeping the women apart. It was like an obsession.

As other rules weren't getting the same kind of attention, I could feel that at least part of it stemmed from homophobia.

At the final debrief, I told them I thought they were putting their energy in the wrong place. What if they shifted their focus to trying to figure out what the women needed to be safe, and providing that? They were never going to stop women from forming romantic and sexual relationships, but they could do more to prioritize keeping everyone safe.

The expectation from corrections is that we can take a group of human beings, put them in a confined space, and expect them to steer clear of emotional and physical involvements. Clearly, that is unrealistic—even under the threat of punishment prisons confer. Relationships will form, and under the constant stress of prison life, they will undoubtedly be stressed.

As in community-based residential drug and alcohol treatment facilities, the rule against relationships in prison is explained as a way to prevent harm. And in many cases the intense feelings that arise with romance can be a problem: jealousy, control, and hurt feelings can certainly provoke harmful emotional and physical behaviors. The women I interviewed who had served longer sentences tended to eventually avoid romantic relationships on the inside, because they learned they didn't want to risk "drama."

Furthermore, prisons are not structured for healthy relationships: you have to be hiding, sneaking around, going against the rules, wondering if the people around you are going to rat you out. There is no privacy, even if one of the partners is released, as mail is read and phone calls monitored. If you've grown up in a family with significant conflict, you are likely accustomed to conflict in your relationships. If you have been in an abusive relationship prior to incarceration, you may be experiencing shame and trauma, which will likely affect your next partnership.

For people to experience anything other than a challenging romantic relationship in prison is nearly impossible. Yet it is a testimonial to the intense human need for relationship that many women do figure out how to find comfort in each other through romantic and sexual connection. I have borne witness to romantic connections that have been restorative and supportive to women. I know partnerships that formed on the inside and lasted beyond the release of one of the partners, then beyond the release of the other. Even shorter-term relationships can offer meaningful connection to help women along their path.

Sexual expression among women, even those who identify as straight or heterosexual outside prison, is a complex issue. I have heard various perspectives on how women connect romantically and sexually while incarcerated. I think this speaks to the incredible fluidity of sexuality and sexual identity.

One interviewee told me she was straight and homophobic when she entered prison, but over time began experimenting with another woman sexually. Living now in the outside world, she prefers being in relationships with women. Another told me she entered prison as "a proper gay" and avoided getting involved. She saw many platonic companionship relationships that became sexual over time, as well as a "power couple" who stayed together long term and didn't get harassed by the prison staff. I also heard descriptions of relationships that replicated all-too-familiar abuse dynamics.

Sensationalized, homophobic media portrayals of predatory lesbians and "gay for the stay" narratives do nothing to capture the true complexity of incarcerated women's romantic and sexual experiences. People who have not experienced incarceration would do well to remember the complex nature of all romantic partnerships.

Each relationship is unique and has the potential to both help and hurt the individuals involved, sometimes at the same time. Relationships among incarcerated women will happen. Viewing them as a problem to be solved compounds the harm of the prison experience and diminishes the humanity of the women involved.

Mentors, Networks, and Friends

Although some like Angela experience a real sense of family within their community, there are a number of ways women connect with each other that are more accurately called *mentorships*, *networks*, and *friendships*. I've often seen relationships where an older woman who has been living in prison for a while takes a couple of younger women as her responsibility.

A great deal of the healing happens in spontaneous and informal ways. It is often difficult to find a quiet and somewhat confidential place to talk.

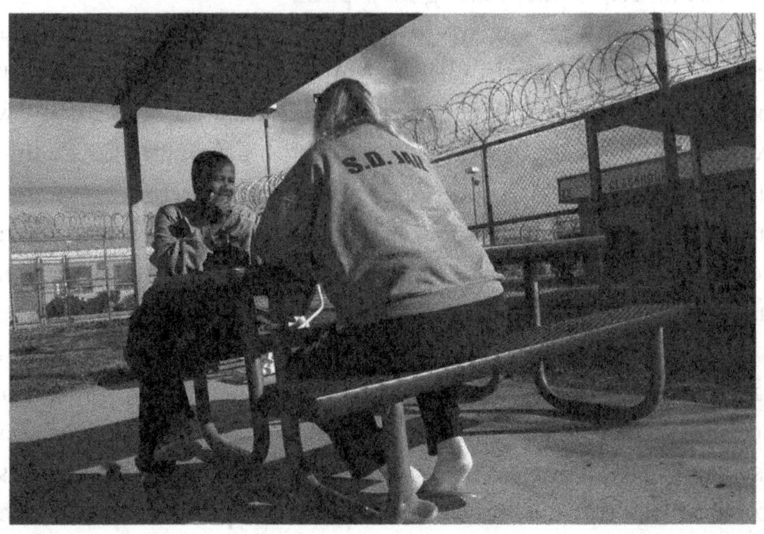

Source: Michele Zousmer.

These are intentional mentorships, where younger women gravitate toward an older, wiser woman who helps them navigate the prison and also helps to set them on a more rehabilitative path.

Linda experienced this type of mentorship when she was incarcerated in an East Coast prison. Linda had known Mrs. Jones on the outside from her years of drug use prior to incarceration, but by the time they met in prison Mrs. Jones had decided on a healthier path for herself, and Linda was grateful to be invited into her circle. "The first time I went in," Linda recalled, "I was petrified. Mrs. Jones took me under her wing and steered me away from all the chaos. She'd tell me not to get involved in all that, just come meet her at the gym. She was my lifeline. She was a mother figure for a lot of women."

Occasionally, as in the case of Kirsty and Beth, a mentorship forms in which there is a difference in experience more than age. Beth and the more prison-experienced Kirsty met while incarcerated in an addiction recovery unit in England. Says Beth: "We've gone on this messy, beautiful, crazy journey ever since. Kirsty is the first one to say she survived really well in prison. I didn't. I was in an institution that I found really traumatizing."

Kirsty recalled that she didn't usually gravitate toward gentle personalities like Beth, but that the day they met in their recovery group Beth seemed to be seriously affected by the conversation. As Beth tells it, "I couldn't speak. I wore my hair long over my face, and I couldn't look people in the eyes because I didn't want to see disgust reflected back."

Kirsty told me that one of the gifts of her own trauma is "the eyes to see the nonverbal. I saw Beth just twitching in this group. She was shouting without saying a word." When the group ended she approached Beth. "I went and I sat down next to her, and I just said, '*I see you.*'"

For Beth, this moment was "like oxygen. It was light. She could see my wounds, and she was telling me it was going to be okay. No one had ever stepped into my world long enough to see all my stuff. In that moment she gave me hope." Years later Beth named her daughter Hope because of how powerfully hope has helped her reshape her life.

"I think that the relationship has always had a sibling dynamic, with every facet that comes with it," Kirsty told me. For Kirsty, friendship with Beth was an opening to compassion that encouraged her to grow as a person. "My life had taught me that the best trauma response was to fight, the best defense was offense, and if you associate yourself with compassion, softness, or any of those things, what that actually means is weakness. Vulnerability is unacceptable because I had twenty-nine years of life teaching me that vulnerability equaled pain. I think that the level of fragility that Beth showed at that time was the thing that opened my heart." Beth confirmed that ordinarily Kirsty "was not gentle, but with me, she was gentle. This created a sense of safety for us both. When she got out, we stayed in touch."

Both Beth and Kirsty eventually transitioned into working in a recovery program out in the community to help other women. In a few years they were in competition for the same job, and the power dynamic in their friendship shifted. Beth got the job over Kirsty, which was a surprise to them both. Kirsty recalls, "It was complicated because I wanted the job, but I also wanted it for Beth. It was such a crazy moment and probably the greatest threat to our relationship. If there's an older sister who's supposed to be wiser, it's me! On reflection I understand why Beth was chosen for the job, but at the time I didn't. And I struggled." Beth ended up as Kirsty's manager.

Rather than let resentment build, they chose to sit down for a "courageous conversation" about how they felt, how they were communicating, and what kind of friendship they wanted to have going forward. They were both experiencing big changes in their lives, with Beth trying to get pregnant and Kirsty getting married, and they decided their friendship was a priority. They put their focus on keeping their bond healthy, and they have remained dear friends through all the changes.

Interviewee Patricia also made a lasting friendship with a woman she called "beautiful inside and out." They shared a small two-person cell. A lover of poetry and art, Patricia taped pages from books and magazines to the walls of the cell to keep her mind occupied. The cell was small enough that they had to take turns if they wanted to walk for exercise. "I would be on the bed reading for hours while she walked and walked, having to look at the stuff I put on the walls," Patricia told me. "My friend used to call me a 'poem pusher,'" she recalled, laughing. "She said, 'You don't push religion, you push poems,' and it's true! Whoever loves me is going to love poetry, but she used to hate them."

Patricia's friend is still incarcerated, so they maintain connection mostly through phone calls, especially when COVID-19 placed restrictions on visitation. Patricia reports that her friend credits their friendship with teaching her to love poetry and art and had even gotten a tattoo of the poem "Invictus" by William Ernest Henley. (Tattooing happens often in prison, clandestinely, with something they can sharpen and ink from a pen.) A nineteenth-century poem famously recited by Nelson Mandela to inspire courage in prison, the last stanza of the poem reads:

It matters not how strait the gate,
How charged with punishments the scroll,
I am the master of my fate,
I am the captain of my soul.

Reflecting on the friendship, Patricia was thoughtful. "It's amazing to me how your own passions, those things that were beautiful and inspiring to you outside of prison, can help become a lifeline for other people," she said. "My friendship with her has continued to be an anchor for me, and I help her too. We still anchor each other."

Of course, not everyone finds their way into deep, supportive relationships inside. I think there are many reasons a woman embedded in a resource-sharing network in prison still might not develop close personal ties. For some, like Liz, years of trauma and violence made it difficult to trust anyone, especially in an environment that fosters distrust on purpose.

Liz told me she could perceive that other women were creating family groups but that she didn't participate. "I was kind of out of that because I never was a part of a family, and so I was never comfortable being a part of any of the cell blocks that I lived in." Though Liz began learning better communication skills and self-reflection in group programming where she felt some safety, she stayed mostly isolated while incarcerated. That was how she had lived her whole life and how she knew to keep herself safe.

Others kept their distance from the women around them because they were still experiencing isolating addictions and trauma symptoms. My interviewee Sarah told me that while she experienced acts of kindness, like someone saving her a seat in the cafeteria, it wasn't until she was leaving prison that a woman was able to get through to her in a deeper way. "I was leaving, so I was giving away my books," she told me. Sarah is Native American and so was the woman she was giving books to. "She looked in my eyes and said, 'You deserve the best. You matter.' And at thirty-eight years old no one had ever told me something like that."

Because this touched Sarah so deeply, she listened to what was next: "She told me to look up a contact of hers, a Native American spiritual leader who was working at a nonprofit in the city where I was going to be paroled." When Sarah was released, she made the call. Her path to sobriety and reconnection with her culture began there. When remembering this connection, Sarah smiled and said, "I'm still in contact with her, and whenever she hears me telling this story, she's like, You're still telling that story? and I say, 'Yeah. It changed my life.'"

Medical and Mental Health Care

The scariest thing in jail and prison is to get sick.

—**Patricia**, *personal interview*

AFTER MULTIPLE INTERVIEWS with justice-impacted people, somatic psychotherapist Lalo Piangco Rivera wrote that "health care in the prison system was viewed by many as a last resort to be avoided at all costs due to the lack of concern or regard received during treatment and the potential risks associated with being treated" (19).

The women I interviewed, across locations, echoed this understanding of the medical and mental health systems in jails and prisons. While I will highlight a few programs or individuals who were able to reduce harm, the general and widespread understanding of justice-impacted women is: Don't go to sick call, prison-speak for letting an officer know you're sick, unless you absolutely have to. A large problem is that many do find they have to, especially during the course of a longer sentence.

Some prisons have a medical facility on site. Some must bring their residents out of the facility to a hospital for anything other than basic routine appointments, which requires plans and funds for staffing, transportation, food, and other concerns. Although the Bureau of Justice Statistics does not update as regularly as researchers would prefer, as of 2016 we know that nationally, fully half the people held in state and federal custody reported ever having a chronic condition, with increased prevalence of diabetes and high blood pressure compared with those in the general public (20).

Adverse Childhood Experiences and Incarceration

People come into prison at higher risk of physical and psychological problems than those who are never incarcerated. In addition, data reveal more health issues for women in prison than men. Although each individual has their own constellation of risk factors, understanding why incarcerated women present with a high incidence of medical issues can start with the Adverse Childhood Experiences (ACE) study. The ACE study has transformed the delivery of human services, helping people to understand the connection between things that happened before age eighteen to later impacts in life.

The original ACE study was a collaboration between San Diego Kaiser Permanente hospital researchers and the Centers for Disease Control and Prevention. From 1995 to 1997, over seventeen thousand people completed a 10-question survey about their childhood experiences before age eighteen and then a survey about current health status and behaviors.

Adverse childhood experiences (ACEs) are grouped into three categories: abuse, household challenges, and neglect. For each experience a person has had, they receive one point on the ten-point scale. What researchers found was that as the number of ACEs increased, so did the risk of negative outcomes in bodily injury, mental health, maternal health, infectious disease, chronic disease, risky behaviors, and educational and occupational opportunities (21). The original study, published in 1998, clearly showed a correlation: people's early childhood experiences had negative consequences for them thirty, forty, fifty years in the future.

Study facilitators were very concerned about asking people these questions and didn't want to "open the can of worms." This is a common concern in many places: people are afraid to ask about abuse and trauma. During data collection at Kaiser, a staff person carried a pager for twenty-four hours a day, seven days a week for three years in order to triage any mental health crises that could come up as a result of individuals answering the questions on the survey. Anyone could call and get help if they were distressed. No one did. People had already survived the experiences, and if they had difficult emotions as a result of the survey, they didn't seek help from Kaiser to address them.

In addition to emergency support, Kaiser also offered those with high scores on the scale an hour with a mental health professional. Many of the people who met with the psychiatrists were stunned to be asked about their childhoods and had never told anyone about what had happened to them. Interestingly, the people who took advantage of the hour with a professional decreased their use of medical intervention in the year afterward.

In sum: no one came forward with adverse effects from answering the ACE questions, and those who talked about their experiences with a professional for one hour experienced a seemingly positive impact on their overall health.

I emphasize these two outcomes because of how much institutional resistance I've experienced to implementing trauma programming, in social services in general, but corrections in particular. Time and again, staff claim that allowing incarcerated women space to discuss their feelings with each other will be like opening Pandora's box, sending them all into mental or medical health crisis and overwhelming the systems. Not once has this happened. Still, the institutional response to programming that addresses trauma is predictably the same: we don't want to open that can of worms, because we won't be able to contain it.

For nearly twelve years, no one paid much attention to the ACE study, despite its startling results. Eventually, other researchers began to replicate the findings. It has been run in different countries, states, and communities, some with very different experiences of environmental stressors, racism, historical trauma, poverty, and so on, with tens of thousands of people. The findings replicate over and over again, showing that increased ACEs are correlated with both medical and mental health issues later in life.

When my colleague Nena Messina and her team took the ACE study into a women's prison, they found that justice-impacted women with a score of four or more had higher rates of medical and mental health problems, and those with a score of seven or more were at 980 percent higher risk of mental health issues (22). The impact of childhood experiences on incarcerated women cannot be stressed enough, and our understanding of trauma has to be the foundation from which new solutions emerge.

Figure 4. ACEs among incarcerated women.

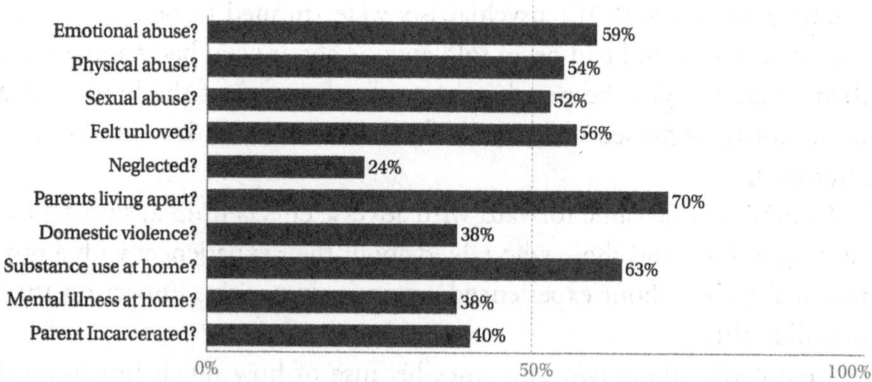

Source: Adapted from Nena Messina and Elizabeth Zwart, "Breaking the Silence and Heaing Trauma for Incarcerated Women: Peer-Facilitated Delivery of a Brief Intervention." *Medcrave Online Journal of Women's Health* 10, no. 1 (2021): 8–10. https://doi.org/10.15406 mojwh.2021.10.00280.

The ACE studies are continuing to challenge our long-held beliefs about medical and mental health by showing them to be totally intertwined. Childhood trauma does not just affect the child; it affects the adult the child grows up to become. This happens sometimes in ways that are not obvious—such as increased risk of diabetes, heart problems, and physical injury—and other times in ways that make grim sense, like addiction, suicide, and violent aggressive behavior, to name a few.

Getting Care Inside

Due to their lived experiences, women coming into prison are already more vulnerable to physical and mental health problems than women in the public at large. Then they are also vulnerable to what happens in a place where good care is not easily accessed.

One prison program coordinator told me a disturbing story about the problem of accessing care. An older long-term resident, with whom she was well acquainted, was ill. The program coordinator visited the sick resident in her cell and became concerned about how poorly she was doing.

"This woman is sick; she needs to see a doctor," the coordinator told the officer in charge of the housing unit. The officer refused, claiming that the resident probably just had the flu. When the program coordinator persisted and pushed the officer to take the resident to the medical office, they sent her to the hospital. There she was diagnosed with sepsis, a serious life-threatening condition that kept her in the hospital for weeks. She came back with severe impairments and continues to suffer the consequences of her illness. If the program coordinator had not advocated for her, she likely would have died.

Medical neglect and violations of residents' rights to adequate care are more common than outsiders know. People who have not been directly impacted by the justice system are sometimes surprised to learn that California's Correctional Health Care Services has been operating under a form of federal supervision called a *receivership* for over fifteen years. A US District Court judge established the receivership as a result of a 2001 class-action lawsuit (*Plata vs. Schwarzenegger*) against the state of California over the quality of medical care in state-run prisons. The court found that the conditions and quality of medical care violated prison residents' constitutional rights via the Eighth Amendment, which forbids cruel and unusual punishment of the incarcerated.

Although the suit was settled in 2002, the state failed to comply with the court's direction, so the court established a receivership resulting in federal oversight in 2005. As of 2020, nineteen of thirty-five California institutions have been returned to state control. The process for facilities to improve their medical care has been stymied multiple times by failures to comply with court orders, arguments over funding of construction projects and staff salaries, difficulty in recruiting and maintaining new medical staff, and more (23). Meanwhile, prison residents continue to need care, weighing the potential consequences of getting in the "med line" at their facility against the consequences of self-medicating.

California isn't the only system that has a history of harming prison residents in the course of inadequate medical intervention. Beatrice, who has been an organizer and activist for over fifty years, received negligent medical care in an East Coast prison and was later able to fight back through the court via one of the only ways incarcerated women can respond to harmful prison experiences: filing an administrative remedy. Beatrice had pain in her leg that kept getting worse. She said she went to sick call, "and they told me I probably pulled a muscle. They told me to stay off it; get some Tylenol at the commissary. But I needed crutches or a cane. I was in so much pain I was wincing and yelling trying to get out of my chair."

Finally, Beatrice's supervisor at her prison job advocated for her to get a more thorough examination. She had a stress fracture in her femur. Due to the flights of stairs she was forced to walk, unaided and in a form of shackling called "black boxing," by the time Beatrice arrived at a hospital in another state (because the closest one was not equipped for the "necessary" security measures), she had a displaced fracture in her hip as well. She required surgery, which could have been prevented had more care been taken in her transport.

Beatrice had tried to get help and was ignored, then harmed outright. Sometimes women don't seek help at all when they are sick or injured, and this compounds their distress as well. When discussing how long some women wait to seek care, Beatrice made the point that medical care often requires a copay. "If you make twelve cents, fourteen cents, twenty cents an hour," she said, "you're going to save up for a phone call home first, and you may wait until your symptoms get worse because you don't have the money to do both a call and a visit to the doctor."

Because of her negative experiences, Beatrice committed to helping other women navigate the system. She began to help the women around her to write up their requests to see specialists for chest pains, lupus, hepatitis C, and other issues. "We had to fight like hell to be treated," she told me. "There were a few physician's assistants who were sympathetic," she remembered. "But then they'd get chewed out for giving out medications that actually helped people if it cost the prison too much money."

Medication is a constant issue in every women's facility. Different jurisdictions do different things with medications. In some states I've seen them use medications we no longer use out in the community. In one juvenile facility I saw usage of expired medication, which has been borne out by other investigations (24).

If a woman had medications prescribed to her prior to her incarceration, there is no guarantee she will be able to take the same ones while in custody, as each jail and prison system has its own rules for prescribing, different lists of approved drugs and generic formulas, and access issues in the pharmacy. Many of the women I spoke to mentioned that when someone in their unit was sick, the others would "make sure they had medicine." Because residents cannot always trust that they will receive the prescriptions they need, they may hoard medications or use their commissary to buy over-the-counter medications like aspirin, then barter or give it to others.

Then there's COVID-19, which ushered in a whole new era of health trauma. Although the interviews that inform *Hidden Healers* reflect prison experiences that were not impacted by the COVID-19 pandemic, I was able to ask questions about its impact through a colleague who received clearance to work with women housed in a California prison during the pandemic.

According to their self-reports, the pandemic significantly dialed up the stress among prison residents. Though the virus infected the prison resident population through their contact with staff—who in California, among other jurisdictions, were not mandated to receive vaccinations—residents felt punished by staff for contracting it. They felt afraid to be around staff and found the staff's behavior to be excessively cruel.

Gone were visits and group programming; all were isolated in their cells. They reported feeling more stress and anger and reported seeing more drug use, mental health issues, and fighting in their communities. The rules changed every day, without clear communication from staff. They were not provided proper protective equipment or cleaning supplies. When someone got sick, they were quarantined without access to community support and without clear follow-up. In short, the pandemic made an already stressful and isolating experience that much more terrifying and lonely. Not to mention lethal: the death rate for incarcerated people in state and federal prisons from COVID-19 was 20 percent higher than for the average American (25).

As we discuss the way medical and mental health staff treat women prison residents, it's important to remember that nationally these include a number of transgender clients, who doctors see often without adequate training. Because we don't have accurate statistics of numbers of nonbinary, gender nonconforming, and transgender people, we do not currently have accurate statistics for the incidence of medical issues within those communities. We do know that trans women housed in men's facilities are at extremely high risk of violence from both residents and staff, which increases their risk of ongoing medical issues.

For trans people, getting competent care outside the prison system is already a significant challenge. In most state prison systems there simply aren't enough trans people per facility to warrant institutional change initiated from the inside, so an incarcerated trans person must seek significant support from nonprofits, grassroots campaigns, and community partners.

Although transgender people in California usually have access to their hormone treatment (although many incidents of harassment during the course of receiving care have been documented), many states do not have specific requirements protecting the medical rights of trans people. In a 2011 conversation between writer blake nemec and Kim Love, a formerly incarcerated trans woman in California, Kim remembered one or two doctors or nurses who "love the girls, and they'll bend over backward to get you what you need. You're lucky if you get one of them. If not, then it's the draw of the dice" (26).

Behavior Management as Mental Health Care

While touring the facility early in my work at an East Coast prison, I noticed one unit that had about twenty-five women asleep in their beds in the middle of the day. When I asked my tour guide why, she said, "They must have all been tired."

I knew something was wrong. Over the course of my week at that facility I was given two more explanations: first, that they were all sex offenders who had to be medicated; then later by another person that they all had serious mental health issues. I knew neither of these stories worked;

these women clearly appeared to be asleep due to medication. Over time I dug a little further and learned that the women had indeed been medicated, on powerful antipsychotics, for behavior control. These were women who talked back, who asked why, who refused to comply. They were given a medication that contained them.

When people first enter custody, they usually have a mental status exam. What the corrections counselors are looking for are signs that a person has a high risk of self-harm, suicide, or violence. They call this an assessment of risk, but it is about a resident's risk of mental disintegration or being aggressive/violent inside the facility, not a standard mental health evaluation. The assessment is done from the perspective of smooth running of the institution, and women are classified according to the risk they may pose to the operation.

Jackie, who gave birth in prison and now advocates for incarcerated women from outside, remembered that "if you were in any way suicidal, they'd throw you in a room by yourself with a paper gown on and a camera on you 24/7. That's their intervention. Their solution is to make sure you don't die so they don't have a lawsuit. It's not about caring."

Prison staff prioritize behavior management over individualized care, and the consequences of this can be disturbing. At another West Coast facility, I worked with my colleague Barbara Bloom to help with a large assessment. This facility housed girls (and uncounted nonbinary and trans youth) and was touting what wonderful mental health services they had.

We had some graduate students perform file reviews, and the results amazed me. The residents were on medications that had nothing to do with their most recent diagnosis. They had as many diagnoses, and were on as many medications, as the number of mental health professionals they had seen. The facility thought that many doctors, and many visits, constituted high quality of care, but they were not providing quality care because there was no continuity. Several girls in one of our focus groups reported feeling overmedicated and "like zombies."

Even when prison residents are getting in to see a mental health care practitioner like a social worker or psychiatrist, they know they are seeing someone who ultimately answers to the institution, and that can have consequences in both their individual case and the aggregate.

For example, I see borderline personality disorder (BPD) disproportionately diagnosed in women's prison mental health systems. I have some resistance to the diagnosis of BPD anyway because historically it has been used almost exclusively for women. My professional opinion is that many of the people diagnosed with BPD, if not most of them, are trauma survivors who would be better served by a diagnosis of complex post-traumatic stress disorder (C-PTSD). In a prison setting this is no small claim, because personality disorders are treated very differently than disorders like depression, anxiety, and PTSD.

Historically, the belief about personality disorders, especially BPD, is that they are untreatable. Therefore, once a woman is diagnosed, the thinking is that there is nothing more that can or should be done for her. Jackie told me she received a BPD diagnosis upon arriving to prison, and she saw many other women receive the same. "Everybody has it, apparently," she quipped. "It was my first time in prison, I was a train wreck, I was detoxing off heroin, and suddenly I and everyone around me had borderline personality disorder. So we're beyond help."

I think the overdiagnosis of BPD allows prisons to avoid providing treatment and services to women who could benefit from them. Serious stigma is attached to the diagnosis: people with personality disorders are seen as difficult, hard to work with, unable to change, and so on. While claiming to be providing access to mental health care via diagnosis, prison authorities can use personality disorders as explanations for the behavior of incarcerated women that lead to more restrictions and punishment. This constant negative messaging harms residents and shores up evidence for the institution that there is nothing that can be done for the women inside; they're incorrigible, and the prisons have the diagnoses to prove it.

While my main concern here is that incarcerated women must navigate inadequate and, in many cases, criminally negligent medical and mental health care systems, it is worth pointing out that most jurisdictions struggle to staff their medical teams. There is especially a shortage of qualified mental health practitioners willing to work in prisons and jails. In general, the stereotype of a doctor who works in a prison is that they are not a good one and couldn't get a better job elsewhere. It is a low-status job in the medical field.

In addition to this belief, for those who may be considering a job inside, barriers could come from two seemingly opposing political directions: some may hold tough-on-crime beliefs about incarcerated people deserving less in the way of treatment and care, whereas others may believe that working in the system contributes to mass incarceration.

This means that sympathetic, trained practitioners may avoid serving incarcerated women because gaining employment in the state or federal system feels like becoming part of the problem (27). The women I interviewed offered occasional anecdotes about practitioners who "cared," but those stood out against a backdrop of poor treatment that ranged from neglect to outright abuse.

Pharmaceutical companies have begun to pay more attention to corrections as a market, where not only currently incarcerated people need medication but the formerly incarcerated may continue to use the same medications after they are released. Given the high number of people who must rely on doctors serving prisons and jails, it follows that major pharmaceutical companies are now tailoring conferences, sales pitches, free samples, and lunches for corrections (28). Meanwhile, the horror stories I still hear from women seeking care on the inside have changed very little.

Untangling the Difficulties in Medical and Mental Health Care

There is no such thing as a "healthy" prison. Women enter prison at higher risk of medical and mental health issues. In general, it is difficult for incarcerated women to get staff to pay attention to their medical symptoms, and if they do receive medical care, it's often inadequate or even causes more harm.

I have seen women who were diagnosed with cancer too late for treatment to be effective. I have seen women on powerful antipsychotics, who were never experiencing psychotic symptoms in the first place. Getting an accurate diagnosis and then the right medications, not to mention seeing a specialist when needed, is terribly difficult. Mental health care is often more about behavior management than it is about healing or support.

However, we should not make the mistake of presuming that all of these challenges are specific just to the prison setting.

Many societal inequities contribute to the systemic issues we see inside. Many incarcerated women already distrust doctors because of the history of racism in medical research and practice, and their experience with medical professionals inside the correctional system does not repair their trust in any way. Most of them did not have access to good medical care on the outside prior to incarceration, because they were experiencing poverty and family stress. Beatrice noticed that some of the women she helped to file paperwork requesting visits to specialists had never navigated a medical system before and were inexperienced at self-advocacy.

Overall, the way medicine is practiced in prisons contributes to justice-impacted women's sense that their lives are not of value to those who are in charge of them. So they care for each other, making soups from commissary rations, sharing medications and remedies, and checking in with each other when illness sets in.

Aging in Custody

Prison is not meant for old people.

—**Betty**, *personal correspondence*

THE DATA CONFIRM something incarcerated people have been saying for years: being imprisoned shortens your life. Over the years I noticed that incarcerated women seemed to age more quickly. It was visible in their hair, skin, and teeth. The combination of inadequate medical care, poor diet, and all the stressors of the environment made them visibly older than their chronological age. Studies confirm that institutional aging has significant impact: prison residents who are chronologically fifty years old are physiologically closer to sixty, with increased health problems associated with older age (29).

Currently, we understand that for every year spent inside, two years of life expectancy are lost (30). This means that a sentence of ten years has the potential to shorten a person's life overall by twenty years. That is the harshness of the experience. That is the urgency of change that is needed. That is one reason why everything from in-prison harm reduction efforts to large-scale abolition campaigns are ongoing despite the obstacles. We are sentencing people not just to serve time but to die younger as a result—to miss out on opportunities to heal, reconnect, and create meaningful experiences in their older years.

The United States imposes the longest sentences of anyone, anywhere. In Germany a long sentence is fifteen years, and it is rare. In the Netherlands a sentence over four years is rarely issued. In a meeting with a delegation of criminal justice officials from Uzbekistan, I was told that no woman, regardless of her crime, would serve over fifteen years. Their theory is that if you haven't helped her in fifteen years, there is nothing more you can do. They were horrified by our long sentences, life sentences, and death sentences.

In the United States, life sentences are common, and many states maintain restricted or no opportunities for parole. These practices persist despite years of research indicating that longer sentences do not deter crime. In fact, the data reveal that people age out of crime. This means that even those who believe that imprisonment is an appropriate response to certain acts of harm must face the fact that keeping people in prison for decades does nothing to reduce harm.

Figure 5. Aging Population.

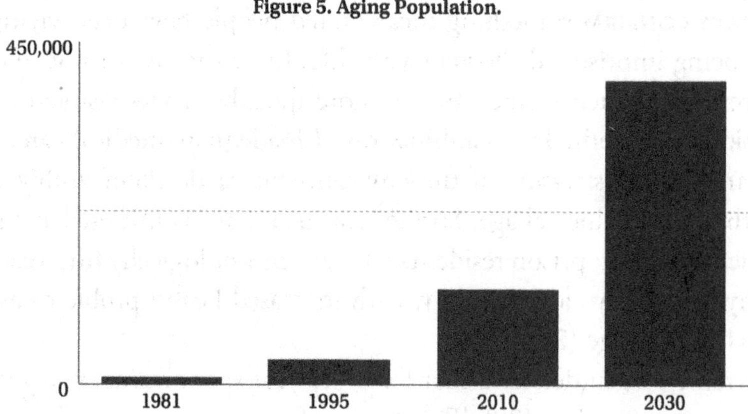

Source: Adapted from American Civil Liberties Union (ACLU), *At America's Expense: The Mass Incarceration of the Elderly* (2012). https://www.aclu.org/files/assets/elderlyprisonreport_20120613_1.pdf.

The prison population is aging, and it is a serious issue both for individuals experiencing it and for policy. From 1999 to 2016, the population of prison residents over the age of fifty-five increased by 280 percent (31). People over fifty are the fastest-growing population in prison, not because they are getting incarcerated later in life but because they have been serving long sentences since their teens, twenties, and thirties. Tough-on-crime policies of the 1980s and 1990s, especially mandatory minimum sentences, have resulted in the aging prison population we have now.

This brings with it an increase in medical and mental health costs, as people over the age of fifty-five are much more likely to need support for loss of eyesight or hearing, dementia, arthritis, and other common developments. Long sentences also mean that women can expect to go through menopause in prison. People who experience menopause in prison,which includes some transgender men and nonbinary, genderqueer, and gender nonconforming people across the spectrum housed in women's prisons because of the sex assigned on their birth certificate, have to rely on the expertise and support of those living with them. In 2018, 25 percent of incarcerated women were age forty-five and older, and yet there are rarely any sources of educational or medical support for the symptoms of menopause.

Sometimes there are even extra punishments for women experiencing menopause symptoms. For example, a woman in a prison in a southern state told researchers that when she experienced a hot flash, she got a write-up for rolling up her sleeves and pant legs (32). Most of the common nonmedical remedies for menopause symptoms are not available or are against policy: wearing layers, access to cool drinks, extra supplies for heavier blood flow, frequent showers. For women serving long sentences who entered prison years before their menopause and who never received adequate health care or education about their own bodies, the onset of symptoms can be very scary. Once again, they rely on each other for information and support.

In my conversations with Gina Fedock, the previously mentioned professor and researcher, we spoke about how often incarcerated women do not receive the help they need from their institutions, particularly for the onset of disabilities associated with aging. Most women have jobs inside the prison because that is how the prison keeps functioning. If you are working inside the prison, in general you do not get decreased responsibilities, much less retirement from working, as you age. This means that a prison job could be done by a twenty-five-year-old or a sixty-five-year-old, and both would be expected to complete the same required amount of labor in the allotted time. Manual labor jobs like janitorial work are proportionally much harder on older women than younger women.

Gina told me that in the midwestern women's prison where she had been conducting research, there was a special wing for women who were disabled or of advanced age. "It's the other women inside who help them get around," she said. "We have deaf and hard-of-hearing women, blind women, women with other disabilities, and they are housed separately, but they are completely neglected by the facility. They receive their support from the other women around them."

Imagine being hard of hearing and trying to decipher what a corrections officer (CO) is telling you to do and knowing that there are severe consequences for seeming insolent or reluctant. Gina told me that having other women to interpret was "crucial, absolutely crucial" for communication between COs and residents with hearing loss. The women housed in the wing for disabled and aging residents are nearly all serving very long or life sentences, experiencing medical issues that were not present when they were first incarcerated.

Dementia, Alzheimer's Disease, and End-of-Life Care

If options for mental and emotional health care are typically inadequate to the needs of incarcerated women, this this is especially true for the onset of Alzheimer's disease or other forms of dementia. The behaviors associated with midstage Alzheimer's—hoarding, refusing to bathe, trouble dressing, and difficulty in communication, to name a few—are easily interpreted by staff as "maladaptive behavior" that requires more behavioral control. A woman may be punished for these behaviors in ways that exacerbate them. If she is unable to visit with family who know her well, or if she is isolated and segregated from the other residents who have been helping her, her condition can worsen considerably.

Some prisons have opted to train younger residents to help care for aging people who are experiencing Alzheimer's and other forms of dementia (33). This has been lauded by the National Institute of Corrections as a potential solution to the issue of an increasing population of dementia-sufferers in custody, even a win-win, as those who are trained as carers will have gained "valuable, marketable skills."

Similarly, one western state has funded a community provider to implement a new program in one of the state prisons. In this program, women with long or life sentences are being trained to provide hospice care inside the prison. Hospice care can involve anything that helps make a dying patient more comfortable: changing bedclothes and diapers, washing a person's body when they are no longer ambulatory, giving them ice chips to soothe mouth dryness, holding their hand. In the prison program case the care is nonmedical, with women taking turns visiting, reading aloud, comforting, and caring for their prison mates who are terminally ill or near death.

Such programs allowing residents to care for each other are good and bring benefits to all involved. While recognizing that, however, it's critical to highlight that these programs are versions of what residents have long been doing, against official rules and for no pay. Indeed, the hospice program modeled its services on the care women have historically and unofficially been providing their terminally ill prison mates all along. When we zoom out and see how prisons can package these programs as evidence of successful interventions, and then take credit for work that residents have already been doing for each other, it reveals these "win-win" programs in a more troubling light.

I would like to be clear that I have never met a woman who was content to die in prison. In fact, as they age the notion of dying in prison becomes particularly painful. Many women have said to me, "Oh my God, I don't want to die in here." It is a measure of the desperation aging women face in prison, then, that the highest percentage increase in deaths by suicide inside prison is in the over-fifty population.

Aging people have particular needs, which prisons were simply not designed to meet, and often they don't try. Aging women have different needs than aging men. For transgender and nonbinary prison residents, there is currently no gender-inclusive means of addressing any of the medical and emotional needs inherent to aging. The older a resident gets, and the more they are confronted with mortality, the more distressed they become about the possibility of dying while incarcerated. Training programs that would allow residents to provide nonmedical hospice care to other residents are a small step toward acknowledging the deep human need for comfort and connection at the end of life.

Celebrating Special Days

There was this young woman who came to my support group every week, and one week she told us all it was her birthday. The following week she told us the people on her tier made her a birthday cake and got her commissary food. No one had ever done anything for her on her birthday before. It was the first birthday cake she'd ever had in her life.

—**Linda**, *personal interview*

AS MENTIONED, IT may be easy to assume that scarcity of resources would result in a lot of stealing. And stealing does happen, more commonly in jails (where women live for shorter periods of time) than prisons. However, from what I've learned in my work with incarcerated women, stealing from another resident in a women's prison is a serious offense in the social system, which requires a response—a confrontation or negotiation—and it is not as common as outsiders presume.

Much more common is for incarcerated women to figure out ways to share with each other. I've consistently been impressed with the level of creativity and resourcefulness I've seen in women's prisons: the creation of useful and even beautiful things from items people with more privilege don't notice, like cardboard, tissue paper, and empty plastic bottles. I've mentioned the inventive way women turn commissary corn chips into tamales, and now I'd like to highlight the ways incarcerated women use what's available to them to help each other celebrate their special days.

Something from Nothing

It is important to remember that although on paper prisons and jails are required to provide basic needs such as food, personal hygiene items, clothing, and shoes, it doesn't always happen. There is no individuality when it comes to basic needs; you are presumed to have the same needs as everyone else in the facility.

During her first few days in a facility, a woman may be given a small bar of soap but no shampoo or toothbrush. She may be issued a "temporary" uniform that ends up being what she wears for months. Many of the items that most people would consider basic needs must be bought through the commissary system, and many women do not come into prison with money on their books. They must work an extremely low-wage prison job to afford stamps, pens, extra sanitary pads, and so on. In the artificial world of the prison economy, it should be no surprise that a resident-run market for "contraband" personal care items usually arises.

In addition to their scarcity, the items a woman receives from commissary are simply not the same quality as what people in the free world would buy in a store. Commissary items are often manufactured for and sold directly to prisons, and the quality is generally not good. They are also not reliably available. It's one thing to be without a necessary item—say, shampoo—if you can anticipate that it will be available next week. It's another thing to have no idea when shampoo will be available, or if the officer in charge will make sure you get the shampoo you ordered before they run out. Also, the shampoo that eventually comes in may be a formula made for white women's hair, which isn't what you ordered in the first place. Incarcerated women often have to decide what they are willing to do—barter, trade, do favors—to get what they need.

This is the context in which women become not only inventive with the materials they have access to, but conscious of each other's needs. They become attuned to the importance of finding things to celebrate;

to the need for each person to feel that they are valued and special. Celebrating holidays is one of the important ways incarcerated women preserve their sense of identity and culture. Most interviewees told stories about their entire unit celebrating Thanksgiving and Christmas together, but there were many other special days: birthdays, graduations, and some just for fun.

The women make decorations to help celebrate many special occasions. Here we see the theme of Christmas. An important thing to understand is that they have few resources or supplies. They learn to use anything and everything they can find to repurpose. Their creativity is amazing!

Source: Michele Zousmer.

Holidays Inside

Unless she is in jail for only a short time, it is likely that an incarcerated woman will have at least one birthday inside. Many of the women I've spoken to describe traditions for celebrating birthdays in their unit, tier, or block. They may make cards or gifts, create dishes from their saved commissary items, and have a party in their common space.

Beatrice remembered that all of this had to be done in semisecret. "It's hard being imprisoned away from your family on your birthday," she said. Beatrice spent fifteen years in prison, so she saw many birthdays come and go. She had vivid memories of birthday celebrations during her time in prison: "It was against the rules, but you know, we'd decorate the birthday person's cube, the artists would draw little happy birthday cards. We'd get some contraband stuff out of the kitchen and make a good meal. We'd make a cheesecake out of Laughing Cow cheese and lemons and cook it in the microwave. Somebody always had to be watching to make sure that a CO [corrections officer] wasn't coming to snatch it away. We'd knit and crochet little things, and then we'd have to hide them because they were contraband." Because keeping these little handicrafts was prohibited, Beatrice remembered, incarcerated women were supposed to immediately send them home.

The scarcity of resources in prison makes the gift of a new item of clothing, a book, or art supplies especially precious. Patricia remembered the importance of receiving a brand-new sports bra for her fortieth birthday. "In jail you got recycled clothes," she explained. "I had underwear that were clearly stained, and bras that had turned gray. So somebody was able to get a hold of a new sports bra and gave it to me for a birthday gift. I just remember looking at it, thinking, Wow, it's so crisp and white, and it's new, and it's mine."

Geri also told me the story of a particularly meaningful birthday gift she received from her roommate. While serving a forty-year-to-life sentence, Geri worked incredibly hard to prove that she deserved a chance at clemency. Although she kept information about her potential release private, she turned fifty while in prison. She told me that her roommate, who was also serving a life sentence, organized a fiftieth-birthday celebration for her.

"She made me a really special bracelet," Geri recalled. "She knew that purple and green were my favorite colors. She said that she believed all along, as I did my time, that I would not do forty years. She said, 'This is a bracelet from a lifer. I'm giving it to you, and when you get out you have to give it to another lifer.'" Geri treasured the purple-and-green bracelet, and when she was granted clemency and released, she gave it to another lifer just as she'd been asked to.

Small tokens of care and moments of shared positive feeling can take on huge meaning for women living in prison. I was surprised when Patricia told me, "Truthfully, I love being free, of course. I love being with my family. But the best Christmas memory that I have is being at the honor dorm doing karaoke."

The honor dorm represents preferred housing in prison, which women can earn with good behavior. Still, I've heard so many women speak about the pain of Christmas inside, separated from loved ones, I needed Patricia to explain how it could be the best. "I just remember having this overwhelming sense of community," she said. "We were there for each other in the darkest times, and for a short moment, we were singing together, all completely fulfilled in our unity, and allowing ourselves to be truly happy. I mean, we were singing karaoke, singing awfully, singing off pitch, and just enjoying every minute of it."

Two women painted a mural on butcher paper of children making a snowman in the snow. "We had an all-day Christmas event inside the dorm to force people to leave their rooms," she recalled. "We had a gift exchange first thing in the morning, and people had spent weeks making their gifts. They saved Doritos bags, washed them, and turned them inside out to make bows for wrapping paper."

"The love that went into each action we took that day made it so special," Patricia reflected. "There was so much more thought that went into everything than there is on the outside. We didn't take anything for granted, and we knew that feeling connected was the most important thing."

Graduation Day

There is such wisdom in taking action to feel connected, recognized, and unified in spite of the prison. In addition to birthdays and holidays, graduations are a very special day for women living inside a prison, and they find ways to mark the occasion. In 2010 I was invited to speak at a graduation in the Rockville, Indiana, women's prison, which would be filmed for a show called *Breaking Down the Bars* on the Oprah Winfrey Network. I'd been going inside that facility for many months for the filming of this seven-segment docu-reality show and was honored to be a part of the graduation.

A group of about twenty women were getting their GEDs, some were getting their associate degrees, and a few were completing their bachelor's degrees through a local college. They wore caps and gowns, and their families were seated in rows while the graduates sat up front with a platform and podium for the speakers, just like it would have been staged on the outside. I remember the children being so, so excited to see their mothers get up and get a diploma. There are many barriers in place preventing women from showing their family, especially their children, that they can do something of value while in prison. It's not what children usually hear or see, so that graduation ceremony meant a great deal.

During the ceremony, I was struck by the degree to which certificates of completion and graduation ceremonies were important signs of hope.

A few years later, when we organized the first graduation for women who had completed the *Beyond Violence* pilot program, this point was driven home again for me. There is a large purple lotus flower on the cover of the *Beyond Violence* workbook and facilitator's guide. One interviewee who had been through the program told me, "I can still see that purple lotus in my mind. When I was struggling, I'd look at that book and remind myself there was going to be more to my life."

Because the twenty-session program was designed to be peer facilitated, our first group of graduates had completed both the program and a facilitator training. When the graduation began, I noticed that the group had made purple tissue-paper flower centerpieces for the tables. They had also made purple graduation caps out of construction paper, along with ceremony programs with a quote from the *Beyond Violence* guide.

This had all taken an incredible amount of planning and use of their own resources. They did it for each other, to celebrate their accomplishment and to reinforce the importance of doing something new, something restorative, together.

Today we continue to have graduations for all the programs, complete with caps, gowns, and certificates. The women design the graduation program and include speakers who have graduated from each group.

This is photograph of a group of women who completed the program and are graduates.

Source: California Department of Corrections and Rehabilitation.

Residents of the prison are invited to attend in order to learn more about the program and to support their graduating friends. Each group selects a graduation speaker from their group to be part of the ceremony.

Source: California Department of Corrections and Rehabilitation.

Just Because

Although birthdays, holidays, and graduations are clearly reasons to celebrate, sometimes we all need to have a special day just because. However, any special holiday meal, movie night, or other recreation that is organized by the prison is conditional and can be taken away at any time. It is not part of corrections culture to offer residents a reason to feel special and cared for. For Lisa, this was the impetus for a new idea.

Lisa, the woman who came to prison later in life and was the recipient there of unexpected acts of kindness, told me she looked around at the "hardcore women" she was living with and thought, "They need a little princess in their lives." She got the idea to throw a "princess party." "I went to the cops and told them I'd wax the whole hallway if they'd give me a little bit of extra floor wax for me to do our room," she told me. "Then I asked them if I could borrow one of the small TVs. I told them I want to have a princess party, and I need to make sure the floors are clean. I want to put all the mattresses on the floor, put a little TV in there, and have snacks." In a stroke of luck, Lisa got an okay from the guards.

Next Lisa went to the program director. "I asked if I could have some construction paper and some glue and some glitter to make some tiaras," she said. "They were like, *What?* I said, 'I want to have a princess party, and we all need tiaras.' So I made six tiaras with pink construction paper and glitter. I invited my roommates to a princess party! We made spread—that's the flavoring from Top Ramen, Squeeze Cheese, a can of jalapeños, and a little bit of mayonnaise mixed together. We ate it with chips and watched *Catfish* on the little TV."

Lisa told me that after the first princess party, word spread quickly, and many other women in the prison asked if they could come to the next one. "The cops made me stop because it got to be too many people wanted to come. But that was my most fun memory."

Lisa's princess parties illustrate the way positive experiences are always conditional inside prison. I attended one graduation for women on condemned row—California's newer name for death row—where the warden told me I had to wear a stab vest or leave. On principle I wasn't going to wear the vest, since I didn't believe there was any need for it. But when I was told I would have to leave, I decided it was more important for me to be present for the graduates, so I relented.

Birthday celebrations, although important and uplifting, always held an edge of sadness, in part because they had to be done mostly in secret, and without a person's family or friends on the outside. The fact that incarcerated women find the resources and energy to celebrate special days together shows me, once again, the incredible power of their will to manifest safety, care, and healing for each other when everything around them is telling them they can't.

REMEMBERING THOSE WHO DON'T SURVIVE

There is a lot of mystery around death on the inside of a prison. The way data are taken varies by jurisdiction, and all facilities are motivated to record as few deaths as possible to prevent lawsuits and bad publicity. When a woman dies in custody, the next of kin she has selected is notified and asked if they want to make arrangements at their cost. They have a limited time to decide. If they decline or don't respond by the deadline, each prison has a contract for burial or cremation with a local mortuary.

Here, we honor the women whose stories were not told.

Many of the women I interviewed had lost a friend to suicide or overdose inside. Not all interviewees volunteered a name or story, but the experience was painfully common. We do know that institutional responses to suicide attempts reflect racist disparities: data suggest that inside prisons, Black women are less likely to receive health care after a suicide attempt than white women (34). We do not need high numbers of deaths to know that something is wrong. We also know that every loss reverberates deeply throughout the prison, affecting everyone for years to come. The women inside remember those who do not survive.

Here, we acknowledge the many women whose lives ended without sufficient support for their suffering.

Some women told me they saw their friends die from medical neglect. Beatrice remembered arguing with a corrections officer for a woman who was on oxygen provided by cannisters that held enough for just thirty days. "She was running out of oxygen," Beatrice recalled. "I fought for her to get more, and the CO told me, 'She's using too much.' I said, 'Are you nuts? She's breathing!' and then I went to see a lieutenant, because I wanted him to know that she was about to die on his watch." When Beatrice's friend did die of her disease, Beatrice grieved, feeling that with greater compassion, more could have been done.

Here, we remember the women who died due to neglect while in custody.

Linda remembers Mrs. Jones. "She was a mother figure. She took care of people."

Jackie remembers Cassie. "She had a baby. But when she got picked up again, she just couldn't deal with the despair."

Jackie also remembers Kristen. "I was close with her. She had been through so much."

Robin remembers Glenda. "She watched out for me. She knew I didn't know what I was doing."

Beth remembers her friend in restrictive housing. "She was a prolific self-harmer. She died because the security officers had to walk over five minutes away to get the keys to her room and didn't get back in time."

Patricia remembers Booty. "I didn't know her well, but she dated a friend of mine. No one knew why she died."

Lisa remembers Ruthie. "She was kind to me when others weren't. She was one of the nicest people I've ever met in my life."

I remember Larretha, who had a promising future in basketball and was killed soon after her release.

Women who die in custody or under parole supervision are made invisible. Incarcerated women may not receive accurate or adequate information if one of their own community inside gets very ill or dies. We on the outside do not have adequate information about women who die shortly after being released either. These were also common stories from interviewees. Recently released women are at high risk of overdose, suicide, and many medical problems. They are also at high risk of becoming victims of violence and abuse.

When we remember the women who did not survive incarceration, we remain mindful of the ultimate lack of respect incarcerated women live under. Every single one of these women is a reminder that we must confront, name, and take responsibility for the conditions that harm them. We must further acknowledge the impact their deaths had on the women around them.

Here, we honor the memories of those who did not survive.

PART THREE:
The Journey Home

Gate Fever
The Work of Reentry
Healing after Incarceration

What do people want in prison? They want to be out. Women often build a fantasy about leaving prison. They imagine what it will look like, feel like, what they'll do, what their kids will do, what will happen to the relationship they were in before. A big story can get created about leaving, a hopeful and beautiful story. It's going to be great. They can hardly wait; they will finally be reunited with a happy family.

The way women fantasize about getting out can be disconnected from the realities of their lives, but the dream is a mode of survival. It is a sustaining dream, but it is not the same as making practical plans for what you will need when you leave. Most prisons do not offer enough supportive transition services, and reentry services for recently released women are inconsistently available across different state systems.

Practically, what this means for women leaving prison is that the stigma and difficulties of incarceration do not end when their sentence is over. One small example comes from an East Coast facility that would release women with their possessions in a white garbage bag. The women were given a few tokens for public transportation and dropped off at a transit hub where everyone knew what the white plastic bags signified. They literally carried the humiliation of the prison experience with them as they reentered the outside world.

Another example comes from a West Coast prison where many women exiting the facility were sent to a residential community program. They would arrive to the program shackled, in a sort of muumuu dress issued by the prison, and no underwear. They had no underwear because they'd heard they would be issued new underwear in the residential program, and there was a shortage at the prison. Of their own volition, they left their underwear behind for the other women who needed it. Their journey home would begin with a brand-new level of vulnerability.

The journey home is what incarcerated women long for, but when it finally comes it can bring with it a host of new challenges without needed support. Many women find that they are unable to reconnect with friends or family after their release. This is why I say that women who find their way toward stability, healing, and community after incarceration are beating the odds stacked against them. The following discussion addresses how women prepare to leave prison and what happens to them on the outside once they do.

Gate Fever

Waiting in line for medical, I was held with two lifers, and both of them said to me, "Honey, make this your last trip. This is not how you want to live your life. Do whatever you got to do to not come back here. This isn't living. Go live your life."

—**Lisa**, *personal interview*

I DON'T CARE if a woman is in jail for ninety days or in prison for fifty years, the best practice would be to start preparing her to leave from the day she enters. This is not what happens.

After being incarcerated, there is so much that women need to learn about what it takes to go home. Like most of us, they don't know a lot about how the legal system works. So many things happen behind closed doors, in a language only lawyers and judges speak. A case file may be hundreds of pages. Once they are inside and situated, it is other incarcerated women who begin to help them understand what the law says and, sometimes more urgently, what the prison rules are and who enforces them. They may have negotiated a sentence in a plea bargain, but the way that sentence translates into actual months and years inside is not always obvious.

Incarcerated women experience confusion around sentencing and release dates, in part because the prison and jail systems are grounded in a shocking amount of randomness, judicial and correctional discretion, and inconsistency. In some states, whatever your sentence is, you automatically serve only half. In others you are expected to fulfill your entire sentence.

There are two types of sentences, determinate and indeterminate, which either specify a distinct amount of time or a range of time (such as twenty to life). Some systems allow for "good time," where an incarcerated person can earn a sentence reduction for participating in programs and avoiding write-ups from staff. Sometimes a system will release people earlier than expected because of overcrowding or other judicial interventions.

On the other hand, women can get time added to their sentence for rule violations and the like. Often, this takes the form of removing good-time credits or barring individuals from good-time-earning programs as a disciplinary sanction. In general, women considered higher risk, women with restrictions due to physical or mental health, and women in restricted housing are prohibited from earning good-time credits.

In addition to release on parole, there are a number of other ways women can leave prison: supervised release to a drug treatment program, release from a commuted sentence, or changes in the laws that affect their time, such as a retroactive sentencing law change that bumps a felony down to a misdemeanor. While advocates organized campaigns to pressure prisons to release more people due to COVID-19, reports indicate that there were actually *fewer* people who received parole hearings and approvals in 2020 than in 2019 (1).

Going Up for Parole

The possibilities affecting the length of a prison sentence are overwhelming and arbitrary, and this means that women sometimes aren't particularly sure of when they are eligible to go in front of a parole board, if they are in a state that allows parole. A lack of remorse and an insufficient plan for staying sober and out of trouble post release are often given as reasons to deny parole.

However, the criteria for getting "deemed suitable" for parole are not transparent. The word *suitable*, used across the United States, has always grated on me. It is insulting. People who are "suitable" for parole are not allowed to discuss in their parole hearing how systemic racism, poverty, substance use disorders, or abuse brought them to prison. The main requirement is that they must show "adequate remorse" for the mistake they made. It is yet another way the system focuses on individual harm instead of systemic issues. In addition, "suitable for parole" does not begin to acknowledge the wisdom and creativity incarcerated people could share in the community. And if a woman is not deemed suitable, it will likely be years before she has a chance to try again.

Even if a board grants a person parole, that decision can be reversed, in some cases by an appeal or a decision by the governor. Parole boards are often composed of political appointees with varying degrees of expertise in the issues that incarcerated women face. In 2020, sixteen states had passed laws that significantly reduced discretionary parole, making it nearly impossible for incarcerated people to use the parole system. According to Prison Policy Initiative, "State paroling systems vary so much it is *almost* impossible to compare them" (2).

I was once asked by the parole board in a midwestern state to create a new program for women who were sentenced due to violent crime. I planned a visit to speak with them. At the time I was naive about this part of the system. I thought I was going to have a thoughtful conversation with empathetic people who had a high degree of understanding about how people get into prison. Instead, the board told me they were uncomfortable with how many women cried at their board hearings, and could I write a program that would make it so the women wouldn't cry? I was shocked.

I reminded the members of the parole board that, number one, they held an incarcerated woman's life in their hands. They didn't know much about trauma, so I told them that 90 percent of the women who came to see them have been abused multiple times, usually by men who held a lot of power over their lives. There are many different ways people respond to trauma, and so, given that the level of fear women feel coming into that room would likely be very high, some of them would dissociate and not seem present. Others may cry. In fact, I told them, crying seemed to me a perfectly appropriate response to the pressures of the situation. Needless to say, we had difficulty coming to an understanding and I learned a great deal that day.

You may assume that incarcerated women who have the possibility of parole are given some way to prepare, but it is more likely that they aren't. In some prisons there are programs or workbooks for women to engage with if they are eligible, but more often than not preparation is done in less formal ways, within supportive groups of other women.

Star, the formerly incarcerated woman who now helps others with their reentry, told me about mock parole board hearings she and her friends would stage for women who were getting ready to "go to board." "Sometimes the staff would let us go into the dayroom when it was supposed to be locked down for cleaning, so we could use a table and chair," she remembered. "We would have two people be commissioners for the person who was going to board, and then one of us would be an officer. We would really try to set it up the way we'd seen it, with notepads so the commissioners could write things down."

These mock boards were filled with realistic details, such as the commissioners asking the parole hopeful to speak up if they were mumbling. The person in the room who had actually been to see the parole board would do some coaching, Star recalled. "We'd say, 'You're slouching, sit up, make eye contact, don't fidget, even if you have to sit on your hands. If they ask you a question about why you did something, like get in a fight, make sure you answer the question they are asking you, but then project how you'll do it differently in the future too.'"

Star and her group helped each other to see that they were likely going to be nervous and defensive at their board hearings, and they needed to be able to stay calm, be honest, and show that they had reflected on their own behavior. "They have a script," Star said, "so we had to have one too. You tell them: if the same circumstances were to happen today, here's how I would deal with it differently."

The preparation for parole board hearings didn't stop with rehearsals. Star remembers helping each other with paperwork, such as the necessary certificates of completion of programs, a written post-release plan, a written set of causative factors, and a description of a current support network. "We really got going," she said, "just in the unit, doing it ourselves."

Preparing to go in front of the parole board was a way for Star to see herself going home. "Once you go to board the first time, something changes," she told me. "It's just an energy or a whisper, but it's hope. It's unwavering. If this is what I have to do to get out, then this is what I'm going to do." Once the finish line is in sight, women can become extremely motivated. Rose told me that in the prison where she was living in the early 1990s, "we called it 'gate fever.' *Get me out, get me out, get me out.*"

When the Law Changes

Angela, mentioned earlier as a peer facilitator for the *Beyond Violence* program and participant in a tight family unit inside prison, had received a twenty-five-to-life sentence via California's aiding and abetting law. This law was used for years to incarcerate people associated with violent crimes via proximity or social contacts, even if they had not participated in the violence. Many women went to prison with life sentences due to this law. When the law changed, it would have been helpful to notify incarcerated women who may benefit from the change, but that is not how the system works. Angela told me she would not have been released from prison if another incarcerated woman hadn't notified her that the law changed.

"Amy's a genius," Angela told me of the friend she made inside, who had been incarcerated since age sixteen. "She could be a lawyer if she wanted to. We got permission to communicate once I got moved [to another facility], and one day I got a letter from her that says, 'Hey, there's this new legal case, I think that it might help you get out of prison early.'" Indeed, this was the case that ended up undermining the aiding and abetting law under which Angela was sentenced.

Like most incarcerated women, Angela did not have a lawyer because she couldn't afford one. Amy's work on Angela's case was welcome help and the only help available. "She had done my initial appeal for me, so she knew my case. She was just a beautiful human being trying to help people. She told me to send her some information she needed, and she would write me a new appeal."

At this point, fear got the better of Angela and she procrastinated. "I was afraid something would go wrong, and they would give me more time, not less." Before long Amy sent her a nudge in the form of a letter, dated only two days earlier. (Normally, mail took two weeks to arrive in the prison.) In it, Amy reminded Angela that the deadline was quickly approaching.

"At that moment I said, 'You know what? Forget it, I'm just gonna do it,'" Angela recalled. "'Whatever happens, happens.' And I sent her what she needed. She did the paperwork and filed it for me just in time."

Amy's efforts resulted in a ten-year reduction to Angela's sentence and an opportunity for her to go in front of a parole board just a few months after her resentencing. Under her original sentence, the earliest Angela could have been released on parole would have been 2022. Instead she was released on parole in 2014 and now works as a drug and alcohol counselor and life coach.

"Had it not been for that sisterhood that we created up there, where would I be?" Angela reflected. "I wouldn't have known there was a chance for me to get out. I was in a place where people weren't that into the law library. I would still be there trying to get out today. That's the importance of forming these relationships. They become your community, your network, and everybody has something different to offer."

The Work of Reentry

When I got out, I tried to find a job. It took me a year and a half. I'm relatively intelligent and have a good work ethic, but nobody could hire me because of my record.

—**Beatrice**, *personal interview*

IT IS WINTER in the Midwest. It is snowing, windy, and very cold. A uniformed officer leaving her shift sees a woman who has been released leaving the jail in a thin sweater and pantyhose. Worried about the woman getting frostbite, or freezing to death, the off-duty officer stops the woman and asks her to come back inside to get some more appropriate clothes. They go inside, and the off-duty officer asks the on-duty officer what's going on. He shrugs and says, "We give them whatever they came in with." She tells him to go to the closet and find the released woman some boots, pants, a coat, hat, and gloves. She reminds him that they have things for people to wear if they are leaving without adequate clothing.

When the off-duty officer told me this story, it clearly illustrated how the punishment of imprisonment continues, even as a woman is released from prison or jail. Although this woman was lucky that the off-duty officer intervened, the intervention should not have been necessary. The message to the woman being released was clear. Her life wasn't worth a trip to the storage closet.

This story stood out to me, but there are many such stories. An East Coast prison used to release women after midnight to a bus stop, knowing the buses didn't start running until five in the morning. Unless they were able to get in touch with someone who could help them, recently released women spent their first night of freedom on the street. In time, a colleague of mine developed reentry services for women exiting that prison, providing a toll-free number for them to call for a ride so they wouldn't be out all night alone.

Why wouldn't the prison change its practice? They received money from the state for each woman they housed each day. So a woman released after midnight could be counted for the following day, and the prison would receive their three dollars for her food without having to give the woman a meal. It is common for people to be released at all hours of the night for bureaucratic reasons, without regard for their safety. Groups of people being released and driven by bus into town may get transported late at night because that is when the buses are not otherwise in use.

Although it is the day an incarcerated woman most looks forward to, her release date is not always reliable or even knowable beforehand. A woman may believe she is getting released on a Friday and set up a ride for herself, only to find out she isn't getting released until Monday, long after her ride has come and gone, because of a paperwork issue.

When I talked to Brandi, who spent twenty-eight years inside what you may remember her calling the "gated community," she was shocked the day her sentence commutation happened. She had filed her paperwork two years before. The day her sentence was commuted, she was "in sweats, hair in a ponytail with a hairnet on, covered in apple juice because I'd been peeling apples for a pie. I got called to the program office, and I didn't know why, so I just walked up there like that. It was surreal. There was a group of us who had all received a commutation, and I was still in my hairnet."

People who are not system impacted often do not understand how the punishment of imprisonment continues, often long after a person is released. In some very important ways, once you've been in, you're never really out. For many recently released individuals, the next stop after release is a highly supervised period of time on parole. Every state in the United States has a different set of parole requirements and rules, and post-release supervision is different in other countries, but a woman is usually under some level of supervision after release.

The conditions of parole are numerous and strict, often including such rules as meeting with a parole officer monthly, not associating with others on parole or co-defendants, getting a job within a certain time period, not traveling more than fifty miles, abstinence from substance use, and more. Truth be told, many of us would have difficulty pulling off a successful parole. Without a car or supportive friends to help, the challenge becomes all the greater. Nearly 20 percent of recidivism cases are due to parole violations, not new crimes (3).

A Lack of Services

Think about the word *reentry*. We use the same word to refer to people returning to Earth from outer space. It is about returning to the world after a disorienting, life-changing experience. It encompasses everything: housing, education, a job, family reunification, continued treatment for substance use disorders or mental health concerns, medical care—everything. Reentry should be about asking the question, *What do people need after being released?* and then providing services to aid them in creating independent lives. What is needed for reentry mirrors what women say they needed to avoid prison.

In the focus groups where we gathered data for the National Institute of Corrections' research project *Gender-Responsive Strategies: Research, Practice, and Guiding Principles for Women Offenders*, women said that for a successful reentry they needed housing, drug treatment, education, job skills, and services for domestic violence (4). Across the United States, it must be noted that these are the very same services the women said would have prevented them from being in prison in the first place. We didn't provide them then; now we discuss these same services in the guise of reentry.

Reentry services are absolutely necessary, and yet they are often inadequate to the level of need recently incarcerated women experience. Rose, who spent over a year incarcerated in the United Kingdom and now has devoted her life to aiding women with addictions and trauma, recalled volunteering with a reentry program as "the perpetual addressing of unmet need."

I have seen a few reentry service models that work better than others. They are based on an understanding of the extreme level and complexity of need many people have upon release. In New York there is finally a one-stop shop for women where they can see child welfare, their parole officer, and every agency they must engage with to meet regulations, all in one place. I'm glad for this. However, it is not the same as an individualized plan that assesses and meets the needs of each individual woman. As I wrote in "A Woman's Journey Home," "Each transitioning woman clearly needs a holistic and culturally sensitive plan that draws on 'wraparound services'—a coordinated continuum of services located within a community" (5).

It should be no surprise that the most successful models for reentry support emerge from the wisdom of formerly incarcerated women. Rose, who had struggled to maintain her sobriety after her release, developed a gate-pickup program to make sure that women getting out of prison had a person waiting to take them to a place free of relapse triggers. Kim Carter, who wrote "A Note from a Hidden Healer" at the beginning of this book, developed a model in the Time for Change Foundation that offers housing and individualized assistance to address each woman's individual needs.

Unfortunately, there is often very little funding for reentry programs from the government, or even from seemingly aligned sources like feminist groups. Kim Carter told me the most difficult group to secure funding for is formerly incarcerated women. Her services were originally funded for women experiencing homelessness, many of whom also happened to be formerly incarcerated.

Years ago, Catholic Charities used a model for people coming out of prison that was based on the model used for refugees. The belief was simple: people who have just been released from prison need everything. They may not speak the "current" language or understand major changes to the cultural landscape that happened while they were inside. They may have no personal possessions, no pots and pans, no bed, no change of clothes, no place to stay, no family in the area. They may have an abusive partner lurking in the background, or children, both of which make it more difficult for them to create new, safe living arrangements. Although wraparound services are clearly what is most needed, they are also the costliest, so women receive patchwork and insufficient support, while the demands placed on them post release are very high.

On parole people are legally required to return to the community where they were arrested. Moving to a different county is possible for some, but it takes ingenuity and resources and is ultimately up to the discretion of the parole officer. This means that a recently released woman is often required to confront all the same dangers and triggers in her community that contributed to her incarceration. It means that she needs to move to one place even if her children or people who support her are in another.

One of my interviewees, Serena, has lived experience with addiction, recovery, and incarceration that prepared her for the work she has been doing for nearly twenty years. She supports women by using principles of harm reduction, providing support groups, and teaching somatic practices like tai chi. In her work she has observed many women on their reentry path, and she conceives of reentry as getting knocked back down to the bottom of Maslow's Hierarchy of Needs.

In brief, Maslow's hierarchy describes five levels of human need, with the most urgent physiological needs for survival as most foundational, and the next most urgent needs building up from there: safety, love and belonging, esteem (of both self and others), and self-actualization (realized potential). The idea is that the basic physiological needs of food, water, shelter, and the like take on heightened importance for a person when they are not being met.

Though we know that prisons often do not adequately meet people's needs for warmth, cooling, nutrition, and safety, the basics that *are* provided—indoor bed to sleep in, enough food and water to survive—are better than what some had coming in. With their first-tier needs met, these people may be able to newly open up to their need for love and belonging. "I think that's one reason why so many people say they found God in jail!" Serena said. "It's why they can form meaningful relationships and care so much about their kids and families. They're psychologically, emotionally, spiritually free to entertain love and belonging."

For these individuals, Serena believes, release from prison pulls that "bottom tier of Maslow" right out from under them, tumbling them right back down into survival mode: where am I going to eat tonight, where am I going to sleep. Even a woman's progress in self-help programming can be swept away. "You can't worry about your kids, you can't worry about your relationships," Serena reflected. "You have to survive." From Serena's perspective, this tumble to the bottom happens every time a person is released from prison or inpatient treatment.

Recently released people are living conditionally free lives with strict schedules to keep: meetings to attend and agencies to visit with the risk of violation at every turn. If she doesn't have a car, a cell phone, and good organizational skills, a woman will have a difficult time getting everywhere she needs to be on time. Even if she has a place to stay and help getting a job, someone exiting prison has a significant emotional adjustment to go through.

Brandi, released after twenty-eight years, found that the world outside had changed so much she was in shock. "When I got picked up, I almost fell out of the car when I saw the bridge toll to Treasure Island in the San Francisco Bay was six dollars," she recalled. "I was like, Are you buying the island? Are you out of your mind? When I went to prison, a hamburger and fries was $1.99. Now it's $10.99. I thought, Well, I'm never eating out again."

In an even more serious example, she remembered how her years inside affected her ability to socialize post release. At a barbecue in a park, she experienced a big anxiety trigger. "I'm standing there, I have a hot dog in my hand, and I see these people running toward me. And it literally freaked me out. Because in the 'gated community' when someone's running toward you, they're running *at* you. But they weren't. It was a park; kids were running, and they just ran on by. But my heart was beating ninety miles an hour, and I had to walk away."

Experiences like this are common and speak to the way prison itself creates more trauma in the lives of incarcerated women. Post release, Brandi found that "crowds and traffic were just totally overwhelming to me. I felt like I had stepped into another dimension." She was shocked at the way the homeless population had exploded in the city where she lived, and within a few months she began to work as a service provider, in time becoming the director of a large site for people with disabilities and medical fragility who are experiencing homelessness.

Meaningful Work

For Brandi, like most of the women who offered stories for this book, lived experience has been an interpersonal asset in the line of work they entered because they are advocates or direct service providers. However, for most formerly incarcerated women, having to "check the box" on a job application (indicating they have been convicted of a felony) means they never get called back for an interview.

Lisa, who organized "princess parties" for her unit while she was incarcerated, had been working in corporate America prior to her incarceration. Once she was out, she tried to return to work. "I have a pretty stellar resume for my field," she said. "I had top-notch jobs, a proven track record, great references, and nobody would hire me. Not one. I stopped checking the box after a while because I had kids to feed. I was desperately trying to get any job."

Like many women who leave prison when they are older, Lisa found that ageism compounded the prejudice employers feel against formerly incarcerated people. Once she stopped checking the box on her applications and colored her gray hair brown, she was able to get hired. She worked her way up in the company she works for today.

Even though they are often legally required to disclose, formerly incarcerated women are afraid that being honest with potential employers about their history will negatively affect their chances of being hired. Many of the jobs they are more likely to get are low paying, so they may need to work more than one to make ends meet. Of course, in this situation sex work and the drug trade make sense for survival, and many women find them the best of a terrible array of options. Some of the women have very clearly said, "The pimp and the drug dealer are the only ones waiting to provide a living wage when I leave prison."

Reentering the free world after living in a prison is overstimulating, confusing, and often very difficult. In addition to the process of learning a new way of life, recently incarcerated women are often experiencing physical health problems and emotional adjustment issues. They have been living in a situation of unhealthiness and forced dependency, then thrust into a condition of extreme vulnerability with a huge burden of responsibility. The injustice of this situation is profound. Those who end up working in advocacy and service provision use their freedom to help other women navigate the difficulties of incarceration, reentry, and reunification with children.

Healing after Incarceration

Universally, we know that when there are wounds on the body, what we need is care. Why is it that the wounds that we can't see are treated with putting people in cages?

—**Beth**, *personal interview*

A GOOD FRIEND of mine who was incarcerated many years ago told me the biggest problem is that you can get out of prison, but you can't get prison out of you. She was one of the many who told me that after all these years, she still remembers her prison number.

People who have been incarcerated are going to carry that experience with them all their lives. Patricia, the interviewee who came to prison with a PhD, told me it took about forty-five days to calm her nervous system after she was released. "I would get so startled by every noise, and the world was too big for me," she remembered. She remembered the constant fluorescent lighting. "They never turned it off," she said. "There was this bright light constantly on you. To this day I have to cover my head to sleep, even if it's dark, because in those five years I learned to feel safe if I had my head covered. I never used to do that."

Because of her training in psychology, Patricia is able to describe her experiences with a high level of expertise. However, expertise is not the same thing as healing. Patricia is in therapy to process how the experience affected her and to receive support for her continued healing. Not all women released from prison are able to access professional support, but pursuing some form of healing from the experience does matter.

Hypervigilant body states and difficulty adjusting to life outside prison are common, yet still not everyone acknowledges that incarceration is a traumatic experience. The best reentry programs that support basic needs often have some form of therapy or support group, but rarely is it labeled as a place to specifically process the difficulty of incarceration itself—in part because some parole conditions forbid reentering women from having contact with others who have criminal histories. A 2020 report from the Vera Institute revealed that reentry service providers are generally not asking their clients about trauma and wouldn't know what to do if someone disclosed victimization (6).

Given that (i) nearly every woman who finds herself in prison has a prior history of trauma and victimization, (ii) many of them will encounter some form of new trauma while living inside the prison, and (iii) the fact of living in a prison is itself a terrible experience, often traumatic or triggering without any added incident, the current lack of attention to healing after incarceration is unconscionable.

As with many traumas, the suffering and shame associated with incarceration are difficult to discuss. No formerly incarcerated person can be guaranteed that a counselor, psychologist, group leader, or social worker will treat them respectfully when they talk about their experience. Many formerly incarcerated people simply don't talk about prison. The struggle to meet one's own basic needs after being released is enormous. The new challenge of continuing to recover and heal once released can be daunting for women who began their healing path while they were still in prison.

Moving along the Spiral

In my work, I use the image of a spiral to help women think about and deepen their understanding of recovery and healing. The *downward spiral* represents addiction and/or trauma. When a woman has an addiction to alcohol or other drugs (or compulsive behaviors with food, sex, gambling, relationships, shopping, etc.), she is caught in a downward spiral.

The line through the center represents the object of her addiction, and it becomes the organizing principle in her existence, constricting and limiting her life.

The downward spiral also represents the limitations and constrictions that trauma can create in a woman's life. *Constriction* can include a person pulling away from relationships and becoming isolated, stuffing feelings, feeling afraid of people and places, and so on. Here, the line represents the traumatic event(s). It, too, can become an organizing principle in her life.

Figure 6. The spiral.

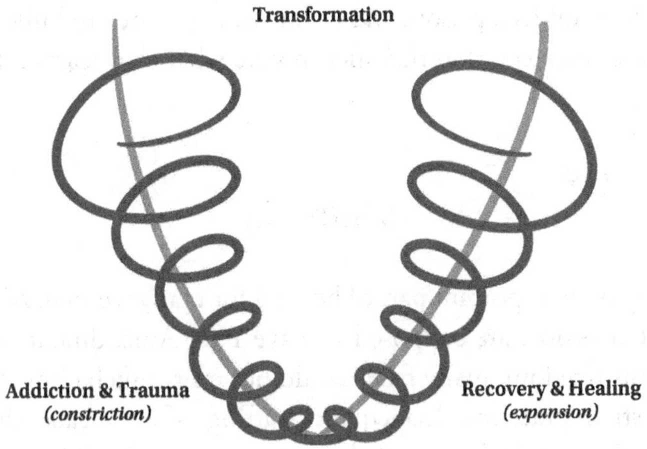

Transformation

Addiction & Trauma
(constriction)

Recovery & Healing
(expansion)

Source: Stephanie S. Covington.

The *upward spiral* represents the process of recovery from addiction and healing from trauma, in which a woman's life begins to expand. The line through the middle of the upward spiral still represents addiction and/or trauma. These life experiences are never gone; major life experiences stay with us all our lives. Yet recovery and healing are possible. The word *transformation* lives at the top of the spiral. Recovery and healing can begin on the inside, if opportunities align well for a person. If that person can continue her recovery and healing process on the outside, it's possible for her to get to a place where she can say, "Who I am today is not who I was."

Every incarcerated person will have something to heal from, whether they ever feel safe enough to discuss their life inside prison or not.

The women I spoke with found all manner of ways to continue their healing process after being released. Some formed groups online using Facebook and other platforms, where they talk about their experiences and support each other in their lives. Some pursued counselor training to share with others. Some devoted their time to substance use disorder treatment. Others created service organizations that supported other recently released women, went into housing advocacy, or developed their spiritual practices.

All of the women I spoke to have been consciously engaged in their own recovery and healing, despite the obstacles. With the help of other women, they survived prison, and today they continue to build meaningful lives after incarceration that incorporate what they learned from their experiences.

Spirituality

Spirituality is an important part of healing for many women. Although all incarcerated people are supposed to have First Amendment protections for religious freedom, many facilities do not exert much effort to support non-Christian practices. Inadequate staffing often means church and temple services could be canceled at any time. Sarah told me that while she was a resident in a West Coast women's prison, there was no female Native American chaplain, and thus she was not offered any kind of culturally competent spiritual care. She remembered that the Jewish chaplain advocated for Native American women and tried to support them.

With the help of another incarcerated woman, Sarah was able to connect with a Native American activist and spiritual leader who helped her to find community and connection after her release. Although she has always been tribally enrolled, she told me that her deeper connection to her own culture happened through the healing she was able to do after prison. "I made my regalia, which is my outfit to dance in," she told me. "And you have to be sober to wear that buckskin dress. Becoming a dancer was really important to me. I was so thankful to be chosen."

Eventually, she returned to the prison where she had been incarcerated to offer a Native American ceremony to the women inside. "I'd go in there every other weekend, to show the women that this is possible. It is possible to leave there and be good again. It meant so much to bring in all the items we use—the dress, the buffalo skull. We were singing together, and they were having a moment where they could act like there were no walls."

Through her own healing, Sarah has stayed motivated to keep bringing hope to others. "I never thought I'd be a counselor," she said. "But now I've taken this role, giving back on a constant basis." Some years after her experience sharing the ceremony with Native American prison residents, Sarah moved to a different state, got married, and now works with horses doing equine therapy. "I believe in the ceremony," she said. "I wouldn't be here today without it. There's no way I would have believed in where I am today. So when I work with people now, I tell them to trust the process, and if I can make it, you can make it."

Freedom Comes in Many Forms

Although some women are helped by traditional paths like individual therapy and recovery groups, others need to find a different way. Geri told me she has found new freedom in learning to become a DJ. She celebrated her fiftieth birthday while incarcerated, and now free at sixty years old, she makes original beats.

Geri inspires herself and others to continue asking the question, What does "free" look like for you? She told me, "I know what I freed myself from. Each and every one of us has something that maybe we're holding on to or may make us feel sad or hurt or frustrated or irritated, these different things that we go through in life that we want to break free from. So what does that look like for you? I want people to be free from the inside out." She shares her music online through social media and has inspired other women to pursue creative passions, no matter their age.

Devoting oneself to helping other women heal after being released from prison isn't every formerly incarcerated woman's path, but it happens frequently enough that I want to underscore what an achievement it truly is. Here are examples, just among my interviewees for this book:

Serena has developed a recovery program that incorporates harm reduction principles, and runs online groups for formerly incarcerated women with membership in the hundreds.

Linda is a certified level-four teacher of the Breath-Body-Mind techniques, a method for working with trauma survivors, and has shared the practice with people all over the world.

Kirsty and Beth work with women dealing with substance use disorders at the recovery program they both went through after their release from prison in the United Kingdom.

Brandi is the director of a site that serves people experiencing medical issues and homelessness.

Liz is a certified addiction counselor providing services to women in the community.

Robin directs a women's recovery home and works with a dance performance project for incarcerated women.

Beatrice and Jackie are both advocates with the Sex Workers and Allies Network, a harm reduction organization.

Amy is an activist for Black liberation and works with nonprofits and community members to change policy and get emergency funds to people who need them.

The other women I interviewed are also contributing to their communities, either through their vocation, volunteering, or simply by being examples of self-awareness and healing. All of them bring depth and wisdom from their lived experience to their families and communities. Their leadership is valuable, and they deserve to be seen, acknowledged, and appreciated.

PART FOUR:
What We Can Do

Envisioning Alternatives
Do One Small Thing

Our current criminal legal system is designed to shame and punish people, to tell them that they are bad people, and to lock them up and throw away the key. It represents a total shift to instead decide that when harm is caused, everyone involved needs care, attention, time, and space to heal. However, for any meaningful change to happen in the way we address harm, the first thing the general public will have to do is hold a complex reality: people who cause harm are often victims themselves.

The next realization will also be huge. We will need to understand that punishment, institutional order, and weaponized security are not the same thing as rehabilitation, connection, and safety; in fact, they are at odds. This is why it is important to practice envisioning alternatives. We need to make changes at all levels, beginning with immediate relief of institutional harms and moving always toward a fundamental restructuring of how we support each other in community.

When harm is caused, we want a place where people can come and get better. We want a place where people can make changes, which isn't possible without adequate care and support. That is a very different mindset than wanting a place where we can take people so they can be punished for doing bad things. It is such a different mindset that I've found most of the people I talk to have difficulty imagining it.

After we practice envisioning alternatives to our current system, we will discuss what it looks like to join in the work of making change. The formerly incarcerated women I interviewed did not achieve safety and self-reliance overnight. They had to put in work, connect with a community, and change their beliefs about what was possible for them. They are engaged in an ongoing process. If they can do it in their own lives, we can do it within the life of our public systems. Everyone has the capacity to do one small thing and to do it consistently—and that is the next step in our journey.

Envisioning Alternatives

For a lot of us, we did so much harm to our communities, and we know you can't unring that bell. You can't make up for it. So we try to do something now, to help the next person.

—**Brandi**, *personal interview*

IN 1999 MY colleague Barbara Bloom and I presented a paper at the American Society of Criminology titled: "Gender-Responsive Programming and Evaluation for Females in the Criminal Justice System: A Shift from What Works? to What Is the Work?" When we say, "What works?" we are referring to the way programs and services for incarcerated women are usually evaluated on a single criterion: recidivism. If a program reduces recidivism, then corrections says it works. We found this to be a wrongheaded approach, for many reasons. At the top of the list: keeping a narrow focus on recidivism does nothing to change the conditions that send women to prison in the first place.

We suggested that people in the field begin to ask themselves instead, "What is the work?" This question opens up new possibilities for supporting women's needs before, during, and after incarceration. It creates twin goals of finding better ways to both prevent and respond to harm. In that paper, we suggested four areas of focus: prevention, do no harm, gender-responsive services, and community support. These were big ideas at the time.

In 2024 my perspective has grown, but the conversations I'm having are disappointingly the same. People working in corrections often claim that it is difficult to get incarcerated individuals to change, but in truth, it's the culture, structure, and industries of our criminal legal system that defy change. The United States is addicted to punishment, and it is time to quit. We need an entirely new vision for how we respond to harm.

Reforms Aren't Enough

I used to believe that if I could just get the right approach, the barriers to women's recovery and rehabilitation inside the prison systems would shift. It may be surprising, then, for me to say that I now see reforming the criminal legal system is a way of keeping it the same.

When I first began working to create programming for women and visiting them inside, all I saw were things that could change, things that should be fixed, that would make life a little better in the immediate sense. Eventually, this took on the quality of repairing an older car. You can fix something here or there, but then the next thing breaks, and you begin to think, *Should I keep putting money into this?* And one day you realize it is truly not fixable. It took me a long time to understand that the system as a whole has to allow a certain amount of reform in order to stay the same. There are a lot of people still replacing parts of the car, because they benefit from the illusion that they are keeping it running.

Every move we make to change the way we do things has both foreseeable and unintended consequences. For example, when a facility gets shut down, we may celebrate the end of its use to harm incarcerated people, but often those people just get shunted off to other facilities, sometimes even farther away from their families and support networks. Shutting down one facility doesn't change the prevailing philosophy of punishment.

One sad example of this comes from California, where many youth facilities are being shut down. On the one hand that's a step in the right direction: using supportive services and community solutions instead of incarceration is necessary for youth who are experiencing trauma, mental health struggles, substance use issues, and homelessness.

However, a friend and colleague of mine who works with youth in custody there reports that many of the youth in those facilities have severe mental illness and exhibit violent behavior. They need services and a safe place to be, but other facilities will not accept them and there is no plan for them. California will *look* progressive on paper, because they are no longer incarcerating youth at high rates in the old facilities, while young people will continue to be underserved or sent to adult prisons.

Just as closing facilities is seen as a reform, so is opening new facilities. But new facilities built in the United States are most likely an expansion of the system and not focused on reducing prison populations at all. This is why prison abolitionists and even many reformists oppose the building of new prisons and jails, even when they may represent an updated upgrade from facilities that are in disrepair. Although touted as larger, safer, and state of the art, new facilities are a way for politicians to get the best of both worlds: points for being humanitarian (This facility is much cleaner and safer!) *and* points for being tough on crime (Your neighborhoods will be cleaner and safer!).

Angela shared a realization she had while she was employed in the clerk's office at the prison where she was incarcerated. "When I went to my first clerk job, they had a map of all the state prisons on the wall … I think about thirty or so," she recalled. "But they had about twenty more new projected prisons throughout the state marked on the map." Fortunately, the tide turned in government, and those new prisons were not all built. But the map stayed with her.

"I'll never forget that," she said. "I was looking at that map, thinking, *How would you find that many criminals?* These prisons would hold hundreds, even thousands of people, so what are you going to do to fill all those beds?" For Angela that map was a wake-up call. "Nobody's safe out there because they want you in here. Their goal is to keep those beds full. They make a lot of money to babysit and to be mean to people. If you are in the prison business and you truly care about rehabilitation, that belief is going to put you out of business."

As many advocates have noted, both the for-profit prison industries and large government contracts for states create incentives for expansion, not reduction, in the prison population overall. For example, surveillance through ankle monitors is often touted as a reform, when it has actually expanded the number of people under carceral control. Effort toward prison expansion is happening outside the United States as well. The government in the United Kingdom has made a decision to hire 2000 more police officers. Because of that, they are going to add 500 beds to the women's prison system—because if they have more police, that means there will be more arrests, and they will need more beds in prison. This is such disturbed logic.

In addition to the ways "prison reform" often equates to expansion of the system, "prison reform" can also look like commissions doing studies. The best way to keep something stagnant is to set up a task force. In a poignant example, a colleague and I were hired to assess the programs for a state's system for youth. We knew that another of our colleagues had done an assessment about five years earlier, and when we met with the director we could see that older report on a shelf behind him. We looked through it and realized that everything in that report still needed implementation.

"You don't need us!" we told the director. "Everything that needs to be done is right here, from the assessment you paid for five years ago." But the new director wanted a new assessment, so we spent nearly a year and a half developing clear recommendations. Shortly after we finished a new director came in, and a new group was brought in to do a new assessment. The system could keep saying they were looking into making change without ever implementing any recommendations that would have actually affected the way the system was run in the state, or the daily lives of the girls and young women who lived in their facilities.

Even the concepts of becoming trauma informed or gender responsive have been emptied of meaning and impact. This is my field, and I will continue to work for gender-responsive and trauma-focused care for incarcerated and formerly incarcerated women, but I can see how my and others' work has been diluted by corrections departments that want to look better without actually doing better. Jurisdictions may get first-level training, but without reinforcing it or creating real change, they simply check the box on a form that says they've been trained in trauma-informed care and ignore follow-up trainings.

At the same time, we must acknowledge that change that is superficial on the system level may still be profoundly affecting on the individual level. For example, it is not unusual for me to suggest that staff stop yelling at women and calling them names. Does this fix the system? Of course not. However, on any given day it can significantly reduce the tension between staff and residents. In one custodial setting where I worked, corrections officers attending a *Becoming Trauma Informed* training subsequently created posters with grounding exercises that helped both residents and the staff. It was a seemingly small but impactful change. There is so much immediate need, for each person, and such enormous systemic and institutional issues—we have to work at all levels.

When I am called in to consult at a women's prison that is interested in organizational change, and they want to become more trauma informed or even trauma responsive, I suggest a self-assessment in the form of a *walk-through* as a first step. A small group needs to walk through the facility with each of them role-playing a woman being admitted. Then they note their experience and the specific areas that need to be improved. In order to prioritize what is usually a long list, the first thing I tell them to do is assess for low-hanging fruit. I tell them to pick changes they can make as quickly as possible because it helps their staff to see that they mean business, and it gives the incarcerated women a sense of hope for change.

I suggest they start with easy, immediate changes: repaint a room, clean up the trash, change signage. Looked at from the outside, a person could say, "That isn't real change; all they did was paint a room." Which is true if the process stops there, but that repainted room is never the true goal. Unfortunately, many facilities treat it like it is.

I may sound cynical, and I suppose I am, about the systems that incarcerate people so brutally and for so long. However, I am not at all cynical about *people.* I believe people can change and that past behavior doesn't always tell you what is going to happen in the future. I have long believed that the vast majority of women in prison simply shouldn't be there; I have seen too many women whose trauma and survival behaviors have been criminalized as dangerous.

The truth is, danger from women looks very different than danger presented by men. And for that very small percentage, maybe one in every few hundred incarcerated women, who seem too dangerous to everyone around them to be rehabilitated or reintegrated into society, I think it is important to recognize that we have not yet figured out how to help them.

We haven't yet learned what to do about consistently destructive behavior that is in keeping with basic humane treatment and human rights protections. We don't have the answers for what safety looks like for them or for the people around them. Reforms rely on the belief that incarceration itself can be done humanely, but I do not see that in US prisons—especially in the solitary isolation so many facilities resort to as a form of behavioral control.

In short: I do not think incarceration as we practice it today is appropriate, even for those we consider most dangerous to others.

What Next?

One thing that struck me while interviewing people for this discussion is how difficult it can be for any of us to truly imagine something new that isn't a prison at all. Our biggest need is alternatives to incarceration. Rather than one-size-fits-all policies that continue to erase individuals, each community taking greater responsibility for its own systems may offer us more creative solutions. This is why individuals like Kim Carter and the Time for Change Foundation, as mentioned in "A Note from a Hidden Healer" at the beginning of this book, are so important to learn from. Each participant in the foundation's programs receives a highly individualized set of services. Every community can bring its own strengths to this problem-solving.

One glimpse of a new path forward lies abroad, where certain programs and policies work better than ours to return women to their communities with the tools, skills, and resources they need. In Switzerland and the United Kingdom the public can enter prisons and interact with incarcerated women, during a Christmas market (much like a craft fair in the United States), for example, or at one of the Clink Restaurants discussed earlier.

Christmas market is a major tradition in European countries. This women's prison participates in the tradition of Christmas market in their community. These are some of the things the women make during the year while in prison that are sold to those in the town during Christmas market.

Source: The Swiss Centre of Expertise in Prison and Probation.

When I talk about these programs to people in the United States, they often need to see photographic proof that they exist, and then they tell me, "That wouldn't work here." We have enough people and resources to make significant changes to our methods. The problem is our lack of political will, primarily because of the prejudice we hold against justice-impacted women.

Those seeking to reform the system often hold up Norway's Halden Prison for men as an example of what could be. In fact, quite a lot of money gets spent for US prison administrators to visit it. I've seen no change in our own facilities as a result of these field trips, but it has created conversation. At Halden there are no traditional security devices, and the staff is unarmed. The men's rooms look like decently apportioned motel rooms, and the entire facility was designed with returning to community as the goal.

Here is a typical room for men living at Halden prison in Norway.

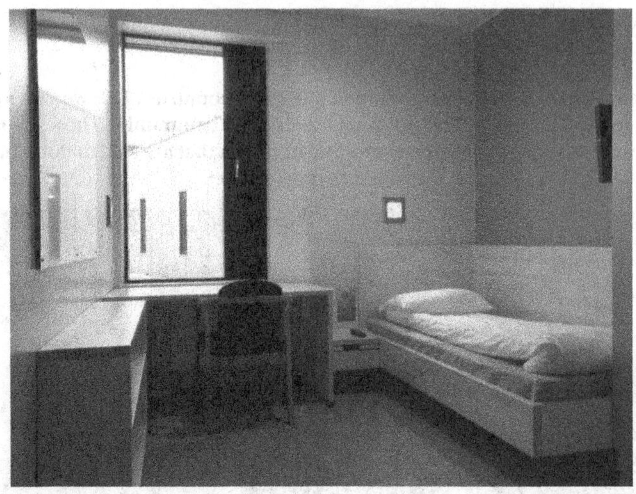

Source: Halden prison.

This is the common area for the men in this housing unit at Halden.

Source: Halden prison.

The people who work at Halden also benefit. Their working conditions are better, which in turn supports a more respectful culture. The recidivism rate from Halden is around 20 percent, compared to 76 percent in the United States. In short: Halden is designed to reduce incarceration overall. Because there is no profit motive governing the decisions, Halden can seek to keep making itself more and more unnecessary. However, it is important to note that the Norwegian system says that Halden works for men and they recommend the Bangkok rules for women's facilities.

In the United Kingdom, the idea of changing the goal from punishment to recovery is beginning to spread. A talk I delivered in 2012 on trauma-informed care for women at an international conference at the University of Cambridge in England led to ongoing work, continuing today, to bring trauma-informed and trauma-responsive care to the twelve women's prisons in England. The success of these programs has in turn led to an expansion of trauma-informed programs in seventeen of England's high-security men's prisons.

This is a Wall of Achievement from one of the meetings of the guide teams for the Women's Estate in the United Kingdom (women's division of the Ministry of Justice). The wall has the Five Core Values of Trauma-Informed and Trauma-Responsive Services as well of the other domains that are part of their Implementation Plan and Goal Attainment Scale. It is a day of celebration of their accomplishments in working toward organizational change.

Source: One Small Thing.

During this work, my colleague and widely respected British prison reformer Lady Edwina Grosvenor suggested that perhaps a prototype of a gender-responsive, trauma-informed prison for women could be the next step. My reply was, "No. We need *alternatives* to incarceration. We need to demonstrate that services in the community are a better answer."

That got my colleague thinking, and she set to work. Today you can read about and even visit the new Hope Street site in Southampton, England, a trauma-responsive community project undertaken by Lady Edwina Grosvenor and the One Small Thing organization. Beginning with a residential community that meets the myriad needs of justice-impacted women, the larger goal of One Small Thing is to redesign the justice system for women and their children from the ground up.

Here is the Hope Street main building. The left side is the café open to the community.

Source: One Small Thing, photo by Fotohous.

Here is the garden with the apartments in the background.

Source: One Small Thing, photo by Fotohous.

Do I think prisons should be abolished? Yes. I am philosophically aligned with the belief that we must totally reenvision how we handle harm caused in our communities. You can't just remodel some of the prisons we already have to make them humane. Even if we did give them all better light, air, room to move, green space, healthier food, and so on—if the culture and philosophy driving the actions of the staff were unchanged, the essential inhumanity would persist.

My time and energy have gone into direct service provision through programs and policy advocacy for incarcerated women, which is not the same thing as actively working to abolish prisons. Because of this, I don't claim *abolitionist* as a title for myself, although my beliefs and work are informed by abolitionists such as Beth E. Richie, Victoria Law, Angela Davis, and Ruth Wilson Gilmore. After years of trying, I do not believe we can reform our way through our current system to arrive at justice. We have a criminal legal system that is impacting people in ways that are incontestably unjust, not because of a bad apple here or there but because the systems are built wrong.

Even if we were able to remodel all our prisons to make them more humane environments with completely different values among staff, we would then face the problem of how many people were not receiving the same level of humane living conditions on the outside. Some worry that creating "healthier" prison environments will incentivize crime, because people who are breaking laws for survival will be offered better living circumstances inside than people in poverty who don't cause harm.

What I see is that countries with more humane facilities, far fewer people inside, and much shorter sentences are usually also working within a broader system of universal health care, greater support for women and children, and a much stronger social safety net—including free higher education and supportive retirement. Our country's failure to keep people safe and to provide supportive services begins long before any individuals are arrested.

At the same time, even as we're working on structural change, I am always encouraging facilities to start the process, start now, and to do something that tells the women living inside that things are changeable. I believe we can do both: make changes that are immediately achievable to support the women living through incarceration right now, *and* work to create something entirely new that offers women the things they've told us they need.

Changing prisons alone is not going to solve the broader social problems prisons reveal, but the situation is so terrible that immediate changes are desperately needed. As we have seen, incarcerated and formerly incarcerated women are already doing the work of mitigating the harms of prison while suffering its impacts. I want more people involved to support them.

Do One Small Thing

There's a lot of examples of these little moments where people can just make your entire day by giving you a pen, a piece of paper, whatever it is. Having somebody give you a cup of coffee meant the world.

—**Linda**, *personal interview*

MY BOTTOM-LINE BELIEF is that life is about being of service. I would like more people to be of service to incarcerated and formerly incarcerated women, and to do that, more people must open their eyes to what is happening. Every aspect of our criminal legal system is flawed. Policing, plea bargains and sentencing, jail time, cash bail, who goes to prison, how the facilities work, parole boards—all of it, every step of the way. When you begin to understand the enormity of the problems, it is overwhelming. Overwhelm can make you want to turn away from the difficulty, rather than walk toward it to help.

Amy, a formerly incarcerated woman with over twenty years' experience as an activist for Black liberation, put it this way: "If you are a person who gets up and goes to work every day, gets Chipotle on Fridays, goes to Legoland with your kids, goes to your Episcopalian church on Sunday, and considers yourself a good person who doesn't cheat on their taxes, it's *still* very easy to criminalize other people, to think they are doing it all wrong. We have to be brave enough to look at the roots of our systems."

Amy has seen how simple it is for good people to think everyone who goes to jail or prison has an individual problem and therefore to ignore the origins and effects of criminalization. As Amy said, criminalization "has destroyed entire marginalized groups of folks who have already dealt with Jim Crow, and redlining, and all the rest." Dealing with our criminal legal system means dealing with all the legacies of institutionalized racism and prejudice against the poor.

The criminal legal systems are big bureaucratic systems in every state and county. In some ways it feels impossible when you think, *What could I do to make any difference?* I believe the important thing, if you are motivated to engage in the work of making change, is to break it down into those things you can do that are sustainable and meaningful for you, and ideally, to do those things in a group, community, or organization. Some people devote their lives. If that is not what you feel strongly motivated to do, you can still engage with change-making in meaningful ways.

Why Start with Women?

In a system that was designed for men, women are still a small percentage of the incarcerated population. It may seem that to get the most impact out of advocacy, then, we should start by working with incarcerated men. However, it has been my experience that when people begin to bring in new information and improve services for women, men also benefit, but it does not work the other way around.

If a program seems to serve women well, people will ask, "Would this also work for men?" But I have found that when we begin by focusing on the majority, we never get anything for the minority. This is another reason why focusing on the needs of trans, nonbinary, and gender-expansive people within the system is so important. Meeting their needs will not only increase their survival and ability to build the lives they want after prison, but also reveal ways everyone's needs could be better met.

We are constantly navigating the priorities of immediate individual needs *and* the enormous need for institutional and systemic change. Are small changes really of value when the bigger issues remain? It's a question that each person must answer for themselves: Is it better to do nothing if you can't get it right by changing it all?

My answer, of course, is no. It is better to do something now. For some people, advocating for change becomes a life commitment. For others, there are many more options than doing nothing. I encourage people to consider making a small change in their routine that can support the needs of incarcerated and formerly incarcerated people, because our movements will be strengthened and gain momentum when more are willing to do one small thing.

Doing one small thing also counteracts the paralysis or despair you may feel when you confront the enormity of injustice and harm in our legal system. Remember, what may seem small to you can have large effects. I have found it important not to minimize what may seem minor to us on the outside, as it can feel major if you are living on the inside.

One example of this comes from the work I did in Black Mountain, North Carolina, after my voluntary three-day stay in the late 1980s. The following year the warden called me about six women with life sentences that her minimum-security facility wasn't equipped for. She asked if I could run a group for them.

I thought to myself, *If I had a life sentence, what would I want more than anything in the world?* The answer was, *I'd want a day off.* It took a lot of work, but I was able to take those six women out of the prison and spend a day with them at a retreat center. North Carolina has beautiful retreat centers all over the state, with big porches and rocking chairs. This particular one had a piano, which during our opening circle one of the participants asked if she could play. As she began to play from a hymnal, we joined our voices together in song. It was powerful.

We took a trust walk in nature, we ate lunch, we made collages. At one point we put the rocking chairs in a circle on the porch and the women slowly started to share. One began to sob. "I can't tell you how often I've thought about rocking chairs, and how I'd never be in one again," she told us. "It's a miracle. Here I am, in a rocking chair out in the woods." The poignance of that small moment has stayed with me for thirty-five years.

Practical Actions

A misunderstanding people often have when they are first alerted to a human rights issue is that "no one is talking about this," or "no one is doing anything to make change." This is generally not true: there are people, grassroots groups, and nonprofits already working on most every issue. You are invited to join them. The following are suggestions for practical actions you can take, but the absolute best action is one you can do consistently that is in alignment with your values and builds strength in your community.

Engage in Further Learning. As Amy said to me, "I want people to begin to look for resources that will debunk and dismantle and unpack what a 'criminal' is and help them examine their fear." In order to facilitate further self-education, you will find a list of organizations, resources, and book group discussion questions in the upcoming pages. Recall that the prison systems in the United States operate quite independently, and their operations are concealed, which is why most people don't know much about them without direct personal experience.

Make a Direct Connection. Joining a pen-pal program and developing a letter-writing connection with an incarcerated woman can make a difference, not only for her but for the twenty or so people she will share her letters with. Writing a letter once a month is not an overwhelming time commitment for a person living on the outside, and the difference it can make is large, especially if you include articles, poetry, and other allowable reading material. Putting a little money on an incarcerated woman's books so she can go to the commissary is a huge support, especially because many women do not have someone on the outside helping them. Finding a pen-pal program is as easy as one internet search for a program in your area.

Hold Elected Officials Accountable. Stay aware of what your local representatives are saying. Find out where they stand on the creation of new jails and prisons, the budget for police, health care for transgender people, support for people experiencing homelessness, and so on. You can find out if an election campaign is funded by the corrections officers' union. You can ask them directly what they are going to do to support reentry programs, or if they have a plan to reduce the jail or prison population in your county or state. Let them know you are concerned about what is happening, even if you do not have a loved one directly impacted by it. That builds the kind of political will that is needed. Pressure on local offices does translate upward.

Work on Policy Change. You can become involved in "ban the box" campaigns (referring to the box applicants must check if they have a felony record) to help reduce stigma against formerly incarcerated people looking for employment. The people most impacted by the cash bail system struggle to afford lawyers and the means to advocate for change, so there are campaigns in many places to eradicate cash bail. If you are interested in legislation and policy, there is likely an advocacy group in your county working on local issues and supporting local cases.

Make Consistent Donations. Many organizations that support incarcerated people and work to change the system are led by people with lived experience, as well as their families and loved ones. Organizations always need resources, and if financial support is the best way you can help, donations are the lifeblood of most organizations helping women because they often have difficulty securing funding. Most organizations also need regular help with practical tasks like making phone calls and stamping letters.

Use What You Already Have. If you work at a university, you can see if there is a partner program helping incarcerated people achieve educational goals and accredited degrees and find out if you can help with access to Pell Grants for incarcerated students. If you work in an office, you can find a program that sends books into prisons in your area and organize donations. You can help develop a culture of reentry employment at your own place of work. There are organizations working on alternatives to incarceration, such as restorative justice, that always need hands. If you are interested in the issue of nutritious food, or supporting the needs of incarcerated LGBTQ+ people, or creating art projects, or teaching African American history, or tutoring Spanish, or leading yoga, any of your interests and skills can be put to use.

If you want to do something, there's a place to do it. Not only are there myriad ways to plug into ongoing work, there are opportunities to learn meaningful new skills and connect with passionate people you may never have otherwise met along the way. Like Kim Carter wrote in the opening of the book, there are brilliant women already leading with solutions. The key is to do something, consistently, that is true to you.

It is so important for people to understand the criminal legal system where they live. It may be easier to believe that the problems are for other people, far away, and certainly the system has hidden itself from view. But as I stated when we started this journey, the prisons belong to us just like our hospitals and schools do. They are part of our community.

People without exposure to the criminal legal system are always surprised that the injustice and abuses are actually happening. They think I am talking about something that happened thirty years ago when I tell a story of something that happened last week. Until you are closely impacted by it, like when a family member or somebody you care about gets into the system, you don't really know what it is like. You can't imagine the challenges. These are closed systems, which is always a problem. We have to take responsibility for them. Staying silent and not doing anything is a form of support for the status quo. If you are not in a position to do larger things, do one small thing. It truly does matter.

Further Learning

THIS SHORT LIST of recommended books, films, podcasts, and visual art is intended to provide accessible support for your continued self-education. There is no such thing as a perfect depiction of the complex world of prison; however, the following offer more realistic and compassionate portrayals along with current thinking and advocacy efforts.

Read

Abolition. Feminism. Now. by Angela Y. Davis, Gina Dent, Erica R. Meiners, and Beth E. Richie (2022).

In this remarkable collaborative work, leading scholar-activists Angela Y. Davis, Gina Dent, Erica R. Meiners, and Beth E. Richie surface the often-unrecognized genealogies of queer, anticapitalist, internationalist, grassroots, and women-of-color-led feminist movements, struggles, and organizations that have helped to define the prison abolition movement and feminism in the twenty-first century.

Arrested Justice: Black Women, Violence, and America's Prison Nation by Beth E. Richie (2012).

Black women in marginalized communities are uniquely at risk of battering, rape, sexual harassment, stalking, and incest. Through the compelling stories of Black women who have been most affected by racism, persistent poverty, class inequality, and limited access to support resources or institutions, Beth E. Richie shows that the threat of violence to Black women has never been more serious, demonstrating how conservative legal, social, political, and economic policies have impacted activism in the US–based movement to end violence against women.

Becoming Ms. Burton: From Prison to Recovery to Leading the Fight for Incarcerated Women by Susan Burton and Cari Lynn (2017).
Becoming Ms. Burton is the remarkable life story of the renowned activist Susan Burton, who affectingly recounts her own journey through the criminal justice system and her transformation into a life of advocacy.

Corrections in Ink: A Memoir by Keri Blakinger (2022).
After she walked out of her cell for the last time, Keri became a reporter dedicated to exposing our flawed prisons as only an insider could. Written with intensity, candor, and shocks of humor, *Corrections in Ink* is not just a story about getting out and getting off drugs, it's about the power of second chances, who our society throws away, who we allow to reach for redemption, and how they reach for it.

Hear Me, See Me: Incarcerated Women Write, edited by Marybeth Christie Redmond and Sarah W. Bartlett (2013).
An anthology of the raw, unvarnished writings of Vermont's incarcerated women as participants in the *writing inside VT* program at Chittenden Regional Correctional and Northwest State Correctional Facilities in northwestern Vermont over a three-year period (2010–2012).

In Search of Safety: Confronting Inequality in Women's Imprisonment by Barbara Owen, James Wells, and Joycelyn Pollock (2017).
In Search of Safety takes a close look at the sources of gendered violence and conflict in women's prisons. The authors examine how intersectional inequalities and cumulative disadvantages are the root of prison conflict and violence, and how they mirror the women's pathways to prison. Women must negotiate these inequities by developing forms of prison capital—social, human, cultural, emotional, and economic—to ensure their safety while inside.

Inside This Place, Not of It: Narratives from Women's Prisons (Voice of Witness), edited by Ayelet Waldman and Robin Levi (2017).
Here, in their own words, thirteen women recount their lives leading up to incarceration and their harrowing struggle for survival once inside.

Jailcare: Finding the Safety Net for Women behind Bars by Carolyn Sufrin (2017).
Thousands of pregnant women pass through our nation's jails every year. What happens to them as they carry their pregnancies in a space of punishment? In this time when the public safety net is frayed, incarceration has become a central and racialized strategy for managing the poor. Using her ethnographic fieldwork and clinical work as an ob-gyn in a women's jail, Carolyn Sufrin explores how jail has, paradoxically, become a place where women can find care.

Orange Is the New Black: My Year in a Women's Prison by Piper Kerman (2011).
Convicted and sentenced to fifteen months at the infamous federal correctional facility in Danbury, Connecticut, the well-heeled Smith College alumna is now inmate #11187-424, one of the millions of people who disappear "down the rabbit hole" of the American penal system. From her first strip search to her final release, Kerman learns to navigate this strange world with its strictly enforced codes of behavior and arbitrary rules. She meets women from all walks of life, who surprise her with small tokens of generosity, hard words of wisdom, and simple acts of acceptance.

Prison by Any Other Name: The Harmful Consequences of Popular Reforms by Maya Schenwar and Victoria Law (2020).
Electronic monitoring. Locked-down drug treatment centers. House arrest. Mandated psychiatric treatment. Data-driven surveillance. Extended probation. These are some of the key alternatives held up as cost-effective substitutes for jails and prisons. But in a searing critique, Maya Schenwar and Victoria Law reveal that many of these so-called reforms actually weave in new strands of punishment and control, bringing new populations who would not otherwise have been subject to imprisonment under physical control by the state.

"Prisons Make Us Safer": And 20 Other Myths about Mass Incarceration by Victoria Law (2021).
Journalist Victoria Law explains how racism and social control were the catalysts for mass incarceration and have continued to be its driving force: from the post–Civil War laws that states passed to imprison former slaves to the laws passed under the war on drugs campaign that disproportionately imprison Black people.

Razor Wire Women: Prisoners, Activists, Scholars, and Artists, edited by Jodie Michelle Lawston and Ashley E. Lucas (2011).
A collection of essays and art by scholars, artists, and activists both in and out of prison that reveal the many dimensions of women's incarcerated experiences.

What's Prison For? Punishment and Rehabilitation in the Age of Mass Incarceration by Bill Keller (2022).
Keller tells the stories of incarcerated men and women who have found purpose behind bars, offers guidance on how to improve our prison system, and makes a powerful argument that the status quo is a shameful waste of human potential.

A Woman Doing Life: Notes from a Prison for Women by Erin George (2010).
This book tells stories of women in prison *from the inside out.* Author and prison resident Erin George draws a vivid and uniquely raw portrait of female life in prison, detailing her own responses to incarceration as well as her observations of prison relationships, death and sickness, reactions from friends and family, and even "cooking" in prison. The text also features poignant stories from other female inmates.

Women Doing Life: Gender, Punishment and the Struggle for Identity by Lora Bex Lempert (2016).
How do women—mothers, daughters, aunts, nieces, and grandmothers—make sense of judgment to a lifetime behind bars? In *Women Doing Life*, Lora Bex Lempert presents a typology of the ways that life-sentenced women grow and self-actualize, resist prison definitions, reflect on and "own" their criminal acts, and ultimately create meaningful lives behind prison walls.

Watch

Sin by Silence (2009, informed by Elizabeth Dermody Leonard's *Convicted Survivors: The Imprisonment of Battered Women Who Kill*).
An important documentary that profiles Convicted Women Against Abuse (CWAA)—the US prison system's first inmate-initiated group, which is led by women—*Sin by Silence* is an essential resource featuring more than two hours of bonus materials, including interviews with experts on abusive relationships, law-enforcement leaders, and leaders in faith-based communities about domestic violence and more.

Tell It Like a Woman (2022, starring Jennifer Hudson).
In "Pepcy & Kim," one of seven segments of this feature film created by women directors, Jennifer Hudson brings to life the redemptive story of Kim Carter, the founder of the Time for Change Foundation (and author of "A Note from a Hidden Healer" at the beginning of this book).

The Unforgivable (2021, starring Sandra Bullock).
This story of a woman leaving prison after twenty years faithfully depicts the struggle to meet the requirements of parole and the traumatic shock upon reentering society.

Unforgotten (Season 2, 2018).
Season 2 of this British crime series focuses on child sexual abuse. The writers demonstrated a rare understanding of the deep impact of childhood trauma on adult lives.

What I Want My Words to Do to You: Voices from Inside a Women's Maximum Security Prison (2003).
This PBS documentary, part of my *Beyond Violence* program, offers an unprecedented look into the minds and hearts of the women residents of New York's Bedford Hills Correctional Facility. The film goes inside a writing workshop led by playwright Eve Ensler, consisting of fifteen women, most of whom were convicted of murder.

Women Behind Bars: Maximum Security Prison with Sir Trevor MacDonald (2013).
This docuseries was filmed inside Indiana's Rockville Correctional Facility and features vulnerable conversations with women who live there.

Listen

One Million Experiments (2021–).
This podcast showcases and explores how we would define and create safety in a world without police and prisons. Through long-form interviews with movement workers across the world who have created community-based safety projects, 1ME expands our ideas about what keeps us safe and celebrates the work already happening to build solutions that are grounded in transformation instead of punishment.

See

The work of Michele Zousmer (https://www.michelezousmer.com/).
Michele Zousmer is a humanitarian and fine art photographer. Her camera gives voice to people and marginalized communities around the world, including incarcerated women. Some of her photographs are included in *Hidden Healers.*

The work of Sara Bennett (https://sarabennett.org/artist).
After eighteen years as a public defender, Sara Bennett turned her attention to photographing women with life sentences, both inside and outside prison.

The work of Yousef Khanfar (http://yousefkhanfar.com).
Yousef Khanfar is an award-winning photographer whose photo-book, *Invisible Eve,* shines a light on the lives of women imprisoned in Oklahoma.

Organizations to Support

THE FOLLOWING ARE organizations that support the needs of incarcerated and recently released women, nonprofits mentioned by my interviewees, and groups that advocate for alternatives to incarceration. This list of organizations (written in their own words) is not exhaustive; new groups emerge all the time. Please use it as a place to begin exploring the world of advocacy for justice-impacted women and nonbinary/gender-expansive people.

All of Us or None (California)
https://prisonerswithchildren.org/about-aouon/
All of Us or None is a grassroots civil and human rights organization fighting for the rights of formerly and currently incarcerated people and our families. We are fighting against the discrimination that people face every day because of arrest or conviction history. The goal of All of Us or None is to strengthen the voices of people most affected by mass incarceration and the growth of the prison industrial complex. Through our grassroots organizing, we are building a powerful political movement to win full restoration of our human and civil rights.

Art of Yoga Project (California)
https://theartofyogaproject.org/
Healing and empowering marginalized youth through mindfulness-based practices. Trauma-informed yoga and art educators deliver our mindfulness-based programming in short- and long-term detention and rehabilitation centers, substance abuse recovery settings, agencies serving CSEC (commercially sexually exploited children), Level 14 facilities (for youth with high psychiatric needs), and schools. Promoting systemic change and healing in our communities requires collaboration at all levels. We partner with county behavioral health, education, probation, judiciary, departments of children, youth and family services, and other community-based organizations.

Black & Pink National (Nebraska)
https://www.blackandpink.org/
Black & Pink National is a prison abolitionist organization dedicated to abolishing the criminal punishment system and liberating LGBTQIA2S+ people and people living with HIV/AIDS who are affected by that system through advocacy, support, and organizing.

Books to Prisoners (Washington)
https://www.bookstoprisoners.net/
Books to Prisoners is a Seattle-based nonprofit organization whose mission is to foster a love of reading behind bars, encourage the pursuit of knowledge and self-empowerment, and break the cycle of recidivism. We believe that books are tools for learning and for opening minds to new ideas and possibilities, and we engage incarcerated individuals with the benefits of reading by mailing tens of thousands of free books to inmates across the country each year.

California Coalition for Women Prisoners (California)
https://womenprisoners.org/
Caring collectively for people in women's prisons, we monitor and challenge the abusive conditions inside California women's prisons. We fight for the release of women and trans prisoners. We support women and trans people in their process of reentering the community.

Five Keys Home Free (California)
https://www.fivekeyshomefree.org/
Home Free is a first-of-its-kind transitional housing program that helps criminalized domestic violence survivors reenter communities and thrive. Here, formerly incarcerated women will experience peaceful and humane transitions—from prison to freedom, from "victim" to "survivor"—while correcting a gross injustice that diminishes our civil society.

Friends Outside (California)
http://www.friendsoutside.org/
Established in 1955 by Rosemary Goodenough, a Quaker and tireless advocate for social justice, incarcerated people, and their children and families, Friends Outside has over fifty-five years of experience working inside institutions and with families and children of incarcerated individuals.

Gays and Lesbians Living in a Transgender Society (New York)
https://www.glitsinc.org/
GLITS has been led to change systemic and economical oppressions of systemic and financial discrimination not only in New York City but also globally when

it comes to our marginal communities. We approach the health and rights crises faced by transgender community members and the sex worker community, holistically using harm reduction, human rights principles, and economic and social justice, along with a commitment to empowerment and pride in finding solutions from our own community.

Insight Garden Program (California)
https://insightgardenprogram.org/
IGP facilitates an innovative curriculum combined with vocational gardening and landscaping training so that people in prison can reconnect to self, community, and the natural world. This "inner" and "outer" gardening approach transforms lives, ends ongoing cycles of incarceration, and creates safer communities.

Just Detention International (United States)
https://justdetention.org/
JDI is a health and human rights organization that seeks to end sexual abuse in all forms of detention. It works to hold governmental officials accountable for sexual abuse in detention; challenge the attitudes and misperceptions that allow such abuse to flourish; and make sure that survivors get the help they need to heal. JDI provides trauma-informed support to currently and formerly incarcerated survivors of sexual abuse via correspondence, hotline, and in-person counseling and art workshop programs.

Legal Services for Prisoners with Children (California)
https://prisonerswithchildren.org/
LSPC organizes communities impacted by the criminal justice system and advocates to release incarcerated people, to restore human and civil rights and to reunify families and communities. We build public awareness of structural racism in policing, the courts, and the prison system, and we advance racial and gender justice in all our work.

Minnesota Prison Doula Project (Minnesota)
https://www.mnprisondoulaproject.org/
The Minnesota Prison Doula Project (MnPDP) provides pregnancy and parenting support for incarcerated people. We provide birth support from trained doulas as well as group-based and individual education and support. The goal is to nurture healthy parent-child relationships and increase parenting confidence and skills. We work with people inside Minnesota's only women's state prison and those held in county correctional facilities. We also support our clients upon release with resources to help facilitate a successful transition into our community.

National Resource Center on Justice-Involved Women (United States)
https://cjinvolvedwomen.org/
NRCJIW is committed to increasing success for women who have been involved in the justice system, providing training, technical assistance, and creating resources for justice agencies on evidence-based strategies for women. NRCJIW maintains a comprehensive library of resources and has played an instrumental role in changing the narrative about women in the justice system.

A New Way of Life Reentry Project (California)
https://anewwayoflife.org/
A New Way of Life Reentry Project provides housing, case management, pro bono legal services, advocacy, and leadership development for people rebuilding their lives after incarceration. We empower and build the leadership skills of formerly incarcerated people, we hire formerly incarcerated people, and we provide cutting-edge organizational leadership that promotes resources for disenfranchised people living in communities that have been marginalized.

One Small Thing/Hope Street (United Kingdom)
https://onesmallthing.org.uk/
One Small Thing's vision is a justice system that can recognize, understand, and respond to trauma. Our mission is to redesign the justice system for women and their children, and we have just opened Hope Street, a pioneering residential community for women and children. We facilitate and fund trauma-informed and gender-responsive programs for the prison and community sectors that consider the individual caught in a cycle of crime and incarceration and aim to humanize their process. Our name reflects the value of those small things—empathy, compassion, respect—and their combined power to make a big difference to the individual and to society as a whole.

PACEs Connection (United States)
https://www.acesconnectioninfo.com/
PACEs Connection is a social network amplifying and supporting the PACEs (positive and adverse childhood experiences) movement by educating people about PACEs science, sharing stories, and solutions. We help communities launch and grow PACEs initiatives, promote trauma-informed and resilience-building practices, and act as an information resource.

The Pathfinder Network (Oregon)
https://www.thepathfindernetwork.org/
The Pathfinder Network provides justice system-impacted individuals and families the tools and support they need to be safe and thrive in our communities. We provide

programs and services for incarcerated individuals through the Oregon Department of Corrections and for parents, children, and families in the community.

Prison Arts Collective (California)
https://www.prisonartscollective.com/
Prison Arts Collective works to expand access to the transformative power of the arts through collaboration and mutual learning that supports the development of self-expression, reflection, communication, and empathy by providing multidisciplinary arts programming in correctional institutions and the justice-impacted community.

Prison Policy Initiative (United States)
https://www.prisonpolicy.org/
The Prison Policy Initiative is a nonpartisan, nonprofit research and advocacy organization producing cutting-edge research to expose the broader harm of mass criminalization and spark advocacy campaigns to create a more just society.

Prison Yoga Project (International)
http://www.prisonyoga.org
Our trainings are informed by our understanding of the unique sociocultural environment of incarceration, social justice issues, and the impact of trauma on the lives of incarcerated people and people working in the system.

Red Canary Song (New York)
https://www.redcanarysong.net/
We are a grassroots sex and massage worker coalition in the United States. There are over nine thousand workplaces across the country with no political representation or access to labor rights or collective organizing. Antitrafficking nongovernmental organizations that claim to speak for migrants in sex trades promote increased policing and immigration control, which harms rather than helps migrant sex workers. We also organize transnationally with Asian sex workers across the diaspora in Toronto, Paris, and Hong Kong.

Sex Workers and Allies Network (Connecticut)
https://swanct.org/
SWAN started in the aftermath of a rash of police arrests and attempts at public shaming of sex workers in the New Haven, Connecticut, area. Activists united and successfully demanded an end to schemes by the New Haven police to conduct stings against sex workers. SWAN continues to push for full decriminalization of sex work and drug use in order to promote the health and well-being of people living and working on the streets. Our commitment to harm

reduction means that SWAN attempts to meet people's most pressing needs without standing in judgment of their choices. SWAN is also committed to the principle of "nothing about us without us": the organization is led by people with lived experience in sex work, incarceration, drug use, and homelessness. One of the key aims of the organization is to bring sex workers into decision-making roles both within the organization and within the city of New Haven.

Sex Workers Outreach Project
https://swopusa.org/
Sex Workers Outreach Project USA is a national social justice network dedicated to the fundamental human rights of people involved in the sex trade and their communities, focusing on ending violence and stigma through education and advocacy. On the national level, SWOP helps build stronger communities and a stronger movement through technical assistance, funding, and direct support and advocacy. On a local level, our chapters address structural, cultural, and interpersonal violence individuals in the sex trade face by working to change attitudes, change policies, and create alternative community-led systems of support.

Time for Change Foundation (California)
https://www.timeforchangefoundation.org/
Since 2002 the Time for Change Foundation (TFCF) has been assisting homeless women and children achieve self-sufficiency by providing housing and necessary supportive services. In response to the housing crisis and effects of mass incarceration and family separation, TFCF implemented an array of evidence-based programs, housing, and trauma-informed approaches to address their needs. Equally important are our leadership development and advocacy projects necessary to bring the voices of those most impacted by punitive policies into policy advocacy and civic engagement.

Transgender Gender-Variant & Intersex Justice Project (California)
http://www.tgijp.org
TGI Justice Project is a group of transgender, gender-variant, and intersex people, inside and outside of prisons, jails, and detention centers, creating a united family in the struggle for survival and freedom. We work in collaboration with others to forge a culture of resistance and resilience to strengthen us for the fight against human rights abuses, imprisonment, police violence, racism, poverty, and societal pressures. We seek to create a world rooted in self-determination, freedom of expression, and gender justice.

Women in Recovery (Oklahoma)
https://www.fcsok.org/services/women-in-recovery
Women in Recovery (WIR) is an intensive outpatient alternative for eligible women facing long prison sentences for nonviolent drug-related offenses. Operated in partnership with the George Kaiser Family Foundation, WIR works closely with the criminal justice system and various community partners to ensure program participants receive supervision, housing, substance abuse and mental health treatment, education, workforce readiness training, and family reunification services.

Women's Prison Association (New York)
https://www.wpaonline.org/
WPA is the nation's first organization for women impacted by incarceration. Our approach is personal. We address the root causes of system involvement, know the data, and are focused on the needs and nuances of individuals. We believe women are the experts in their own lives. We partner with women to use our collective voice and experience to drive change that positively impacts families, communities, and society.

Sources

Introduction

(1) Joanne E. Belknap, *The Invisible Woman: Gender, Crime & Justice*, 5th ed. (Los Angeles: SAGE, 2020), accessed January 4, 2024, https://www.google.com/books/edition/The_Invisible_Woman/CBTnDwAAQBAJ?hl=en&gbpv=1&printsec=frontcover.

(2) Bonnie Sultan and Mark Myrent, *Women and Girls in Corrections* (Washington, DC: Justice Research and Statistics Association, 2020), accessed January 4, 2024, https://justiceresearch.dspacedirect.org/bitstreams/9a8e6938-8fd6-4f67-b561-f47d66867ae1/download.

(3) Aleks Kajstura and Wendy Sawyer, "Women's Mass Incarceration: The Whole Pie 2023," Prison Policy Initiative, March 1, 2023, accessed January 4, 2024, https://www.prisonpolicy.org/reports/pie2023women.html.

(4) Leah Wang, "The U.S. Criminal Justice System Disproportionately Hurts Native People: The Data, Visualized," Prison Policy Initiative, October 8, 2021, accessed January 4, 2024, https://www.prisonpolicy.org/blog/2021/10/08/indigenouspeoplesday/.

(5) Leah Wang, "Both Sides of the Bars: How Mass Incarceration Punishes Families," Prison Policy Initiative, August 11, 2022, accessed January 4, 2024, https://www.prisonpolicy.org/blog/2022/08/11/parental_incarceration/.

(6) Lauren G. Beatty and Tracy L. Snell, *Profile of Prison Inmates, 2016* (Washington, DC: US Department of Justice, 2021), accessed January 4, 2024, https://bjs.ojp.gov/content/pub/pdf/ppi16.pdf.

(7) Stephanie Covington, *Helping Women Recover: A Program for Treating Addiction*, 3rd ed. (Hoboken, NJ: Wiley, 2019), 51–52.

Part One: Entering the System

(1) Cathy Hu and Sino Esthappan, "Asian Americans and Pacific Islanders, a Missing Minority in Criminal Justice Data," *Urban Wire* (blog), Urban Institute, May 23, 2017, accessed January 4, 2024, https://www.urban.org/urban-wire/asian-americans-and-pacific-islanders-missing-minority-criminal-justice-data.

(2) Beryl Ann Cowan, "Incarcerated Women: Poverty, Trauma and Unmet Need," *SES Indicator*, American Psychological Association, April 2019.

(3) Bill Keller, *What's Prison For? Punishment and Rehabilitation in the Age of Mass Incarceration* (New York: Columbia Global Reports, 2022).

(4) Ram Subramanian, Léon Digard, Melvin Washington II, and Stephanie Sorage, *In the Shadows: A Review of the Research on Plea Bargaining* (New York: Vera Institute of Justice, 2020), accessed January 4, 2024, https://www.vera.org/publications/in-the-shadows-plea-bargaining.

(5) Subramanian et al., *In the Shadows*, 2020.

(6) Subramanian et al., *In the Shadows*, 2020.

(7) Carlos Berdejo, "Gender Disparities in Plea Bargaining," *Indiana Law Journal* 94, no. 4 (Fall 2019): 1248–1303, accessed January 4, 2024, https://www.repository.law.indiana.edu/ilj/vol94/iss4/1,1250.

(8) Sultan and Myrent, *Women and Girls in Corrections, 2020.*

(9) Louis Favril, Rongqin Yu, Keith Hawton, and Seena Fazel, "Risk Factors for Self-Harm in Prison: A Systematic Review and Meta-Analysis," *Lancet Psychiatry* 7, no. 8 (August 2020): 682–691, https://doi.org/10.1016/S2215-0366(20)30190-5.

(10) Jamie Grierson, "Self-Harm Among Female Prisoners in England and Wales at Record High," *The Guardian*, January 28, 2021, accessed January 4, 2024, https://www.theguardian.com/society/2021/jan/28/self-harm-among-female-prisoners-in-england-and-wales-at-record-high.

(11) Stephanie Covington and Barbara E. Bloom, "Gendered Justice: Programming for Women in Correctional Settings," Paper presented at the 52nd annual meeting of the American Society of Criminology, San Francisco, CA, November 2000, accessed January 4, 2024, https://www.centerforgenderandjustice.org/site/assets/files/1542/11.pdf.

(12) Sheryl Kubiak, Gina Fedock, Woo Jong Kim, and Deborah Bybee, "Long-Term Outcomes of a RCT Intervention Study for Women with Violent Crimes," *Journal of the Society for Social Work and Research* 7, no. 4 (Winter 2016): 661–679, https://doi.org/10.1086/689356.

(13) Malika Saar, Rebecca Epstein, Lindsay Rosenthal, and Yasmin Vafa, "The Sexual Abuse to Prison Pipeline: The Girls' Story," *Center for Poverty and Inequality*, Georgetown Law Center, 2019, accessed November 30, 2022, https://genderjusticeandopportunity.georgetown.edu/trauma-and-mental-health-for-girls/sexual-abuse-to-prison-pipeline/.

(14) Nena Messina, "The Evolution of Gender- and Trauma-Responsive Criminal Justice Interventions for Women," *HSOA Journal of Addiction & Addictive Disorders* 8 (2021): 070, https://doi.org/10.24966/AAD-7276/100070; Nena Messina and Elizabeth Zwart, "Breaking the Silence and Healing Trauma for Incarcerated Women: Peer-Facilitated Delivery of a Brief Intervention," *MedCrave Online Journal of Women's Health* 10, no. 1 (January 2021): 8–16, https://doi.org/10.15406/mojwh.2021.10.00280.

(15) "Recidivism Rates by State 2022," World Population Review, accessed November 30, 2022, https://worldpopulationreview.com/state-rankings/recidivism-rates-by-state.

(16) Yvonne Jewkes, Melanie Jordan, Serena Wright, and Gillian Bendelow, "Designing 'Healthy' Prisons for Women: Incorporating Trauma-Informed Care and Practice (TICP) into Prison Planning and Design," *International Journal of Environmental Research and Public Health* 16, no. 20 (2019): 1–15, https://doi.org/10.3390/ijerph16203818, 8.

(17) Jorge Renaud, "Who's Really Bringing Contraband into Jails? Our 2018 Survey Confirms It's Staff, Not Visitors," Prison Policy Initiative, December 6, 2018, accessed January 4, 2024, https://www.prisonpolicy.org/blog/2018/12/06/jail-contraband/; Keri Blakinger and Jolie McCullough, "Texas Prisons Stopped In-Person Visits and Limited Mail. Drugs Got in Anyway," *The Marshall Project*,

March 29, 2021, accessed January 4, 2024, https://www.themarshallproject.org/2021/03/29/texas-prisons-stopped-in-person-visits-and-limited-mail-drugs-got-in-anyway.

Part Two: Living Inside

(1) Kirk Mitchell, "Male Correctional Officer at Denver Women's Prison Arrested for Allegedly Attempting to Pimp Women," *Denver Post*, July 5, 2019, accessed January 4, 2024, https://www.denverpost.com/2019/07/05/male-correctional-officer-womens-prison-pimping/; Romy Ellenbogen, "No Consequences after Florida Officers Admit to Sexually Abusing Inmates, Lawsuit Says," *Tampa Bay Times*, September 17, 2020, accessed January 4, 2024, https://www.tampabay.com/news/florida/2020/09/17/no-consequences-after-florida-officers-admit-to-sexually-abusing-inmates-lawsuit-says/.

(2) Devon Link, "Fact Check: Federal Law Makes Sex with Inmates Illegal," *USA Today*, July 3, 2020, accessed January 4, 2024, https://www.usatoday.com/story/news/factcheck/2020/07/03/fact-check-federal-law-makes-sex-inmates-illegal/5360107002/.

(3) Richard Winton, "Former Warden at Female Prison Known as 'Rape Club' Guilty of Sexually Abusing Women Behind Bars," *Los Angeles Times*, December 12, 2022, accessed January 4, 2024, https://www.latimes.com/california/story/2022-12-08/ex-warden-at-female-prison-guilty-of-sexually-abusing-inmates.

(4) Marcela Chavez, "Sexual Misconduct against Women Inmates, Former Officer Investigation Underway: CDCR," YourCentralValley.com, December 28, 2022, accessed January 4, 2024, https://www.yourcentralvalley.com/news/crime/sexual-misconduct-against-women-inmates-former-officer-investigation-underway-cdcr/.

(5) Sara Sullivan, Léon Digard, and Elena Vanko, *Rethinking Restrictive Housing* (New York: Vera Institute of Justice, 2018), accessed January 4, 2024, https://www.vera.org/publications/rethinking-restrictive-housing.

(6) Jewkes et al., "Designing 'Healthy' Prisons," 2019, 9.

(7) Dasha Lisitsina, "'Prison Guards Can Never Be Weak': The Hidden PTSD Crisis in America's Jails," *The Guardian*, May 20, 2015, accessed January 4, 2024, https://www.theguardian.com/us-news/2015/may/20/corrections-officers-ptsd-american-prisons.

(8) "Correctional Officer Life Expectancy," National Institute of Corrections, accessed January 4, 2024, https://nicic.gov/resources/nic-library/hot-topics/correctional-officer-life-expectancy#:~:text=In%20other%20words%2C%20law%20enforcement,years%20for%20the%20general%20population.

(9) Substance Abuse and Mental Health Services Administration, *Substance Abuse Treatment: Addressing the Specific Needs of Women, Treatment Improvement Protocol (TIP) Series*, no. 51 (Rockville, MD: Substance Abuse and Mental Health Services Administration, 2009), accessed January 4, 2024, https://www.ncbi.nlm.nih.gov/books/NBK83257/.

(10) Leslie Soble, Kathryn Stroud, and Marika Weinstein, *Eating behind Bars: Ending the Hidden Punishment of Food in Prison* (Oakland, CA: Impact Justice, 2020), accessed January 4, 2024, https://impactjustice.org/impact/food-in-prison/#report.

(11) Laura M. Maruschak, Marcus Berzofsky, and Jennifer Unangst, *Medical Problems of State and Federal Prisoners and Jail Inmates 2011–2012* (Washington, DC: Bureau of Justice Statistics, 2016), accessed January 4, 2024, https://bjs.ojp.gov/content/pub/pdf/mpsfpji1112.pdf.

(12) Soble et al., *Eating behind Bars*, 2020.

(13) Soble et al., *Eating behind Bars*, 2020.

(14) Soble et al., *Eating behind Bars*, 2020.

(15) Alexa Richardson, "Shackling of Pregnant Prisoners Is Ongoing," *Bill of Health* (blog), Harvard Law, March 4, 2020, accessed January 4, 2024, https://blog.petrieflom.law.harvard.edu/2020/03/04/shackling-of-pregnant-prisoners-is-ongoing/.

(16) David K. Li, "Video Allegedly Shows Woman Giving Birth in Denver Jail Cell Alone, with No Assistance," *NBC News*, August 29, 2019, accessed January 4, 2024, https://www.nbcnews.com/news/us-news/woman-had-give-birth-denver-jail-cell-alone-no-assistance-n1047766.

(17) "Will I Get Furlough if My Loved One Dies while I'm Incarcerated?" *How to Justice*, accessed January 4, 2024, https://howtojustice.org/going-to-prison/loved-one-dies-furlough/.

(18) See the Jean Baker Miller Training Insitute at the Wellesley Centers for Women at Wellesley College for the history of Relational-Cultural Theory. Nearly 100 publications written by JBMTI scholars are available for free download. Accessed January 4, 2024, https://www.wcwonline.org/JBMTI-Site/relational-cultural-theory.

(19) Lalo Piangco Rivera, "The Transcarceral Body: Beyond the Enemy Behind Me—From Incarceration to Emancipation," in *Oppression and the Body: Roots, Resistance, and Resolutions*, Christine Caldwell and Lucia Bennett Leighton, eds. (Berkeley: North Atlantic Books, 2018), 123, accessed January 4, 2024, https://www.google.com/books/edition/Oppression_and_the_Body/eqwpDwAAQBAJ?hl=en&gbpv=1.

(20) Maruschak et al., *Medical Problems*, 2016.

(21) Centers for Disease Control and Prevention, "About the CDC-Kaiser ACE Study," Violence Prevention, 2021, accessed January 4, 2024, https://www.cdc.gov/violenceprevention/aces/about.html.

(22) Nena Messina and Christine Grella, "Childhood Trauma and Women's Health Outcomes in a California Prison Population," *American Journal of Public Health* 96, no. 10 (October 10, 2011): 1842–1848, https://doi.org/10.2105/AJPH.2005.082016.

(23) California Correctional Health Care Services, *CCHCS Receiver Fact Sheet* (Elk Grove: California Correctional Health Care Services, 2020), accessed January 4, 2024, https://cchcs.ca.gov/wp-content/uploads/sites/60/2018/09/Receiver-FactSheet.pdf.

(24) "Washington Women's Prison Healthcare Violations Continue," *Prison Legal News*, January 15, 2007, accessed January 4, 2024, https://www.prisonlegalnews.org/news/2007/jan/15/washington-womens-prison-healthcare-violations-continue/.

(25) "How Many People in Prisons Died of COVID-19?" *USA Facts*, September 20, 2022, accessed January 4, 2024, https://usafacts.org/articles/how-many-people-in-prisons-died-of-covid-19/.

(26) Eric A. Stanley and Nat Smith, eds., *Captive Genders: Trans Embodiment and the Prison Industrial Complex* (Chico, CA: AK Press, 2011), 224.

(27) Nathaniel P. Morris and Sara G. West, "Misconceptions about Working in Correctional Psychiatry," *Journal of the American Academy of Psychiatry and the Law* 50, no. 3 (February 2020): 1–8, accessed January 4, 2024, http://jaapl.org/content/early/2020/02/12/JAAPL.003921-20.

(28) Max Blau, "Pharmaceutical Companies Are Marketing Drugs to Jailers," *The Atlantic*, December 31, 2019, accessed January 4, 2024, https://www.theatlantic.com/politics/archive/2019/12/pharmaceutical-companies-are-marketing-drugs-jailers/604264/.

(29) Hadar Aviram, *Cheap on Crime: Recession-Era Politics and the Transformation of American Punishment* (Oakland: University of California Press, 2015), 124, accessed January 4, 2024, https://www.google.com/books/edition/Cheap_on_Crime/Oe2ADwAAQBAJ?hl=en&gbpv=1.

(30) Emily Widra, "Incarceration Shortens Life Expectancy," Prison Policy Initiative, June 6, 2017, accessed January 4, 2024, https://www.prisonpolicy.org/blog/2017/06/26/life_expectancy/.

(31) Matt McKillop and Alex Boucher, "Aging Prison Populations Drive Up Costs," Pew Charitable Trusts, February 20, 2018, accessed January 4, 2024, https://www.pewtrusts.org/en/research-and-analysis/articles/2018/02/20/aging-prison-populations-drive-up-costs.

(32) Elana Jaffe, Aunchalee E. L. Palmquist, and Andrea K. Knittel, "Experiences of Menopause During Incarceration," *Menopause: Journal of the North American Menopause Society* 28, no. 7 (July 2021): 829–832, https://doi.org/10.1097/GME.0000000000001762.

(33) Aileen Hongo, "Losing Time: Dementia and Alzheimer's Disease behind Bars," National Institute of Corrections, live webinar recording, 53:27, July 28, 2016, accessed January 4, 2024, https://nicic.gov/losing-time-dementia-and-alzheimers-disease-behind-bars-webinar.

(34) Gina Fedock, Rachel Garthe, George E. Higgins, Cashell Lewis, and Amy Blank Wilson, "Health Care Disparities for Incarcerated Adults after a Suicide Attempt," *Suicide and Life-Threatening Behavior* 51, no. 5 (2021): 931–939, https://doi.org/10.1111/sltb.12776, 931.

Part Three: The Journey Home

(1) Tiana Herring, "Parole Boards Approved Fewer Releases in 2020 than in 2019, Despite the Raging Pandemic," Prison Policy Initiative, February 3, 2021, accessed January 4, 2024, https://www.prisonpolicy.org/blog/2021/02/03/parolegrants/.

(2) Jorge Renaud, "Grading the Parole Release Systems of All 50 States," Prison Policy Initiative, February 26, 2019, accessed January 4, 2024, https://www.prisonpolicy.org/reports/grading_parole.html.

(3) Beth Schwartzapfel, "Want to Shrink the Prison Population? Look at Parole," *The Marshall Project*, February 11, 2019, accessed January 4, 2024,https://www.themarshallproject.org/2019/02/11/want-to-shrink-the-prison-population-look-at-parole.

(4) Barbara Bloom, Barbara Owen, and Stephanie Covington, *Gender-Responsive Strategies: Research, Practice, and Guiding Principles for Women Offenders* (Washington, DC: National Institute of Corrections, 2003), accessed January 4, 2024, https://s3.amazonaws.com/static.nicic.gov/Library/018017.pdf.

(5) Stephanie Covington, "A Woman's Journey Home: Challenges for Female Offenders," in *Prisoners Once Removed: The Impact of Incarceration and Reentry on Children, Families, and Communities*, Jeremy Travis and Michelle Waul, eds., 67–103 (Washington, DC: Urban Institute Press, 2003), 88.

(6) Allison Hastings and Kaitlin Kall, *Opening the Door to Healing: Researching and Serving Crime Victims Who Have a History of Incarceration* (New York: Vera Institute of Justice, National Resource Center for Reaching Victims, 2020), accessed January 4, 2024, https://www.vera.org/downloads/publications/opening-the-door-to-healing.pdf.

Author Biography

Stephanie S. Covington, PhD, LCSW, is an internationally recognized clinician, organizational consultant, lecturer, author, and pioneer in the fields of addiction and trauma. For more than thirty-five years, she has created gender-responsive and trauma-informed programs and services for use in public, private, and institutional settings. Her extensive experience includes consulting for and developing programs for numerous US and international agencies and designing women's services at the Betty Ford Center. She has developed programs for women in many criminal legal settings and is the featured therapist on the Oprah Winfrey Network TV show *Breaking Down the Bars*. Dr. Covington has conducted seminars for behavioral health professionals, community organizations, criminal justice professionals, and recovery groups in the United States, Canada, various countries in Europe, the United Kingdom, Mexico, Morocco, Iceland, Brazil, and New Zealand. She has published extensively, including twelve gender-responsive, trauma-informed treatment curricula. She wrote the first manualized treatment program for substance use disorder treatment and authored the best-selling book *A Woman's Way through the Twelve Steps*. Her awards include the Power of One Award from the Association of Justice-Involved Females and Organizations (AJFO), the Believing in Girls Award from the PACE Center for Girls, and the Legacy Award from the She Recovers Foundation. Educated at Columbia University and the Union Institute, Dr. Covington is the co-director of both the Institute for Relational Development and the Center for Gender & Justice, which are located in Del Mar, California.

Book Group Discussion Questions

- After reading *Hidden Healers*, do you feel that reforming our current prison system is still possible? Or do you agree with Dr. Covington that we need a new philosophy and entirely new structures and systems to deal with harm in our communities?
- What about *Hidden Healers* surprised you? Was there anything memorable that you learned?
- What is your relationship to the prison system? Was anything about the criminal legal system described in Part One new to you?
- What are some of the main ways you saw women connect with each other on the inside? How were their connections similar and how were they different from the ways you connect with people you know?
- How would you fare if you had to live inside a prison?
- When you imagine alternatives to incarceration, what comes to mind? What would you build or implement that we don't have now?
- Are you moved to do one small thing, as Dr. Covington suggests? Why or why not? What could your one small thing be?
- How are women in prison represented in media? How do these representations compare to the women whose voices appear in *Hidden Healers*?
- If you were recommending this book to a friend, how would you describe it?

- If not punishment and revenge, what might better bring justice when harm is caused? How should justice feel, and what is the intention of a justice system?
- If this hasn't been your experience, imagine that you currently have a loved one living inside a prison. How might it affect you and your relationship? What challenges might you face as the person living outside?
- What questions do you still have about how prisons work and the women who live there? What do you want to know more about

Also by the Author

- *Awakening Your Sexuality: A Guide for Recovering Women*
- *Becoming Trauma Informed: A Training Program for Professionals*
- *Beyond Anger and Violence: A Program for Women*
- *Beyond Trauma: A Healing Journey for Women*
- *Beyond Violence: A Prevention Program for Criminal Justice–Involved Women*
- *Exploring Trauma+: Brief Intervention for Men and Gender-Diverse People* with Shane Pugh and Roberto Rodriguez
- *Healing Trauma+: A Brief Intervention for Women and Gender-Diverse People* with Eileen Russo
- *Helping Men Recover: A Program for Treating Addiction* with Dan Griffin and Rick Dauer
- *Helping Men Recover: A Program for Treating Addiction* (criminal justice edition) with Dan Griffin and Rick Dauer
- *Helping Women Recover: A Program for Treating Addiction*
- *Helping Women Recover: A Program for Treating Addiction* (criminal justice edition)
- *Leaving the Enchanted Forest: The Path from Relationship Addiction to Intimacy* with Liana Beckett

- *Moving from Trauma-Informed to Trauma-Responsive: A Training Program for Organizational Change* with Sandra Bloom
- *Voices: A Program of Self-Discovery and Empowerment for Girls* with Kimberley Covington and Madeline Covington
- *A Woman's Way through the Twelve Steps*
- *Women and Addiction: A Gender-Responsive Approach*
- *Women in Recovery: Understanding Addiction*
- *A Young Man's Guide to Self-Mastery* with Roberto Rodriguez